Mexico in Crisis

Judith Adler Hellman

HM

Holmes & Meier Publishers, Inc. ● New York

Heinemann ● London

Published in the United States of America **1978** by
Holmes & Meier Publishers, Inc.
101 Fifth Avenue
New York, New York 10003
ISBN 0-8419-0317-4

Published in Great Britain 1978 by
Heinemann Educational Books Ltd
48 Charles Street, London W1X 8AH
ISBN 0-435-83362-6

Library of Congress Cataloging in Publication Data

Hellman, Judith Adler.
   Mexico in crisis.

   Bibliography: p.
   Includes index.
   1. Mexico—Politics and government—1946.
2. Mexico—Politics and government—1910-1946
I. Title.
JL1231.H44   320.9'72'082   77-6468

Printed in the United States of America

To my parents

Contents

Preface

Over the past few years, many people who learn that I have lived in Mexico and carried out research in the countryside have immediately put to me a series of hard-to-answer questions. Those who have traveled in Mexico, even as casual tourists, could not fail to note the contrast between modern urban centers and an apparently backward countryside; between the affluence of some Mexicans and the obvious misery of so many others. During their stay in Mexico City, these travelers have been duly impressed with the skyscrapers, elegant hotels, palatial villas, the broad, tree-lined boulevards filled with late model cars, and the shiny new metro. At the same time they are dismayed to find only a short distance from this attractive, modern core all the sights, sounds, and odors of poverty. For some tourists the contrast is underlined when they are approached by a constant stream of beggars as they make their way along a promenade of shops filled with gay paper flowers, straw donkeys, and marionettes who play guitars and wear oversized sombreros. Often visitors who have taken in this series of contrasting impressions are puzzled and want to know why such dramatic disparities of wealth have accompanied economic development in Mexico.

Another set of questions is posed by those who have studied the Mexican Revolution and have always believed that it represented an example of a triumphant peasant revolution. Such people often ask, "What has happened here? Was the Mexican Revolution betrayed?

Why is it that there are more landless peasants in Mexico today than before the Revolution?"

Yet another series of questions is raised by students of politics who have been led by their readings to regard Mexico as an outstanding example of democracy within a one-party system. These students ask, "How does 'democracy' function in Mexico? How does the dominant party maintain itself in power? What is the meaning of elections in a one-party system? How do various interest groups make their demands known to the country's leaders? And, finally, how can a ruling party 'institutionalize' a revolution?"

In 1968 an outbreak of student unrest and a brutal government response made headlines in newspapers around the globe. With world attention focused on Mexico as the site of the 19th Olympics, and the international press on hand to record the Games, newspaper readers were shocked to learn from their own correspondents that in a single evening more than 300 unarmed demonstrators had been mowed down by army machine guns and that hundreds more had "disappeared" during a summer of violent conflict. What had happened to Mexico's much admired "political stability"? What were the forces involved in this conflict? What were the "grave national problems" that the students were shouting about? Why had the government found it necessary to call in the army? Why was so much force required to put down a student movement?

Obviously these are complex questions, and to find reasonable answers or explanations we need to take a careful look at Mexican political development over the last sixty years. We begin by going back to the Revolution of 1910 to analyze the forces and interests at play in that struggle, focusing not only on the participants and the goals for which they fought, but also on the groups that emerged with power at the end of that conflict. In chapter 2 we look at this new political elite, its economic base, its interests, and the political party it established. We then analyze the structure of the party both as it appears on paper and as it functions in reality. The third chapter concerns the development policy the ruling elite has formulated and implemented since 1940. We are particularly concerned here with the consequences this policy has had in human terms. In chapters 4 and 5 case studies of a peasant and a student movement highlight the mechanisms employed by the ruling party to maintain itself in power, and the ways in which opposition to the system is expressed. The final chapter is an examination of the prospects for change in

Mexico, either by reform under official party leadership or as a result of the overthrow of the existing political system.

When I began work on this book in 1970, there were few sources in English which addressed these issues in a straightforward way and attempted to cut through the elaborate mythology which surrounds the Mexican Revolution and the Mexican political system. Much of what North Americans had written about contemporary Mexico was laudatory and focused on the political stability and economic growth facilitated by the one-party system.[1] Flattering comparisons were made with the disorder and stagnation that characterized other Latin American countries, and the persistent economic inequalities and social injustice in Mexico tended to be downplayed with references to the "incomplete" or, even more positively, the "ongoing" nature of the Mexican Revolution. Reading these studies, one wonders if these observers were afraid of offending their Mexican friends or the Mexican government, or if their perception of the Mexican situation was such that they actually found little to criticize. In either event, the violent explosion of 1968 generally caught these scholars in an intellectual bind because nothing that they had written about Mexican politics suggested either the possibility or the cause of an outbreak of this dimension, nor the naked armed repression and mass imprisonment of political opposition that followed.

Since 1968, students of Mexican politics appear to have been emboldened, and there is a much greater tendency to "tell it like it is." This is what I have attempted to do. In so doing, I have no fear of offending gracious and respected Mexican friends because it has been their expressed desire that I write about these issues as objectively and revealingly as I can.

I would like to thank Eric Wolf and Gerrit Huizer who long ago encouraged me to undertake this project. My friend and colleague, Liisa North, contributed invaluable comments and advice on each draft of every chapter. Giorgio Cingolani provided provocative criticism and showed me how research on Mexico can be carried forward while sitting for a summer in a library in Italy. I am very grateful to Professor Mario Einaudi and to the directors and staff of the Fondazione Einaudi in Turin for affording me the opportunity to proceed with my work while my husband carried out his own research at that institute. I would like to express special appreciation to Cynthia Hewitt de Alcántara and Sergio Alcántara Ferrer who introduced me to rural Mexican politics in 1967, and read and criticized the early chapters of this book in 1973. Russell Chace provided valuable comments on the section dealing with the Revolution of 1910. Through every stage of this work I relied heavily on the analytic skills, theoretical knowledge, common sense and encouragement of my husband, Stephen Hellman. All of these people have been extremely generous with their time and their help, but are in no way responsible for the instances when I was too stubborn to heed their advice.

My greatest debt is to countless Mexicans who, with patience and tolerance, have allowed me to interview them. Men and women inside the government and engaged in opposition, individuals above and underground, members of elite groups as well as peasants and workers, have all contributed to this book by their interest in my project and their willingness, and in some cases, eagerness, to have their point of view included in this study of Mexican politics.

1. The Revolution

> . . . If for the ardour of an easy triumph, if
> for wanting to abbreviate the struggle, we
> cut out of our program the radicalism
> which makes it incompatible with the pro-
> gram of the specifically bourgeois and con-
> servative parties, then we will have done
> the work of bandits and assassins, because
> the blood spilled will only serve to give
> greater strength to the bourgeoisie. . . .
>
> Ricardo Flores Magón
> January 19, 1910

The Mexican Revolution was a brutally violent political and social
upheaval that ravaged the Mexican countryside for more than a
decade. The Revolution still stands as the bloodiest conflict ever witnessed in the Western Hemisphere. In terms of the proportion of
population lost, this was the most violent revolutionary struggle ever.
For in 1910 Mexico counted a population of only 14.5 million
people. And during the struggle that followed the outbreak of
fighting in October 1910, as many as one and a half million Mexicans
lost their lives. The appalling death toll on the battlefield, the lack of
medical care for the wounded, and the routine execution of captured
soldiers decimated the revolutionary armies.

The civilian population suffered grievously. For nearly a million "noncombatants" the Revolution brought death by starvation, disease, exposure, or execution. Villages were burned or flooded by federal troops. Crops were destroyed and peasants were taken as hostages, or summarily shot as "examples" to their fellow villagers. Thousands fled across the northern border into the United States never to return to their native land. By 1920, a total of 8,000 different villages had completely disappeared from the map as a direct result of the Revolution.[1]

The Revolution was touched off by a group of landowners and intellectuals centered in the North of Mexico. These men sought to overthrow Porfirio Díaz, the general who had seized power by military coup in 1876 and ruled Mexico as a dictator for more than thirty years. In his place they hoped to establish a liberal democracy in which presidential succession would be determined by the principle of "effective suffrage and no reelection." Led by Francisco Madero, a politically progressive landowner, the northern revolutionaries were a heterogeneous conglomeration of sectors of a number of different social classes, each with its own grievances against the Díaz regime and its own set of demands to press.

Both the style and substance of Díaz' politics had provoked deepseated resentment among substantial portions of the North's elite. These landowners, industrialists, mine owners, and merchants were prepared to take up arms in 1910 because their economic and political advancement had been thwarted by the Díaz dictatorship. The penetration of the Mexican economy by foreign capital had been pushed by Díaz to the degree that on the eve of the Revolution more than two-thirds of all investment came from foreign sources.[2] Díaz had invited foreign capital to finance the construction of Mexico's railroad system and had offered all kinds of monetary inducements to reduce the risk of investment. "In sweeping away the web of resistance which had inhibited foreign capital in the past and in enforcing the peace and security for such capital, Díaz assigned a role to foreigners in Mexico's internal economy which has very few parallels in the history of modern states."[3] American ownership of land, railroads, mines, banks, and industries was particularly marked in the North of Mexico, a situation that frustrated the economic ambitions of the northern Mexican bourgeoisie.[4] And apart from Díaz' encouragement and generous concessions to foreigners, the President had reserved economic and political opportunity at the top for a small, favored elite made up of the men who had come to power with him in the 1870s and their descendants. Members of the northern bourgeoisie who were excluded from this closed circle felt economically and politically emarginated. As the dictatorship provided them no institutional means by which to effect a transfer of power to themselves, these men readily aligned themselves with the intellectuals who called for the overthrow of the regime.[5] Thus the revolutionary armies of the North included this elite component of men who were fighting to oust the narrow group of Mexican and foreign capitalists in whose hands economic and political power had concentrated.

The northern armies also incorporated members of the middle classes—clerks, teachers, professionals, small businessmen, small and medium-sized farmers, estate overseers and ranch foremen—a group whose advancement was also blocked by entrenched elites. Opportunities for employment for the educated middle class had not expanded during the Díaz years at a rate rapid enough to absorb those seeking white collar and professional jobs.[6] And middle class northerners resented their exclusion from the closed circle of government where all appointments were controlled by Díaz and his henchmen. Furthermore, the economic recession which began in 1905 and reached crisis proportions in 1909 heightened middle class discontent as it caused further contraction of the already limited opportunities for social and economic mobility open to these people. Thus when the call to Revolution came, a substantial proportion of this middle sector cast its lot with the revolutionary forces.

The mass base of the Revolution in the North was formed by workers, miners, agricultural laborers, peasants, cowboys, shepherds, muleteers, and drifters. Before the Revolution this sector had been characterized by a pattern of horizontal mobility; according to the work available men moved back and forth among various jobs on the estates, in the mines, in the factories or across the border in the United States. But the years of recession and depression immediately prior to 1910 simultaneously eliminated most of these alternative work opportunities. And the northern working class and peasantry, whose economic condition was already precarious at best, found themselves squeezed even harder.[7]

The goals articulated by the revolutionary leaders of the North were as diverse as the social classes participating in the struggle. The middle and upper class Liberals were calling for political reforms to broaden the base of political participation, for anticlerical legislation to curb the power of the Catholic Church, and for nationalistic legislation to impose state control over foreign investment and owner-ship. They were concerned with putting an end to some of the more glaring abuses of the Díaz regime: forced military conscription, suppression of the press, the total neglect of public education, and the maintenance of order through the use of the brutal *rurales,* a militia of mercenary soldiers.

While the call for "social justice" and "democracy" articulated by Liberal politicians appealed to the mass base of revolutionary soldiers, the peasant and worker combatants had goals of their own. These goals corresponded to the workers' and peasants' needs and exper-iences and were not always well understood by their middle and upper class leaders. Workers were concerned with winning the right to organize, guarantees of decent working conditions, adequate pay and job security, the abolition of the company store, and other basic labor rights. Peasants had demands which varied according to the type of work they did and their relationship to the land. Agricultural laborers who worked for wages on commercial estates had grievances that closely resembled those of workers: demands for higher pay, better working conditions, and so forth. Sharecroppers and renters wanted land of their own. They wished to be free of the obligation to return to a landlord in cash or kind a large proportion of their produce. And those peasants who were tied to traditional estates sought relief from the burdens of debt peonage.

At the same time that we can identify separate sets of demands made by elite, middle, and mass sectors incorporated within the revolutionary movement of the North, we must also distinguish this ideologically heterogeneous northern movement from the clearly peasant revolution which developed in the south-central region of Mexico in the state of Morelos. The revolutionary front that emerged in Morelos was a unified, ideologically coherent movement of land-less peasants fighting under the leadership of men and women of peasant origin.[8] In this area of Mexico, peasant villages had held title to communal lands from the period of the Spanish conquest until well into the second half of the nineteenth century. The "Liberal Reforms" of the 1850s and '60s were designed to transform these peasants into yeoman farmers working individual family farms. But the reforms had the effect of permitting large commercial land-owners to gain control over the communal village holdings. Deprived of the basis of their livelihood, the peasants of Morelos and other central Mexican states were forced to relinquish their status as independent small holders and attach themselves as peons or serfs to the large estates of the commercial landowners who had gained control of the village lands. This process of land alienation had greatly accelerated during the Díaz years. Thus, when word of the outbreak of Revolution in the North reached Morelos, the peasants quickly rallied to the cause. The fight to overthrow the Díaz regime promised to provide the opportunity to reclaim land from the Díaz favorites who had progressively usurped the peasants' holdings. In this respect the goal of the southern revolutionary front was a radical one in that its implementation would have required the total transformation of the land tenure system which existed in 1910. Yet, at the same time, the southerners' demand was an archaic one: the peasants of Morelos were fighting for the restoration of village lands and the return to a traditional order of communal agricultural exploitation. Their vision of revolution had little to do with the demands of the northern elite or middle classes. It did not even comprehend the aspirations of industrial or agricultural workers who had never had any land of their own either to lose or have "restored." It was a limited vision of revolution, but despite its narrow focus, it was a compelling vision for the tens of thousands of peasant men and women who left their wretched homes to join the Revolution in Morelos.

The Armies of the Revolution

The revolutionary armies that formed in the northern and south-central regions of Mexico are customarily identified by the names of their principal leaders. This convention reflects the degree to which personal charisma rather than ideological commitment was the element that drew and held together each of the revolutionary armies. Political adhesion to one army or another was linked to personal loyalties to the leader and his network of allies. It is particularly difficult to discuss the armies of the North without reference to the general who mustered and led the troops, because these movements were so heterogeneous in composition and ideology that, at times, the only common motivation shared by comrades-in-arms derived from personal attachment to their revolutionary chief. Even on the southern front where the Revolution had a clear and coherent ideology, the movement was shaped by the charismatic qualities of its undisputed leader, Emiliano Zapata, whose name came to represent all that the southern peasants, or *zapatistas,* were fighting for.

Born in a peasant village in the state of Morelos, Zapata himself was a horse trainer and trader, rather than a peasant farmer, but his movement fully embodied the aspirations of the peasants of his home region. At the head of an army of 70,000 landless men and women organized in small, highly mobile guerrilla bands, Zapata used the mountains and forests of Morelos as his base of operations. From this tactically advantageous position, he led the fight for the restoration of village lands. As occurs in cases of successful guerrilla warfare, Zapata's followers were not so much an army as a fully mobilized population. The peasant fighters struck swiftly at the federal forces sent into the region to suppress their rebellion, and then retired to their villages, buried their rifles beneath the mud floor of their huts, and resumed their everyday life in the fields. When the enemy penetrated Morelos in search of the "rebel army," they found only peaceful peasants humbly ploughing the tiny parcels of land that were all that was left of their once extensive village holdings. Because Zapata's force was manned and supplied directly from the small villages of Morelos, in the course of the Revolution the entire state was devastated by federal armies using search-and-destroy techniques to flush out the peasant guerrillas.

The loyalty of Zapata's troops was unique in the history of the Revolution. The guerrilla leader lived with a price on his head for ten years. But his followers regarded him with such esteem and affection that no one within his movement gave in to the temptation to betray his leader in return for the cash reward. The passionate loyalty Zapata commanded seemed to grow from his direct and earthy way of dealing with his supporters, and from the fact that he never asked nor accepted any material benefits for himself.

As one peasant who fought for Zapata explained:

> In my judgment, what Zapata was fighting for was just. Porfirio's government took everything away from us. Everything went to the rich, the *hacendados,* those with the power were the masters, and we had nothing. We were their servants because we could not plant or make use of any lands that did not belong to the *hacienda.* So they had us subjugated. We were completely enslaved by the *hacendados.* That is what Zapata fought to set right. . . .
>
> I liked Zapata's plan and that's why, when he came to my village, I went to him. I still hadn't joined but I went up in the hills with *tortillas* and water. . . . I went to see Zapata in his camp. He was in a little house but they wouldn't let me go in. They were suspicious. There were two guards

right in front of the door. I stood at a distance, watching. He was sitting inside with his general staff. And he calls out to me, "What do you have there, friend?"

"Nothing, *señor*. Just my *tortillas*."

"Come in."

"Let's see your *tortillas*: Take them out."

And I gave them all to him. How he liked my *tortillas*!

He and his staff finished them off.

"And what do you have in your gourd? *Pulque*?"

"No, *señor*, water." And he drank it.[9]

While Zapata's leadership was charismatic, and the goals of his movement compelling to his peasant followers, the Revolution of the South never succeeded in attracting any sizable degree of non-peasant support. Throughout the years of struggle, Zapata was able to count upon the adhesion and collaboration of a group of urban and rural radical intellectuals. These men helped Zapata formulate his *Plan de Ayala* and other proclamations and programs calling for the breakup of the large estates and the restoration of lands to the peasant villages. But apart from these intellectuals, Zapata seemed unable to understand or reach urban Mexicans. Thus a serious limitation of *zapatismo* lay in the movement's inability to broaden its appeal or move beyond the land question to other issues that concerned industrial workers. Another limitation was that Zapata and his people constituted an effective fighting force only when they fought on their home ground, the mountains of Morelos. When they ventured beyond their own territory, the *zapatistas* were like fish out of water. This is what happened when they marched on Mexico City. Cut off from their supply base, the guerrillas could not hold the Capital, and so they returned to their mountains to continue the struggle to defend the lands they had already won.

While the *zapatista* guerrillas held off federal troops in Morelos, on the northern front Díaz' soldiers clashed with a large number of different "revolutionary armies," each with its own charismatic leader who gave his movement a specific social and political character. Among these armies, three in particular played determining roles in the course of the Revolution.

The army led by Venustiano Carranza, a large landowner, was a conservative force among the revolutionaries. During the Díaz years, Carranza had served as a senator of the Republic. But when the call to Revolution came, Carranza armed the peons of his own *hacienda,* put together a small army, and joined the fight on the side of Madero. Carranza's force was called the "Constitutionalist" Army, and its leadership was provided almost entirely by middle class liberals. These men fought for political reforms that would alter the worst aspects of the Díaz dictatorship, and would replace the despotism of Díaz with a narrowly based "constitutional democracy." But the *carrancista* leaders hated and feared the revolutionary groups that fought for radical social change just as much as they had resented the oppressions of the Díaz regime. [10]

Fighting on the same side with Carranza were the troops of General Alvaro Obregón. Obregón was the son of a once wealthy rancher who had fallen on hard times. As a young man the general worked at a variety of trades—mechanic, salesman, sugar miller, and others—before returning to ranching. This background gave Obregón experience with people, places, and ideas somewhat outside his own social milieu, and helped him to identify with some of the more radical social goals of the Revolution. In particular, his experiences enabled him to understand the grievances and aspirations of workers, and his ability to attract a working class following would eventually alter the course of the Revolution. "Obregón was by no means a socialist, but favored nationalist legislation and agrarian and labor reforms which would, at one and the same time, curtail United States encroachment, break the power of the great landed families, and widen the opportunities in the market for both labor and his kind of middle class." [11]

In 1912, inspired by the ideas of Madero, the liberals, and the radical intellectuals, Obregón gathered a group of 300 fellow ranchers into a fighting force "that came to be known as the Rich Man's Battalion." [12] Apart from the small and middle scale commercial farmers who joined this band, teachers, tradesmen, white collar professionals, and a variety of other middle class elements were attracted to Obregón's cause. The ranks of Obregón's force, as elsewhere in the North, were filled out with miners, cowboys, industrial and agricultural workers, and peons from the huge *haciendas* of the northern states.

Undoubtedly the most able of all the northern generals, Obregón was a student of military strategy and in the course of the war proved himself a master tactician. He studied the progress of the Great War in Europe, and applied in battle what he had learned of modern trench warfare. Of all the northern generals Obregón was perhaps the man best qualified for leadership.[13] He was a flexible, well-disciplined person who was able to understand goals beyond his own self-interest.

The last of the most important revolutionary armies was the "Northern Division" led by the famous bandit-turned-revolutionary, General Pancho Villa. Villa's origins were as humble as Zapata's. He spent his youth laboring as a peon on a large *hacienda*; then, after a brief career as a mule driver, Villa lived for twenty-two years as a cattle rustler and bandit. By the time the Revolution broke out, he already enjoyed a widespread reputation as a Robin Hood who stole from the rich landowner to give to the poor peon. Villa was not an ideologically sophisticated man. But in a good fight between the old dictator in Mexico City, supported by the rich landowners, and the new liberal leaders from the North, Pancho Villa cast his lot with Francisco Madero and the revolutionaries.

John Reed, an American journalist who travelled with Villa's army as a war correspondent, described the bandit this way:

> His reckless and romantic bravery is the subject of countless poems. They tell, for example, how one of his band named Reza was captured by the *rurales* and bribed to betray Villa. Villa heard of it and sent word into the city of Chihuahua that he was coming for Reza. In broad daylight he entered the city on horse-back, took ice cream in the Plaza—the ballad is very explicit on this point—and rode up and down the streets until he found Reza strolling with his sweetheart in the Sunday crowd on the Paseo Bolivar, where he shot him and escaped. In time of famine he fed whole districts, and took care of entire villages evicted by the soldiers under Porfirio Díaz's outrageous land law. Everywhere he was known as The Friend of the Poor. He was the Mexican Robin Hood.[14]

Villa recruited his forces from the cowboys, miners, small ranchers, bandits, gamblers, and drifters of Chihuahua State. In the other armies of the Revolution, the women and children of soldiers normally travelled along with the troops, often because their homes had been destroyed, or their lives so totally uprooted that they had nowhere else to go. As a result, the movement of revolutionary forces often resembled the migrations of whole populations rather than an army on the march. But Villa often persuaded his troops to leave their women and children behind, and he instituted a technique of rapid, forced marches and surprise attacks that were the key to his military success. Most of Villa's troops were men who had lived half their lives in the saddle, and 40,000 strong, the Northern Division comprised a formidable cavalry. Indeed Villa's most impressive military victories were achieved with daring cavalry maneuvers, while his most disastrous defeats, toward the end of the Revolution, came when he failed to understand the limitations of a cavalry attack used against an entrenched army protected by barbed wire and machine guns.[15]

The social goal closest to Villa's heart was free public schooling. Unlike Zapata, who enjoyed the benefits of two years of primary education, Villa was illiterate until the age of 46 when socialist intellectuals, imprisoned with him in the Mexico City penitentiary, taught the passionately eager general the rudiments of reading and writing. Villa never lost the illiterate's overwhelming faith in the power of education to erase injustice and social inequality. From the Villa camp John Reed wrote, "Often I have heard him say: 'When I passed such and such street this morning I saw a lot of kids. Let's put a school there.' "[16] In this haphazard fashion Villa established more than fifty primary schools during his reign as military governor of Chihuahua State.

Apart from his commitment to education, Villa's concern with social reform was sporadic and ill-defined. His movement had no clear political ideology and his army was so amorphous that it provided a home for any opportunist who sought to penetrate its ranks.

> More a force of nature than of politics, the *villista* party was commotion rampant. These northern drifters could give their populism no real point. Cowboys, muleskinners, bandits, railroad laborers, peddlers, refugee peons, the *villistas* had no definite class interests or local attachments. And to certain ambitious operators . . . this disorder was an opportunity. . . . Villa was the very incarnation of irregularity, and his men took him as a model.[17]

Although his movement was originally allied with the forces of Carranza and Obregón, distrust, rivalry, and, ultimately, betrayal by Carranza led Villa to break with the conservative and moderate northern generals and to identify himself with the radical demands of the *zapatistas*. Nevertheless, we cannot say that Villa's concept of revolution was as fully developed or as radical as Zapata's. For, even at the height of his military strength, Villa never attempted to seize landholdings and distribute them to the landless in a systematic fashion as Zapata had done in the South. Villa often gave away tracts of land in the same generous spirit that he distributed thousands of pesos of the currency he printed himself in the basement of the Governor's Palace in Chihuahua City. But neither Villa nor the generals who fought under him were much interested in establishing the legal bases or the mechanisms for a full scale land reform program. For one thing, the arid expanses of the North did not lend themselves to parcelization and distribution in small lots. For another, given the low level of political consciousness that characterized Villa's officers and troops, the large estates that were seized by the *villistas* tended to remain in the hands of Villa's generals. These men used the estates to create an upper class way of life for themselves, becoming a landed elite in their own right with interests directly opposed to those who demanded land reform.[18]

Years of Conflict and Bloodshed

These were the principal forces that made the revolution against the old regime. Díaz' institutional structure, sclerotic and decayed after so many years of rule, fell to pieces more quickly than any of the protagonists would have thought possible. And only a year after the fighting began, Francisco Madero, head of the liberals, took office as the Revolution's first President.

But Madero proved incapable of controlling the forces he had unleashed. A weak-willed, inconsistent idealist, Madero was unable to provide firm leadership or to reconcile the contradictions between conservatives like Carranza and radicals like Zapata. In all fairness, it is difficult to imagine that the strongest and most able of politicians could have satisfied the demands of so many different forces fighting for so many different goals. Madero certainly was unable to play this role, although he struggled bravely. Unfortunately he never really understood the passions he had kindled with his call to revolution. He never understood the overpowering hunger for land that had filled the ranks of Zapata's army with desperate, landless men and women. Madero wanted to give full democratic rights to the people at a time when such niceties as votes and electoral contests were largely irrelevant. He expected that he could govern with mercy and humility at the moment that the reactionary forces were plotting his overthrow.[19] Madero did not appreciate that he needed the armed support of the revolutionary forces to consolidate his control over the Mexican state. For Madero the struggle had successfully concluded when he took his seat in the presidential chair. Díaz' army, administration, and Senate were left intact while the new President attempted to delimit the content of the Revolution and to contain the revolutionary forces that had emerged.[20] Madero implored his allies to lay down their arms and accept the revolution that he would construct. But none of the principal generals had enough confidence in the new regime to disband his army without some concrete assurance that the new Revolution would reflect his own concept of what a revolution ought to be.

Madero also faced strong opposition from the United States government. President William Howard Taft was initially sympathetic to Madero's government, but as soon as he realized that Madero had no intention of granting special concessions to American capital nor taking measures to protect American property in Mexico, Taft withdrew his support.[21] To make matters worse, the American ambassador to Mexico, Henry Lane Wilson, was closely linked to American financial interests which were in direct competition with those of the Madero family. Accordingly, Wilson became "a fanatical enemy of the government to which he was accredited," and did everything in his power—which was considerable—to bring that government down.[22]

Ambassador Wilson proceeded to create panic among American citizens in Mexico, sending thousands fleeing from the Republic, and on the Ambassador's advice, 100,000 American troops were massed on the Mexican border. Wilson then brought to the Embassy the leading counterrevolutionary conspirators, Felix Díaz, nephew of the deposed dictator, Bernardo Reyes, and Victoriano Huerta, and assisted them in formulating their plot against Madero. Four days later Madero and his closest associates were dead, the sinister Huerta had assumed the presidency, and Wilson gleefully dispatched the news to Washington that "a wicked despotism has fallen."[23]

But the United States government was now headed by Woodrow Wilson. And the new American President was reluctant to recognize Huerta because it was clear even in Washington that Huerta's government was despotic. Ambassador Wilson was recalled and replaced, and a new type of U.S. intervention began. The new American policy in Mexico involved arms sales to favored revolutionary factions, arms embargoes against revolutionary forces unacceptable to U.S. business interests, and the seizure of the port of Veracruz at the cost of some two hundred Mexican lives.[24]

With Madero gone, the fighting began anew. In March 1913,

Carranza sent forth the call to rebellion to avenge the death of Madero and overthrow Huerta. The revolutionary armies united to crush the counterrevolution of Huerta, and their strength was such that Huerta's reign in Mexico City was relatively short lived. He managed to control Mexico for eighteen months, from February 1913 to July 1914. Then Huerta was driven from power by General Carranza who had finally emerged as the dominant force among the armies of the Revolution.

Another six years of bloodshed followed. Carranza's appropriation of the Revolution was challenged by Zapata and Villa and later by Obregón. The various armies of the North split and reunited along new lines. In the North, where the revolutionary troops had always lacked a clear political orientation, former comrades-in-arms now rode against one another in battle. Soldiers surrendered to an enemy force one day and, as a condition of their release, took up arms the next day to fight under a new general. Betrayal followed betrayal, and most of the principal revolutionary leaders died at the hands of assassins and traitors.

When the bloodletting came to an end in the early 1920s, the veterans returned to their villages and towns to find that there was not much left to come home to. The Mexican economy was in shambles and thousands of miles of roads, bridges, and railroad track had been blown up or torn out. The telegraph and telephone systems as well as public utilities were so seriously disrupted that they had to be completely reconstructed.[25] Mining, the most important industry in Mexico before the Revolution, was now in decline.[26] Production of all staple crops, particularly beans and corn, was down to about half of the prerevolutionary yield. In 1924, for example, less corn was harvested than in any other year during the previous two centuries.[27] Cattle that had not been slaughtered on the spot to feed the troops of the revolutionary armies were often rounded up and driven across the U.S. border, where they were traded for arms and ammunition. *Hacienda* buildings, sugar and cotton mills, and crops had been burned to the ground, and where large estates were left more or less intact, landowners often refused to sow their fields for fear that revolutionary forces would reap the harvest. As a result of this severe dislocation in cattle raising and agriculture, food prices soared. Widespread starvation prompted food riots in cities throughout Mexico, and each day hundreds of peasants and urban poor died of malnutrition.[28]

After more than a decade of fighting that intimately touched the lives of millions of people, the old order of the Díaz regime had been overturned and a series of governments—some reactionary, some conservative, some moderately progressive—had followed in rapid succession. But the great mass of Mexicans were economically no better off than before the Revolution. Workers still labored long hours for pitiful wages under miserable conditions. And those who had joined the revolutionary armies to fight for land had not witnessed the fulfillment of the promise that "the land would belong to the tiller." After so many years of hardship and destruction, a comprehensive land reform program was not to be initiated in earnest until the late 1930s. Although workers and particularly peasants constituted the bulk of all revolutionary combatants and casualties, the Revolution did not bring them the economic, political, and social status for which they had fought.

The "triumph of the Revolution" did not alter their low status because the politically conscious peasantry and working class were not the sectors that emerged victorious in the Revolution. On the contrary, the gains made by peasant armies, like those led by Zapata, were undermined or neutralized by the manipulations of politicians like Carranza who represented the aspirations of landowners, industrialists, and a highly mobile and ambitious middle class. While the workers and peasants were the principal actors in the revolutionary drama, while it was mostly their blood that was shed, there was no point during a decade of conflict when peasant troops or workers' battalions, fighting under peasant or working class leadership, were able to seize and hold national power.[29] By 1920 Zapata had been treacherously assassinated. Pancho Villa had been defeated in battle, and his once powerful army of 40,000 reduced to an ineffectual force of a few thousand. In addition, as we have noted before, many of the *villista* generals (and even some of Zapata's men) who had begun the Revolution as popular leaders, used the spoils of war to enrich themselves. As a result of this tendency, those peasant or working class leaders who were not eliminated in the course of the Revolution often acquired middle class characteristics and middle class interests and were quickly assimilated into the new ruling class.

The New Ruling Class

By the end of the Revolution the leadership of Mexico had fallen into the hands of Carranza and the men closest to the old general, and a new ruling coalition had formed. The coalition was composed of (a) the new elite of recently landed revolutionary generals, (b) industrialists and businessmen who had prospered during and immediately after the Revolution, and (c) members of the old land-owning oligarchy who had become aware that they could pursue their prerevolutionary interests and preserve much of their prerevo-lutionary status by declaring their adherence to the new regime.

Not every family that had enjoyed social prestige and economic and political power before the Revolution was able to hold onto its former position. Some of the old landowners lost everything in the Revolution. Some died in the course of the war, and many others chose to emigrate to Europe or the United States. But a remarkable num-ber of these families survived with their property more or less intact, and some of the most economically powerful were able to further enrich themselves under the new order.[30]

Old money was joined by new wealth amassed during the Revo-lution and the period of physical reconstruction that followed. Reconstruction offered the growing community of capitalists a wide variety of opportunities for investment and profit.[31] Friends and relatives of the successful revolutionary generals grew rich, some-times overnight, on highly lucrative government contracts.[32] In addi-tion to the reconstruction of the communications network and the initiation of public works projects, a variety of industries introduced before the Revolution developed rapidly in the 1920s and 1930s. Mining picked up and petroleum production soared.[33] Iron, steel, cement, paper, textiles, shoes, beer, tobacco, soap, sugar refining, and flour milling were all expanded from their prerevolutionary base, while new enterprises—among them metal goods, window glass, and foodstuffs—developed for the first time during this period of eco-nomic recovery.[34]

The emergence of a new capitalist class, or "industrial bour-geoisie," and the consolidation of this group's political power has been described by Andre Gunder Frank.

> The viable economic base of the more aristocratic upper class was de-stroyed by the Revolution. But many of its members and their wealth survived. Their money was invested in finance, commerce, industry and later again in agriculture; and the ex-aristocrats became the nucleus of the new bourgeoisie. Their ranks were soon supplemented by their erstwhile enemies, the individual beneficiaries of the same Revolution, many politi-cians and generals among them. As their economic position became con-solidated, so did their political power.[35]

The interests of the new bourgeoisie differed, of course, from those of the old aristocracy. The new group possessed a modern capitalist orientation and looked to the commercialization of agriculture, industrialization, and a minimum level of government regulation in order to promote their modern financial, commercial, or industrial enterprises. It was hardly as if nothing had altered since the days when Mexico was controlled by Porfirio Díaz and his coterie. On the contrary, the social and economic changes wrought by the Mexican Revolution were extensive, and they laid the basis for a modern and industrialized Mexico. But it is important to understand that the changes that were produced by a decade of conflict were changes most appropriately summed up in the term "bourgeois revolution"—a transformation reflecting the interests of those people in a society who control capital and the means of production, and those people who share in the profits of capital. It was the Carranzas, the Obregóns, and the other representatives of the rising Mexican bourgeoisie who gave ideological character to the political order that emerged from the Revolution. Although the Mexican Revolution was made by peasants and workers, it was in no way a "popular revolution" since neither the peasants nor the workers gained effective power, nor did their representatives come to control the state. As we have noted, for all their sacrifices the peasants and workers in fact got very little immediate benefit from the Revolution. The benefits they did receive came in the form of legislative guarantees.

The expressed goals of the popular forces that had participated in the revolutionary struggle were written into a new Constitution of 1917. This constitution became the one legacy provided by the Revolution to the worker and peasant combatants.

The Workers' Legacy

It is one of the ironies of Mexican history that the great legislative breakthroughs for the Mexican working class were made during the period when the dominant *politico* in Mexico was General Venustiano Carranza—hardly a figure one would be tempted to describe as a great friend of the working man. The labor legislation that came out of the Mexican Revolution was, in its day, the most progressive body of labor guarantees on record anywhere in the world. Yet, ironically, the very fact that such laws were produced was due to the political and strategical needs of a conservative on his march to national power.

Although Carranza was a conservative within the revolutionary coalition of the North, the general made his first overtures to labor as early as 1914. At that point in the Revolution, Carranza's forces (led by Obregón) had taken Mexico City, ousted the reactionary Huerta, and installed Carranza in the National Palace. But Carranza found himself in a very precarious military and political situation. In September 1914, Zapata had renounced Carranza because of the latter's lack of concern for land reform, while Pancho Villa, who had once figured among Carranza's outstanding divisional generals, had met secretly with Zapata and agreed with the guerrilla leader that Carranza could never be trusted with the leadership of the Revolution.

Carranza countered by calling Villa and the other "Constitutionalist" leaders to Mexico City to discuss the program for the new *carrancista* regime. But Villa and his forces refused to meet in territory controlled by Carranza, and so the proceedings were moved to the northern city of Aguascalientes and the meeting became the Convention of Aguascalientes. This city rapidly filled up with Villa's troops and, against the express wishes of Carranza, the *villistas* brought Zapata's representatives into the convention hall. Among the *zapatistas* was one of the greatest orators of the period, Antonio Díaz Soto y Gama. Proclaiming Zapata as the heir of Karl Marx, St. Francis of Assisi, and Jesus Christ rolled into one, Díaz Soto y Gama explained to the delegates the basic goals of Zapata's movement.[36] Speaking with great eloquence, he persuaded the convention to accept the principles of Zapata's *Plan de Ayala,* a blueprint for radical agrarian reform that Zapata had already put into practice in the areas of Morelos State that he controlled.[37]

Carranza chose to ignore the results of the convention, dismissing the meeting as an inconsequential pack of *villistas* swayed by a bunch of hot-headed *agraristas.*[38] But Carranza was in serious political trouble. Only a month or so after his loss of face at the Convention of Aguascalientes, Zapata's forces, dressed in their loose, white peasant clothes, enormous sombreros, and heavily armed, marched on Mexico City. And when the Morelos peasants reached the capital, they were joined by Pancho Villa's Northern Division. This display of military strength forced Carranza to remove his troops to the port of Veracruz, on the Gulf of Mexico. Desperate for military support to counter the challenge of the *zapatistas* and *villistas,* Carranza turned to the working class for the military clout that he needed.

To recruit the support of workers, Carranza sent his ally, General

Obregón, to negotiate an agreement with the labor unions of Mexico City. Obregón, always skillful in appealing to workers, persuaded the union leaders to send their members to the front in separate units called "red battalions." Carranza, in turn, gave union leaders his permission to proceed behind the lines, "to agitate and organize the workers in the districts reclaimed from the enemy."[39]

In return for support on the battlefield, Carranza issued his Decree of December 12, 1914. In this document Carranza openly acknowledged the insufficiency of the narrow political goals which had been the rallying cry of the liberals who unleashed the Revolution in 1910.[40] Carranza had finally realized that the scope of the Revolution had to be enlarged if it were to express the social and economic aspirations for which the peasants and workers were willing to fight. And, therefore, in the Decree of December 12 Carranza stated his intention "to establish a regime which will guarantee the equality of the Mexicans among themselves; . . . legislation to better the condition of the peasant, of the worker, of the miner, and in general of the working classes. . . ."[41]

With the Decree of December 12, Carranza attempted to reassure organized labor that progressive labor legislation would have top priority for any government he might head. He promised that his administration would give attention to the "just claims of the workers in any conflict arising between them and employers." Although Carranza was anything but wholehearted in these gestures towards the working class, Alvaro Obregón, Carranza's divisional general, had in fact maintained close ties with organized labor and Obregón played a key role in winning labor support at this critical time.[42] It was Obregón, for example, who expropriated the Mexico City Jockey Club and presented the building to the labor unions as a headquarters for their central organization, the *Casa del Obrero Mundial* (House of the Workers of the World). The "Casa" had been established as a training, organizational, administrative, and propaganda center for the entire Mexican labor movement. When Obregón and the other *carrancista* agents first approached labor leaders to bargain for their support, there was great dissension among the membership. Once the decision to support Carranza was taken, many workers individually deserted their union battalions to join the struggle under the leadership of Villa or Zapata.[43] But even with a substantial number of workers leaving the red battalions to fight with the revolutionary forces of Villa or Zapata, Carranza's army, reinforced by the influx of workers, militarily overwhelmed both the *villistas* and the *zapatistas.*

Since the support they had given to Carranza proved important to his ultimate success, in 1916 organized labor looked to the general to make good his promise of progressive legislation for the working class. In November of that year, delegates from all over the country met in the central Mexican city of Querétaro to draft a new constitution. Once again, it was Carranza who called together the convention, and once again he tried to pack the meeting with his own people by excluding the representatives of his political enemies, Zapata and Villa. This time Carranza felt reasonably confident that his own people and his own political line would dominate the proceedings from start to finish. The delegates to the convention shared an ideological perspective that has been described as "corporate liberalism."[44] They accepted private capitalist enterprise as the system that would prevail in Mexico, and they differed fundamentally only to the degree that they supported or rejected the principle that the state should play a strong regulatory role in the process of capitalist development. This disagreement became evident in the final months of 1916 as delegates quickly grouped themselves into two opposing factions: the moderate liberals or "reformists" who supported Carranza and rejected state intervention, and the radical liberals, or "jacobins," who identified themselves with the more progressive General Alvaro Obregón and pushed for an active regulatory role for the Mexican state.[45] Among these radical liberals were a group of revolutionary leaders who had fought with Carranza's armies, but whose deepest sympathies lay with the agrarian cause of Zapata. The *agraristas* at the convention were determined to see the principles of Zapata's *Plan de Ayala* incorporated into the constitution itself.

After several weeks of infighting and political intrigue, the radical liberal faction gradually gained the upper hand, and the more conservative *carrancistas* were forced to give way on the most crucial issues.[46] Carranza presented to the convention his own proposals for the new constitution. Carranza's draft was a conservative document, emphasizing restraints on the power of government, and sticking closely to the precepts established sixty years earlier in the old Constitution of 1857. His proposal offered no program for land reform, specified no restraints on the power of the church, and offered few specific guarantees to labor.

But the jacobins fought back, and while the final draft of the

constitution adopted six weeks later included about three-fourths of
the 132 articles originally proposed by Carranza, the document that
emerged was far more radical in both spirit and letter from the proposals Carranza originally had in mind.[47] The radical liberal members of the assembly were determined to extend all the existing
guarantees to workers and to state them explicitly in a separate
article dealing exclusively with labor. The result, Article 123 of the
Mexican Constitution, was, as we have noted, the most progressive
piece of labor legislation in any country of the world of 1917.

First, the Article established the power of the government to intervene in labor relations in order to promote conditions favorable to
the workers. It guaranteed the right to organize unions and the right
to strike. These rights were to be enjoyed by workers employed in
public service, as well as those employed by private enterprise. Article 123 established an eight-hour workday and carefully limited over-
time. Well defined limitations on child labor were set, and the
principle of equal pay for equal work regardless of sex was laid
down. A provision for maternity leave and limits on physical labor
for pregnant women were included in the legislation. The authors of
the Article were careful to state explicitly that

> The minimum wage for workers shall be *sufficient to satisfy the normal
> material, social and cultural needs* of a head of family and provide for the
> compulsory education of the children. In every agricultural, commercial,
> manufacturing and mining enterprise, *the workers have the right to share
> in the profits.* . . . A social security law is considered of public utility, and
> shall include disability insurance, life insurance, insurance against unem-
> ployment, sickness, accidents and the like. . . .[48]

The Constitution established employers' liability for labor or work
accidents, and it required that every worker enjoy at least one day of
rest each week. All wages were to be paid in legal currency rather
than merchandise or credit at a company store, and three months'
severance pay was due any worker laid off his job. In addition,
"employers must furnish workmen with comfortable and sanitary
dwelling places. . . . They shall also establish schools, clinics and
other services necessary to the community when factories are not
located in inhabited places. . . ."

Both state and national governments were required to enact specific labor legislation in conformity with the guidelines laid down in
Article 123.[49] Through these provisions and the requirement that all
state labor codes conform to these constitutional principles, the radi-

cal liberal drafters meant to insure that the working class would receive the full share of the revolutionary legacy that belonged to them.

The Peasants' Legacy

The dominant radical group responsible for the progressive labor legislation was every bit as determined to provide both the constitutional principles and the mechanism through which the peasants could take possession of the land for which they had fought. Article 27 of the new Constitution established the nation's ownership of all land and water resources, all forests, minerals and other products of nature. In Article 27 the radical liberals were able to lay down the conditions for expropriations of private holdings by the state. The key passage is as follows:

> The nation shall at all times have the right to establish regulations for private property which the public interest may dictate, such as those regulating the use of natural resources for conservation purposes or *ensuring a more equitable distribution of public wealth. With this end in view, the necessary measures shall be taken to break up the large estates;*[50]

In addition to restricting land ownership on the part of the church and foreigners, Article 27 provided for the restoration of land to peasants who had been despoiled of their communally held properties before the Revolution, and the distribution of land to "population centres that lack land and water, or do not have them in quantities sufficient for the needs of their people. . . ." These grants were to be made from the expropriation and distribution of the land holdings of "adjacent large properties."[51]

In summary, the Constitution adopted in 1917 provided both the most progressive array of guarantees to labor known anywhere in the world at that time, plus the legislative basis for the widest scale land reform program in history. The radical framers of the Constitution left the hall in Querétaro deeply satisfied that within the framework of a capitalist system they had secured for both workers and peasants the legislative foundation for the economic and social justice they had sought in the Revolution.

Unfeasible and Unenforceable Legislation

Unfortunately the mere stroke of pen on parchment could not transform the aspirations of peasants and workers into reality. Two very basic problems stood in the way. The first was the nature of the legislation itself. The second problem was the conflict between the goals expressed in Articles 27 and 123 and the social, economic, and political interests of the men to whom the task of enforcing that legislation would fall.

With the best of good intentions, the radical liberals at the Constitutional Convention had drawn up a set of labor laws that unfortunately did not relate to the social and economic conditions of Mexico in 1917. Deeply influenced by the advanced proposals of European and North American labor movements, the authors of Article 123 adopted as their own some of the most progressive ideas that were current in capitalist countries at that time. But Mexico was far from comparable to countries like Britain and the United States in terms of her political and economic structure, industrial base, capital reserves, and the level of political consciousness and organization of her work force. Mexico had just emerged from a war that had divided the working class and peasantry and had devastated the economy. The men who wrote Article 123 made the mistake of trying to institute laws appropriate for societies in an advanced stage of development in a country that was recovering from war and had only just embarked on the road to capitalist development.

Thus, for example, it was unfeasible to place sanctions on child labor in an economy so backward that families relied for their survival on the pitiful wages received by children. Likewise, the establishment of minimum wage was equally unrealistic in a period when there were relatively few factories and millions eager to enter the industrial work force. Progressive labor legislation is a luxury that belongs to a fairly advanced stage of development. The problem for Mexicans was how to *arrive* at the point where progressive legislation could even be considered. And yet the labor code written into the Constitution presupposed that this stage had already been reached. As always, when abstract principles clash with an unpleasant reality, it is the unworkable, if admirable, principles which fall by the wayside. Thus, it is no surprise that Article 123 was not taken very seriously either by the postrevolutionary political leaders, nor the industrialists and businessmen who were to build Mexico's industrial base. Had they attempted to apply these impressive humanitarian laws to the conditions that then existed in Mexico, the capitalist development that these powerful groups desired would have been impossible to achieve.

In contrast, the Constitution's agrarian legislation did not conflict with the goal of capitalist development in Mexico. On the contrary, the long-term effects of land reform may encourage capitalist development. Land reform programs generally break down traditional structures, stimulate efficient utilization of land resources, move people from the backward agricultural sector into the cities where they provide a pool of cheap labor for the factories, and create internal markets for the goods of industry. The problem with Article 27 was not that it clashed with the long-run needs of capitalist development, but rather that it conflicted with the short-term, immediate interests of the men who came to power at the close of the Revolution.

The radical liberals who dominated the Constitutional Convention were never in a position to enforce the legislation they had written. It would be General Carranza, a landowner and industrialist, who would assume the presidency in 1917, and to him fell the task of enforcing the Constitution. Once Carranza was elected President, the fortunes of both peasants and workers took a turn for the worse. Carranza, who had actively sought the support of labor, now turned his back on the working class, which only three years earlier had turned the tide in his favor. The labor leaders he had once courted with promises of favorable legislation were now the victims of brutal government repression. In 1923, Carleton Beals described Carranza's administration in this way:

> ... the revolutionary elements were one by one eliminated and supplanted by politicians and unprincipled militarists. The enlightened constitutional provisions were ignored or malconstrued ... land was not distributed except in certain states where it was forcibly torn away at the first opportunity, labor not only did not receive the protection accorded it by the constitutional code, but its organizations were openly persecuted.[52]

Obstacles to Land Reform

Carranza's relationship with the agrarian movement was one of the darker stains on his political career. At the point in the Revolution when he feared the growing power of Zapata's forces in Morelos, Carranza attempted to undercut Zapata's appeal to peasants with generous overtures and concessions of his own. Thus in 1915, Carranza issued the Decree of January 6, a document that restated some

of the main points of Zapata's *Plan de Ayala*. Ironically, it is Carranza's decree that is generally taken as the *formal* beginning of the
great Mexican land reform. But, in fact, once Carranza felt secure in
his power, he turned his back on the peasants, just as he did with the
working class. He used workers' battalions to combat peasant armies,
and in 1919, Carranza personally arranged for the assassination of
Zapata and other radical peasant leaders.[53] Shortly before he was
assassinated, Zapata himself denounced Carranza's betrayal of the
peasantry in an open letter published in March 1919.

> You have betrayed the agrarian reform and taken over the *haciendas* only
> to give the property and its proceeds to your favorite generals . . . a group
> of friends are helping you enjoy the spoils of war: wealth, honours, busi-
> ness deals, banquets, luxurious and licentious feasts, drunken carousing,
> orgies of ambition, of power and of blood. . . . The hopes of the people
> have been turned to scorn. . . .[54]

On the basis of his previous record, the *agraristas* felt nothing but
despair when Carranza was installed in the Presidential Palace. Although progressive legislation was on the books, without the support
of the federal government there was little hope that politically weak
and divided peasantry could successfully petition for land grants in
accordance with the procedures stipulated in Article 27. And government support would not come as long as Carranza, a landowner himself, remained in power.

And so, despite official acceptance of agrarian reform as a main
tenet of the Revolution, sporadic land distribution took place on
only a token scale over the next twenty years. Although militant
agrarista organizations survived in some areas of Mexico,[55] the
armed opposition of landowners was usually sufficient to repress
these peasant movements in their efforts to force the application of
land reform legislation.

The landholders' opposition to the implementation of agrarian
reform took a variety of forms. The most brutal was the use of
private armies or police forces called "white guards." The white
guards, conservative peasants in the pay of the landlords, specialized
in the assassination of *agrarista* organizers and the destruction of
crops and homes belonging to peasants bold enough to seek land
grants under the agrarian law. Because the land reform law stipulated
that only peasants living in "population centers" of a certain size
were qualified to petition for land grants, the white guards often

scattered the population of whole villages by burning houses, diverting river waters to demolish adobe huts, or by killing off so many villagers that the number required for the petitioning process would not be reached. If these methods failed, landowners blacklisted those peasants who had enrolled their names on an agrarian petition, and these unlucky peasants would have to leave the region to find work.

In their fight against land reform, the landowning class found an ally in the Catholic Church. In September 1922, a peasant league in the state of Durango filed the following report with the Archbishop of the state:

> Father Reyes of Gómez Palacio is so violently anti-*agrarista* that he refused to administer the last rites to Eulalio Martínez, merely because, in life, he had been an *agrarista*.
>
> Father Santiago Zamora of Mapimí sustains on every occasion that taking possession of idle lands is theft, and the government that authorizes it, as well as the peasants and their families who benefit from it, are bandits.
>
> The priest of Nazas, Manuel Gallego, is an avowed protector of the *hacendados* of that region, whom he serves unreservedly, attacking Article 27 of the Constitution within and outside of the church.
>
> Father Margarito Barraza, formerly of the Hacienda of Dolores, now of El Rodeo, has preached incessantly against agrarianism, and has publicly declared that all members of the Agrarian Committee of El Rodeo shall be without benefit of clergy even in the hour of death.
>
> Anastasio Arellano, curate of Peñon Blanco, threatened the Secretary of the Agrarian Committee, telling him that upon all who touched the lands of Pablo Martínez del Río would fall the "curse of God." . . . Father Arellano is sold body and soul to the owners of the Hacienda de Catalina, which has resulted in his possession of an automobile and other properties which do not harmonize with the humility and poverty which Jesus preached.[56]

The effect of the Church's anti-agrarian position was powerful enough in a northern state like Durango, which lacked a strong Catholic tradition. Much greater was the effect of clerical opposition in various western and southern states of Mexico, where the influence of the Church over the peasantry had always been a determining factor in the social and political life of the region.

In 1926-7, Ernest Gruening studied the agrarian problem in Mexico.[57] While travelling in the state of Guanajuato, he interviewed a priest who was attached to a large *hacienda,* and ministered to the community of peons who worked the *hacienda* lands.

"Have these workers been offered their communal lands?" I asked one of them.

"They have not, they do not want them," replied the priest.

"Why do they not want them?" I asked. "It seems strange that anyone should not want something that is given for nothing."

"They would not know how to take care of the lands if they got them," said the priest.

"Why not, aren't they working the land now?" I inquired.

"They could work the land, but they wouldn't know anything about buying and selling, and they would lose the money they had put in for seed and tools if they could ever get enough together to buy these."

A few minutes later, Gruening approached one of the peasants laboring in the fields of the *hacienda,* and the following exchange took place.

"You people haven't received any *ejidos* in this region?"

"No, senor, we haven't."

"Is it because you don't want them?"

"Yes, we want them, but—"

"But what?"

"If we got them, we wouldn't be able to take care of them."

"How is that? Aren't you working the land now? How would it be any different if you were working your own plot?"

"Oh, working the land would be the same, but we poor people wouldn't know anything about selling our product, and we would lose whatever we had paid for seed and tools."

"Who told you that?"

"The boss."

"Anyone else?"

"The padre."

As Gruening's account indicates, the alliance of the priest and the landlord would not have functioned so effectively to block land reform had it not been that a great many peons had accepted and internalized a concept of themselves as inherently inferior and destined by nature to live in servitude. Linked by personal and paternalistic bonds to a powerful landlord, many peasants were reluctant to cast off the ties that bound them to the *patrón* and his estate. In contrast with the agricultural worker who sold his labor for a cash wage, peons who were attached to the *hacienda* and given a hut or a subsistence plot in return for labor enjoyed a kind of security as their reward for loyalty to the landlord.[58] The *patrón* might be a harsh and cruel father figure, but his paternalism was at least a familiar arrangement to the peasant, accustomed all his life to play the role of dependent.

> In the minds of the labor force, the person of the *hacienda* owner—who mediates between them and the outside world—may also come to represent the *hacienda* itself: his well-being may seem a validation of their collective effort. . . . Once such a system becomes established, its functioning may become essential to the feeling of security of those who must live in terms of it. Disturbances of the system, whether due to changes in the position of the worker or of the owner, tend to be felt as threats to a way of life.[59]

Given the security provided by the known, if oppressive, condition of dependent peon, we should not be surprised that many peasants did not push harder to obtain the ejidal lands to which they were entitled under agrarian law.

Yet another barrier to the implementation of land reform was the extensive foreign ownership of land in Mexico. At the outbreak of the Revolution, more than 40 percent of Mexican agricultural land was owned directly and indirectly by American citizens.[60] By 1923, the pattern of land ownership still heavily favored foreigners; approximately one-fifth of all private agricultural property belonged to foreigners. Americans owned the greatest amount (about 41 million acres), followed, in order, by Spanish, British, German, French, and a variety of other foreign landowners and landowning companies.[61] Most foreign landowners enjoyed the full support of their own governments, which were always ready to apply pressure to prevent any change in the land tenure pattern.[62] Like domestic landowners, the foreign companies built their own police forces, maintained close ties with federal forces, and at times went in for sharp diplomatic arm-twisting to protect their property from expropriation.

All of these obstacles to land reform were compounded by the lack of commitment or enforcement at the national level. Although the mandate for land distribution was clear, neither Carranza, nor Obregón, who followed him in the presidency (1920-1924), nor Plutarco Elias Calles, who followed Obregón (1924-1928), had any desire to carry the program forward. These men were or had become large landowners in the North of Mexico, and they were supported by large landowners from all parts of the Republic. It was in their personal interest to leave the large landholdings intact. And these men ruled Mexico until 1934. Indeed, their hegemony over the Mexican political scene was so extended, and so complete, that they came to be known as the "northern clique" or, more solemnly, as the "northern dynasty."

The Northern Dynasty

This group held power for nearly two decades. First came Carranza, who called himself the "First Chief of the Revolution" and exercised political power during four critical years. In May of 1920, Carranza tried to impose his own successor, but he was driven from office by a military junta led by Obregón and Plutarco Elias Calles, a *carrancista* general from the northern state of Sonora. Carranza fled from Mexico City with 50 million pesos of the national treasury, but was assassinated before he could reach asylum in the United States. The junta gave the job of "acting president" to another northerner who remained in the National Palace only six months, just long enough to stabilize the situation so that he could oversee the election of Obregón. Obregón, the general from Sonora who had labored so long in the shadow of Carranza, held office until November 1924. Then Obregón chose his friend Calles to succeed him and, in this way, the hegemony of the northern group was preserved. But when Calles' presidential term was up in 1928, Obregón's ambition led him to commit a very serious political error. Through all the years of military struggle and political infighting, Obregón was the one figure whose power and influence in revolutionary circles had grown steadily. He had tremendous staying power, and he thought he could reassert this power by returning to the presidency. Accordingly, he initiated a constitutional reform that would permit his reelection as president. Notwithstanding considerable opposition, the constitution was amended to permit Obregón's reelection. But before he could assume office, he was assassinated by a religious fanatic, enraged by the constraints that the northern leaders, Calles and Obregón, had imposed on the Catholic Church. "It has been generally accepted that the attempt at reelection created a favorable climate for Obregón's murder."[63]

Calles, whose political ambitions were no more modest than Obregón's, learned an important lesson from Obregón's fight for reelection and the support it cost him. Accordingly, Calles never attempted to take advantage of the constitutional amendment permitting reelection.[64] He determined, instead, to direct Mexican politics from behind the scenes, placing in office a series of puppet presidents directly responsible to him. In addition, he created for himself the title of *Líder Máximo de la Revolución* (Supreme Leader of the Revolution), and from this new position he succeeded in dominating and manipulating the incumbent presidents, while sustaining northern control over Mexican politics until 1934.

Throughout their seventeen years of political hegemony, the northern dynasty displayed considerable unity of purpose. These leaders were preoccupied with the material reconstruction of Mexico and her economic growth along capitalist lines.[65] In the field of agriculture, they were mainly concerned with the development of commercial agricultural exploitation based on large and middle sized properties. For one thing, they were determined to preserve their own large landholdings and those of their friends and associates. At the same time, they were interested in building an agricultural society based on the middle sized family farm that had flourished in the United States. Neither of these interests was consistent with the mandates of the land reform legislation of 1917, which envisioned the division of large estates into small parcels and the provision of a plot for every peasant who wished to farm the land. The contradiction between the "goals of the Revolution" as expressed in Article 27, and the goals of the strong-arm presidents who comprised the northern dynasty simply went unresolved during their period in power. And, of course, the land reform program itself was one of the principal casualties in the confusion over goals and priorities. Even Obregón, who had fought at the constitutional convention for the inclusion of specific agrarian legislation, was not energetic in implementing that policy once he came to power. The following is an excerpt from an interview with a peasant who headed an agrarian petitioning committee during the administration of Obregón. In this report he recounts a trip to Mexico City made by the committee in order to enlist Obregón's help in winning a land grant.

> Obregón offered to help us, the peasants of the Laguna. But when it came to the point, he sold out to the Chamber of Agriculture, which was made up of all the landowners around here.
>
> We went to Mexico City with all the documents they asked of us as proof with which to confront the lawyers of the landlords. I, myself, carried the documents in twelve soapboxes, and guarded them in a room. In them were decisions favorable to us, handed down by the judges in Durango. On their side, the Chamber had all the big lawyers of Mexico City, as well as Joaquín Moreno, the owner of *El Siglo de Torreón*, the

regional newspaper. We had three meetings with them and in the first it was obvious that the lawyers thought that because we were illiterate, we would not know how to defend ourselves, and they would beat us easily. They never imagined that we would present the proof we had from Durango. . . .

We gave the documents to an intermediary who passed them on to the President, Álvaro Obregón. But the lawyers, seeing that they could do nothing *legal* to stop us, slipped some money to Obregón, and accordingly, he did not act in our favor.

In the last confrontation, by way of explanation, they offered us the pretext of a law book, but when they showed it to me, I said to General Obregón, "Don't bother showing me these books of yours because I don't know how to read. I see that they have red covers, but, as for what's inside, we have never bothered much with that."

Then the government offered to pay all the expenses of our stay in Mexico City and the trip back to the Laguna, whilst the lawyers continued slipping money to Obregón.[66]

The Consolidation of National Power

It is difficult to know whether Obregón failed to act on the petition of the Durango peasant committee because he had accepted a bribe, as the peasants claimed, or because the large landlords of the region were too powerful a group to take on. In either case the unofficial policy of indifference or "benign neglect" of agrarian reform continued under Obregón and his successors until 1934. The lack of official support to peasant petitions meant that fewer than 940,000 out of a rural population of almost 12 million received small land grants between 1917 and 1934.[67] During that time Carranza, Obregón, and Calles had other matters on their minds. They were concerned principally with the consolidation of national power. They were preoccupied with the struggle to establish the preeminence of national over regional or local power, i.e. the authority of the president over hundreds of local and regional strongmen who ruled whole sections of the Republic like personal kingdoms. All over Mexico former "revolutionary generals" and their henchmen had established themselves as the political chiefs of various towns, states, or regions where their word became law.[68] Many of those whose power and prestige originally derived from victories in battle now exchanged the title of "zone commander" for that of "state governor." The essentially military structure of power remained intact and the generals at the top, Carranza, Obregón, and Calles, had the job of maintaining control and discipline over the lesser military men, the local bosses. The autonomy exercised by the regional bosses, or *caciques,* threatened to build into a centrifugal force capable of pulling apart the frail unity and peace established after the Revolution.

Thus, during the 1920s and early '30s the energies of the northern dynasty were directed towards building a strong central government. In addition to dealing with local and regional politicians, this meant curbing the power of the Catholic Church and checking the political force of nascent labor and peasant organizations. Above all, the presidents wished to prevent the renewal of armed conflict, an eventuality which was never far below the surface of Mexican politics during these years.

In the aftermath of Obregón's assassination, the need to stabilize the situation, legitimize their power, and extend and prolong the political hegemony of the northern clique was increasingly apparent to Calles. Accordingly, he gradually developed the idea of forming a political party that would provide an institutional framework for centralized rule and might solve the ever-troublesome question of presidential succession. Calles and his group could thus retain power and dictate the policy of the developing nation without running afoul of the "anti-reelection" principle. Calles himself introduced the idea of a new official party that would incorporate militant *agraristas,* labor leaders, military strongmen, regional bosses, industrialists, commercial landowners, merchants, and others—all the divergent groups currently vying for political power—within a single, all-inclusive party structure. [69] In his September State of the Union address, Calles announced his proposal for the National Revolutionary Party (Partido Nacional Revolucionario, or PNR). The PNR was to be a loose coalition of already existing regional and special interest parties. In March 1929, delegates were sent once more to the central Mexican city of Querétaro to participate in the founding of the new party. [70] The PNR was to have a structure flexible enough to permit the enthusiastic coexistence of the incredibly varied assortment of groups that collaborated in its formation. [71] Differences among the interest groups were to be resolved through broad policy decisions, and a heavy emphasis on unity and solidarity over decisive selfishness. Personal differences among leaders were smoothed over with the signing of the Querétaro Pact of Union and Solidarity in

which leaders pledged their willingness to accept the policies and
candidates of the new party, submit to party discipline and eschew
the use of armed force in the resolution of political conflicts.[72]

With Calles' initiative in 1929, an institutionalized structure was
established to resolve the problems of policy determination and
presidential succession. It is often asserted that Calles' principal
motivation in founding the PNR was to perpetuate himself in power;
to provide a mechanism through which he could remain "Supreme
Chief of the Revolution" while appearing to have relinquished power
to a successor. Whatever the designs that motivated Calles' initiative,
the result spelled irrevocable political change for Mexico. The new
official party not only began the process of legitimizing the Revolution, but it also provided the means through which a new "revolutionary" elite would continue in power up to the present time. The
structure of that party and the way it maintains and exercises its
political power are the subject of chapter 2.

2. A Ruling Party Is Formed

> Tacho Somoza, who runs Central America's
> most efficient dictatorship, confided to an
> *Excelsior* reporter last summer that he
> envied the official party and wished he
> had one of his own.
>
> Joseph C. Goulden

Few people observing the motley conglomeration of semi-independent parties, movements, interest groups, and political cliques that was the PNR in 1929 could have believed that it would develop into a unified and enormously powerful political organization. From a frail coalition held together principally by the forceful personality and political clout of ex-President Calles, the PNR evolved gradually towards institutionalization and legitimacy. By the late thirties, the PNR had undergone various changes in its internal structure and had been renamed the Party of the Mexican Revolution (Partido de la Revolución Mexicana, or PRM). By this time the political potpourri pulled together by Calles had emerged as the "official party," a ruling party linked directly to government institutions at local, state, and national levels.[1]

For all his long and checkered career as a military man, politician, and administrator, Calles is probably best remembered by Mexicans in his creative, unifying role as founder of the official party. But once this party was established, the man who did the most to shape its features and set its course was Lázaro Cárdenas.

Cárdenas Comes to Power

When the orange, green, and white sash of office was draped across the chest of Lázaro Cárdenas, few Mexicans realized that the inauguration of this young general from western Mexico would mark a definitive break with the past. Cárdenas had come to the presidency through the familiar route of military service and political loyalty to the northern dynasty. At sixteen he had left his native Michoacán and walked halfway across the Republic to join the forces of General Calles. As a soldier he rose quickly through the ranks of the Constitutionalist Army, and by the age of twenty he held the post of lieutenant colonel; at twenty-seven, he was a general. Calles remembered him as a loyal and dutiful officer, and accordingly, after the Revolution he appointed Cárdenas to serve as governor of Michoacán.[2]

It was during his term as governor (1928-1932) that Cárdenas began to distinguish himself as a progressive force within the Calles camp. He initiated a serious land reform program, distributing 350,000 acres of hacienda lands to 181 peasant villages. He encouraged the formation of peasant leagues throughout the state, and in so doing won for himself the vigorous support of national peasant organizations such as the Partido Nacional Agrarista. Along with his agrarian program, Cárdenas' social reforms, especially the commitment to popular education he demonstrated with his construction of technical schools explicitly designed for Indians and for working class women, earned him the respect of the most progressive men within the PNR.[3]

In the early thirties these progressive elements began to coalesce behind Cárdenas as a candidate for president of the Republic. The politicians who rallied behind Cárdenas were those who were most frustrated by *callista* corruption, by Calles' concessions to foreign capital, and the anticlerical demagoguery and ultrarevolutionary rhetoric used by Calles to cover his regime's failure to provide concrete benefits to the peasants and working class.[4] In Cárdenas, leftists saw a man who was honest, popular, and clearly concerned with social transformation. What made Cárdenas a particularly attractive candidate was that while demonstrating his commitment to social justice, he had managed to retain his legitimacy as a loyal *callista*.

Cárdenas had been one of the key military figures who stood by Calles when the chief's control over national politics was threatened by military coup in 1929. A year later, at Calles' request, Cárdenas had served briefly as head of the official party, and in 1932, as Minister of War in the cabinet of Abelardo Rodríguez, Calles' puppet president. Thus support for Cárdenas' candidacy offered progressives the possibility of shifting the course of national politics to the left while avoiding a head-on clash with Calles and his conservative clique.[5]

Calles considered Cárdenas to be an "extremist," and it is doubtful that the old revolutionary chief wanted to see Cárdenas in the presidential palace. But Calles' party was in crisis, torn by the conflict between conservative and radical forces. In effect Calles was obliged to choose Cárdenas or a man like him in order to defuse the increasingly militant demands of leftists within his own organization and to reduce the pressure from peasant and labor groups across the Republic. With the unity of the party at stake, the *jefe máximo* had no choice but to support Cárdenas to avoid a direct confrontation with progressives. All Calles could do was accede to Cárdenas' candidacy and hope to control the young general once he came to office in the same fashion that Calles had manipulated the men who had served him in the presidency from 1928 to 1934.[6]

But Cárdenas was determined to be his own man, and he soon came into direct conflict with Calles. Again and again the two leaders clashed over the issue of who would be the real head of the Mexican political system, and whose policy would prevail. Cárdenas differed sharply with Calles over the issue of labor's right to organize and strike. By June of 1936, the two leaders had broken publicly over the fact that Cárdenas refused to suppress the strikes that were spreading throughout Mexico as workers, encouraged by the new president's pro-labor sympathies, demanded the full rights guaranteed to them by Article 123 of the Constitution.[7] Calles complained loudly in newspapers and public statements that labor unrest was wrecking the economy and the very stability of the Mexican state was threatened. Cárdenas faced this charge directly, stating:

> If the strikes cause some uneasiness, and even temporarily injure the economy of the country, when settled reasonably, and with a spirit of equanimity and social justice, they contribute with time to making the economic situation more stable, since their rightful solution brings about better conditions for the workers . . .[8]

On the question of land reform, Cárdenas stood firmly by the principle that the land belongs to those who work it. In the Constitution of 1917 he found the concrete mechanism through which agrarian justice could be achieved. Cárdenas clearly meant to throw the full power of his office behind a dramatic, large scale land distribution. Accordingly, he gave encouragement and support to peasant syndicates, leagues and petitioning committees as they organized to press their demand for the immediate resolution of the "Agrarian Problem." If the peasants could articulate their demand for land, Cárdenas would respond with the full authority of his office.

Another area of conflict between Cárdenas and Calles was the issue of foreign investment. Of Calles' position, one observer wrote, "perhaps not since the time of Díaz had any leader made so firm a defense of foreign capital."[9] Cárdenas, on the other hand, was determined to set limitations on foreign ownership of Mexican resources and infrastructure. In the course of his first years as president, Cárdenas locked horns with Calles over this issue.

As Calles felt his power slipping away he regrouped his forces to attack the man he had set in the presidential chair. But Cárdenas outmaneuvered him by organizing the National Committee for Proletarian Defense. Cárdenas brought tens of thousands of workers and peasants into this popular militia, trained to defend his government against coup or insurrection.[10] Under this program, arms were eventually distributed to 60,000 peasants who constituted a "rural reserve," organized to defend Cárdenas and the land they would receive from him.[11] Leaders of the National Committee for Proletarian Defense openly denounced Calles, labeling him a traitor to the Mexican Revolution and as an enemy of the working class.[12] With the backing of a popular militia, Cárdenas began to feel more secure in his position. Thus, when the Calles-Cárdenas split reached its climax in 1936, Cárdenas was able to take decisive action. In the spring of 1936 he learned that Calles was orchestrating an elaborate military coup, and so Cárdenas immediately ordered the ex-president's expulsion from Mexico along with other prominent callistas.

Once rid of Calles, Cárdenas still had to cope with the old callista machine and its supporters throughout the Republic. Calles' strength had rested to a large extent on the backing or reluctant cooperation of regional strongmen.[13] Some of these regional chiefs could be won over to the Cardenas camp by the offer of direct and significant participation in the reform movement of the new regime. In the case of those regional chiefs who would not support Cárdenas, a clear effort was made to deprive them of their peasant following by incorporating their supporters into a unified peasant confederation sponsored by Cárdenas.[14]

The problem facing the President was more than the question of winning the cooperation of regional strongmen or ousting Calles' people and replacing them with his own. Rather, Cárdenas had to build a whole new coalition of support because the policies that he intended to push would inevitably bring down on his head the full opposition of conservative forces in Mexico.

The policies Cárdenas hoped to pursue were not revolutionary; they were reforms aimed at improving, rather than overturning, an existing situation. On this point there was a great deal of confusion on both the right and left during the Cárdenas' years. Cárdenas' speeches and those of his top ministers were full of talk of "state ownership of the means of production," "worker cooperatives," and "workers' democracy as the first step towards socialism."[15] In several addresses, Cárdenas threatened that factory owners who did not comply with the rulings of government arbitration boards would have their property expropriated and nationalized "for the good of the nation." He asserted that it was the role of government to "intervene in the class struggle on the side of labor which was the weaker party." Yet, only weeks later Cárdenas would turn around and state, "The working classes know that they cannot appropriate factories and other instruments of work because they are not, for the time being, either technically fitted for management nor in possession of the financial resources needed for the success of an undertaking of such magnitude."[16] And in February 1936, Cárdenas went on to reassure capitalists that, "The government desires the further development of industries within the nation since it depends upon their prosperity for its income through taxation."[17]

While Cárdenas' rhetorical turnabouts confused his contemporaries, in retrospect it is clear that the policies he had in mind were inspired by the doctrines of socialism, but were in fact piecemeal reforms rather than revolutionary transformations. Cárdenas accepted the division of Mexican society along class lines. He viewed his task as one of "conciliation" among conflicting classes in the interest of "national progress." For Cárdenas, the plight of the exploited groups in Mexican society would be remedied through

political and legal action on the part of the state. Social contradictions would be mediated by the government in such a manner that
the state itself would act to protect the interests of peasants and
workers rather than permit the masses to take justice into their own
hands and eliminate their exploiters.[18]

> Evidently Cárdenas felt that while class conflict certainly existed, for the
> good of the country, class struggle should not be allowed to overflow into
> the liquidation of one of the contendors. And why for the good of the
> country? Simply, because class struggle without restraint was, for him,
> anarchy, and—this was decisive—because he considered the capitalist class
> to be necessary for the progress of Mexico.[19]

Thus Cárdenas was not setting out to destroy the bourgeoisie. He
was, rather, attempting to shake up a social, political, and economic
structure that had grown rigid since the Revolution. He had to force
the bourgeoisie to yield some of its power so that some desperately
needed reforms could begin. Far from building socialism, Cárdenas'
reforms were calculated to improve the conditions of peasants and
workers enough to establish the "social peace," the climate of political stability, which would permit capitalist development to proceed
in Mexico. Cárdenas was interested in fostering a particular kind of
capitalist development; his plan involved heavy government intervention and control in all sectors of the economy.[20] But, notwithstanding the active role foreseen for government, Cárdenas' vision of
Mexican development was essentially a capitalist one.[21] "The
government's design was to develop a capitalism which was Mexican-
owned, tax-paying, and beneficial to the nation."[22]

But even the moderate reform implemented by Cárdenas would
meet with fierce resistance from the interest groups entrenched since
the Revolution. Landowners, industrialists, bankers, and foreign capitalists had thrived during the years that Carranza, Obregón, and Calles
held power. These bourgeois interests monopolized power and privilege in Mexico. They were unwilling to permit even the most modest
reforms (such as piecemeal land distribution or slightly improved
working conditions) much less the more significant reforms (large-
scale land reform and nationalization of foreign-owned petroleum
and railway companies) that Cárdenas wanted to carry out.

Cárdenas was working against incredible odds. Once he took
office, Mexican capitalists began investing abroad or accumulating
their profits in foreign bank accounts. Foreign capitalists began

withholding their funds as fear of labor militancy and possible expropriation of their holdings made investment in Mexico increasingly unattractive. The press, controlled by conservative money, vilified Cárdenas and his administration. The middle class was injured by inflation, frustrated by the feeling that they would be left out of the social transformations directed by this new administration, and profoundly frightened by what they regarded as Cárdenas' communist leanings. The President's support for the Spanish Republican cause and his policy of open immigration of Spanish Republican refugees was taken by middle class Mexicans and devout Catholics of all social classes as proof that Cárdenas meant to establish in Mexico a "godless" state modeled on the Soviet Union.[23] Finally, during these years, fascism was on the rise in Mexico as it was in Europe.[24]

Faced with this array of destabilizing forces, Cárdenas had to move decisively to build a new power coalition to back his regime. His government was threatened by the bourgeoisie, diehard partisans of Calles, organized fascist groups and the specter of economic reprisals by the American and British governments. And he had not yet secured the solid support of socialists, communists, and organized labor groups. This predicament prompted him to make a direct appeal for the backing of workers and peasants.

A New Power Coalition and the Restructuring of the Official Party

To gain the necessary support, Cárdenas moved ahead with a program of liberalizing labor legislation, strengthening peasant and labor unions, and uniting each under the forceful leadership of men he trusted to support his regime. The appeal for the allegiance of the peasants and workers, in many cases an appeal made over the heads of their old guard *callista* leaders, was an essential step for Cárdenas in the formation of the supportive coalition needed to back up his reform administration.

In order to consolidate the support he was winning, Cárdenas set about reorganizing the official party in a way that would strengthen the relative position of the peasant and labor groups. A first step was to draw peasant groups out from under the domination of labor unions and establish them as a separate political force within the party. The separation of peasants from labor was consistent with Cárdenas' policy of never relying completely on the political loyalty of any one group.[25]

Cárdenas' next step was to institutionalize peasant and worker participation in his government by creating a role for the two groups within the official party. In December 1937, Cárdenas dissolved the PNR and called for the formation of a "new" revolutionary party to be named the PRM, the Party of the Mexican Revolution. The reorganized party featured a four sector structure. Each of the party's sectors, peasant, labor, military, and the so-called "popular" sector, were to play an equal role in making national policy. According to Cárdenas' vision of how the new political coalition would operate, the party's candidates for public office would be drawn in fairly equal proportions from all four interest groups. Local party organizations would caucus before any local, state, or national election to determine the number of candidacies to be allotted to each of the sectors.[26] Once the nominees were selected by this process their electoral victory was all but assured as all four sectors closed ranks behind the party's chosen candidate.[27] With peasants and workers chosen by their sector leaders to stand for election on the official party ticket, Cárdenas anticipated that the interests of the masses would be safeguarded by members of their own class who had been elected to public office. By providing for the protection of peasants' and workers' interests and by vastly increasing their influence within the political system, Cárdenas hoped to build a base of support for the land reform program and the nationalization of railroads and petroleum that he would administer during his administration. In short, he hoped permanently to redefine the balance of power in Mexican politics, giving far greater weight to peasants and workers.

The sectoral organization of the official party was the keystone of Cárdenas' new power structure. For this reason it is worth examining each of these sectors more closely.

The Labor Sector

Cárdenas' initiative towards labor was not the first occasion on which union leaders had been asked to lend the support of their movement to a national political figure in return for increased influence in the formation of government policy.[28] As we saw in chapter 1, Carranza had exuberantly pledged that "labor would enjoy special benefits once hostilities ceased."[29] But far from reaping a harvest of special benefits, the workers found that even the most basic rights guaranteed to them under the Constitution of 1917 were ignored by the postrevolutionary governments. The House of the Workers of the World was shut down by government order and its membership and activities suppressed. The House was replaced by a new labor organization, the Regional Confederation of Mexican Workers (Confederación Regional de Obreros Mexicano, or CROM) directed by men loyal to the Carranza regime. When Obregón broke with Carranza, he, in turn, called upon the membership of the CROM to back him in his bid for national power.[30] In the power struggle that followed, the CROM swung its support to Obregón. And yet again, the workers had little concrete benefit to show for their intervention and participation in national politics. The Obregón regime did not provide the working class with the benefits for which they had struggled so long.

Thus when it came time for Cárdenas to make his appeal for working class support, he had to find some way to convince labor leaders that he did not intend to repeat the old patterns of deceit and betrayal. He had to back his rhetoric with some kind of concrete action. But Cárdenas was in no position to give real power to the working class. What he did do was to give government backing to the dynamic Marxist labor organizer, Vicente Lombardo Toledano. Within a year, Lombardo Toledano was able to persuade tens of thousands of workers to organize unions, to join government organized unions, to bring previously independent syndicates into federation with one another, and finally to affiliate with the government sponsored Mexican Workers Confederation (Confederación de Trabajadores de México, or CTM).

The CTM was then to form the base for the labor sector of the official party. Although other labor organizations joined the party independently of the CTM,[31] the giant confederation dominated labor sector politics. With full government support, the CTM continued to expand its base until Cárdenas' administration came to an end in 1940.

"When Cárdenas left office, the CTM lost not only much of its stimulus from the presidency, but also much of its ideological militancy."[32] The rhetoric of "class struggle" was abandoned in favor of an ideology that championed "national unity." The short-lived tradition of militant labor struggle gave way to a policy that stressed collaboration with government and industry to hasten the economic development of Mexico.[33] Thus, throughout the forties and fifties, the CTM led the labor sector into a policy of ever increasing cooperation with government and big business. And as this process accelerated, the more militant labor unions in the Confederation—the mining, electrical, and railway workers' unions—dropped out of the organization.[34]

In the meantime, the CTM was plagued by *continuismo,* the tendency of leaders to perpetuate themselves in office. The CTM committees at national and state levels increasingly dictated the selection of leaders in affiliated unions.[35] With officers imposed from above, union rank and file found themselves powerless to remove and replace leaders guilty of bad management, dishonesty, or abuse of power. The lack of internal democracy within the labor sector was exacerbated by the fact that the old-guard CTM leaders drew ever closer to management and government as they became a monied elite in their own right. Over the years, as the same group of labor leaders continued in office, many amassed personal fortunes so large that their interests began to coincide more with those of big business than with the working class. Eventually workers within the CTM movement began to claim that they were "exploited by their own leadership." As one observer noted:

> Two situations have frequently occurred. First of all there is an alliance of union officials with management for the purpose of speeding up the worker and quelling protests. . . . Secondly, union leadership may abuse workers through the establishment of unwarranted quotas or membership dues [which] benefit leaders personally.[36]

Over the years, such corrupt practices became increasingly commonplace within the CTM. And workers affiliated with the organization are understandably dissatisfied. While the expressed goal of the labor sector has always been the unification of all Mexican workers' organizations under the official party banner, the history of this sector has been characterized by schisms and splinter movements.

The official labor movement has gradually lost its independence as an autonomous interest group.[37] As its leadership has drawn closer to government and big business, the bargaining power of the workers has declined sharply. The role of union leaders has been totally transformed. Instead of bargaining for concessions to labor, they work to assure labor support for the government. Ironically, at the same time, working class support for the government is not even so crucial to the ruling party as it was in the past. As the Mexican political situation stabilized and the threat of armed insurrection against the federal government diminished, the government came to depend less and less upon the potential military aid of the working class.[38] In terms of the balance of power within the official party, this new situation of increased political stability has meant that the influence of the labor sector has declined steadily since its heyday under Cárdenas.

The Peasant Sector

The second group that has suffered a steady decline in political influence is the peasantry. It is both tragic and ironic that the major instrument that has rendered the peasants politically ineffective is the very organization designed by Cárdenas to give the peasants genuine political power.

In June 1935, Cárdenas ordered the formal organization of a peasant sector for the official party. To form the peasant sectors, landless peons, sharecroppers, agricultural wage earners, the owners of small land parcels, and the recipients of government land grants were all incorporated into a single organization, the National Peasant Confederation (Confederación Nacional Campesina, or CNC).

Cárdenas' drive for unification of peasant groups was prompted by his apparently sincere belief that such an organization would come to represent a political force equal to that of any interest group or class in Mexican society. He calculated that millions of peasants, united in a single federation, would prove strong enough to stand up to the power of the landholding class. Whereas the landowning *patrón* had formerly monopolized political and economic power in the countryside, the new National Peasant Confederation was designed to alter that situation. Through the CNC, Cárdenas set out to break the political influence of the great landowners by creating an alternative network to replace or offset the patronage traditionally provided by the landowners.[39] In order to do this, Cárdenas tried to institutionalize a patron-client relationship through which government goods and services would come to the peasantry in return for the peasants' loyal adherence to his own regime.

Once this mutually supportive government-peasant relationship was established, Cárdenas anticipated that the CNC would develop into a compelling spokesman for peasant interests, capable of lobbying for the extension of land reform, agricultural credit, irrigation projects, and improvements in rural welfare such as electrification, schools, and medical facilities. Cárdenas had great confidence in the capacity of peasants to govern their own communities and to pressure effectively for their interests, just as he believed they could successfully cultivate any land grant that they would receive under his agrarian reform program. Nevertheless, he saw a key role for government in guiding and assisting the peasants in meeting the new challenges which would come with political enfranchisement and control of property. For Cárdenas, land distribution was not a unilateral measure taken by a progressive government. The President understood the importance of the political interaction between peasant demands and government response. It was not his place to "bestow" land upon the peasants. To be effective, agrarian reform had to come in answer to a clearly articulated demand on the part of peasants for land that was rightfully theirs. Hence, Cárdenas believed it crucial to create a climate in which peasants could organize politically. And so he promoted an institution which would give a voice to peasant organizations.

Unfortunately, the CNC did not develop along the lines envisioned by its founder. The peasantry never became a political force equal to any of the other major interest groups in the political arena. The men who succeeded Cárdenas in the presidency looked to groups other than the peasants and workers for their base of support. We have already noted that as the official party machine gained full control over national politics, it became increasingly unlikely that the government would ever need to call upon an armed peasant and worker militia to rescue itself from a military *coup d'etat*. Accordingly, the loyalty of the peasantry became marginal to the government, although government support continued to be crucial to the peasantry. And in most regions of Mexico, the mutually supportive relationship between the peasants and their national government gradually disintegrated.

In addition to the decline in the peasants' strategic importance in the years following Cárdenas' regime, the organizational structure of both the CNC and the official party have contributed to holding the peasantry in the relatively powerless position it has occupied to the present day. The membership of the CNC is made up of a variety of different kinds of peasants. Included in its ranks are landless peasants, agricultural wage workers, sharecroppers, *minifundistas,* [40] and *colonos.* [41] The bulk of CNC members, however, are *ejidatarios* [42] who are automatically incorporated into the CNC by virtue of their membership in their own ejidal community. The mass of peasants who make up the CNC's rank and file are supposed to be represented on the local level by a local peasant union or ejidal commissariat (the governing body of the ejidal community), at the state level by the State League of Agrarian Communities and Peasant Syndicates, and at the national level by the Executive Committee and the Secretary General and the CNC.

One basic problem for peasants affiliated with the CNC is that their organization has a rigidly hierarchical structure. The *ejidatarios* who form the main body of the CNC membership exercise direct influence in the organization only in the election of their local officers. These local officers who form the ejidal commissariat have some influence in elections at regional and state level. However, the ballots presented at the State Conventions are accepted by acclaim, while the state itself is prepared ahead of time by state level politicians of the official party. Only at the local level are offices filled by a voting procedure, and oftentimes serious irregularities occur in these ejidal elections. Once every three years, the subtle play of forces at the top level of the organization determines the selection of the secretary general of the CNC. Most other top functionaries are ushered into office by a unanimous voice vote at the state or national conventions.[43]

Because middle and upper level CNC officials are appointed rather than elected, the CNC functionary owes his position of power and prestige not to the peasant constituency he, in theory, is chosen to serve, but to a group of powerful state and regional politicians, many of whom are representatives of the landowning class. Thus the responsibility of the CNC officer is to the politicians who appoint him.

When we look at the way in which CNC operations are financed, we better understand the degree of control that high level politicians are able to exercise over local and regional CNC functionaries. In most states, the regional committees depend for the larger part of their budget on subsidies from the state machine of the official party. Aside from the subsidy paid directly to the CNC by the party, various government agencies pay regular extralegal subsidies to the peasant organization and provide the all-important patronage which further ties the interests of the CNC official to the government and to the government agencies. As both recruitment and financial support in the CNC flow from the top down, the CNC rank and file has no lever of control over its officers.

The relatively brief but secure tenure of the CNC official also contributes to his irresponsibility. CNC office is inevitably a patronage plum for which the recipient has waited many long years. Once installed in his position in the hierarchy, the CNC functionary may have only three years in which to exploit the financial and personal benefits which go along with the job. But, since these rewards can be bountiful, particularly when compared to the lot of the average peasant, to many people the long wait in the patronage line is more than justified by the material opportunities for social and economic improvement available during even a brief tenure as CNC officer.

Thus many of the CNC's problems spring directly from the socio-economic structure of Mexico; specifically, the lack of alternative roads of social and economic mobility open to people of peasant origin. For peasants who have so few avenues for the expression and realization of their personal aspirations, the CNC offers an important opportunity for advancement. The men who have the tenacity to climb step by step up the CNC hierarchy are generally rewarded with social and economic status of which ordinary peasants only dream.

It might seem that under this system of leadership recruitment, the CNC members would at least have the leadership services of a group of quick-witted, dynamic individuals who have managed to push their way to the head of the patronage queue. Unfortunately, however energetic, efficient, and dedicated aspirant leaders of the CNC may be in the promotion of their own careers, overenthusiasm in the representation of the peasant constituency is self-defeating to the rising CNC politicians. It is to be avoided at all costs. This is because Cárdenas' vision of a representative peasant organization has been completely distorted. Over the last thirty years the orientation of the CNC has gradually altered. It has become far more involved in maintaining the status quo of land tenure than in pushing for the extension of the agrarian reform program. Over the same period, it has changed in such a way that it no longer is an organ for the expression of peasant interests. Since 1940 the CNC, like the workers' CTM, has proved to be an instrument through which the government controls the peasantry, rather than a means through which the peasants may exercise a measure of control over their government and its policies.[44]

The Military Sector

In addition to a labor and a peasant sector, the official party of the late thirties featured a sector comprised entirely of military personnel. Incorporation of the military into the party was part of

Cárdenas' plan to reform and reorganize the army and bring it under civilian control. Military intervention or the threat of a military coup had been a constant of postrevolutionary politics up to Cárdenas' day. Enormous political power was wielded by this top-heavy military establishment, which absorbed more than one-third of the federal budget, boasted one general for every 338 enlisted men, and had supplied every president and most of the state governors since the Revolution. Cárdenas was keenly aware that the power of this conservative force would have to be reduced if his reform administration was to survive.[45]

Cárdenas' strategy to subordinate the military to civilian control involved reorganizational measures which he, a revolutionary general himself, was well equipped to undertake. He restructured the army by pushing for greater professionalism: instituting proficiency tests for commanders of all ranks, remedial training for those who failed, and competitive examinations to determine promotion. Placing a ceiling of 55,000 troops on the army and closing down marginal military installations, Cárdenas was able to cut the military's share of the federal budget from 25 percent in 1934 to 19 percent in 1938. All this he accomplished while sweetening the reorganization with pay boosts to officers and enlisted men, increased equipment and uniform allowances, and improved military housing and medical services.[46]

The other key to Cárdenas' plan to control the military was the incorporation of army men into the PRM. In December 1937 he recommended the formation of a military sector for the new official party in which the army would be represented "not as a deliberating body or as a class corporation" which would promote the interests of a "special caste," but as a group of responsible citizens.[47] On the face of it, Cárdenas was proposing to enfranchise military men and bring them into a political process to which their status had previously denied them access.[48] What he in fact accomplished with this move was to force the generals' political activities into the open and oblige them to operate in a political context in which they were constrained to share power with three other organized sectors. "We did not put the army in politics. It was already there. In fact it had been dominating the situation, and we did well to reduce its influence to one out of four."[49] Of course the military chiefs were not fooled by Cárdenas' maneuver, but they saw little alternative to acting out the citizenship role that had been thrust on them.

The life span of the military sector was brief. At no time did the sector participate in official party politics as fully as the other three sectors. For example, the military role was limited in that the sector did not take part in the nomination process at the national level, nor in state and local elections.[50] But even with limited participation, the formal incorporation of the army into the political process succeeded in reducing its tendency to intervene surreptitiously and illegally. In 1941, the same desire for civilian preeminence which earlier had made compulsory PRM membership for military personnel seem a good idea, now led Cárdenas' successor to disband the sector.[51] Soon after his inauguration, Manuel Avila Camacho dissolved the military sector, and its members either left the party to join right wing opposition movements, or were absorbed into the other sectors of the official party. And so, by the early 1940s, the official party was left with the same tri-sectorial structure it retains up to the present day.

The Popular Sector

Given the heavy emphasis that Cárdenas placed on his peasant and labor support, industrialists and businessmen regarded his administration as a terrifying threat to their interests. But, as we have noted, Cárdenas was in no position to destroy the bourgeoisie. He was trying to break their monopoly on political power and bring them under government control. Thus, while carrying forward programs favorable to peasants and workers, Cárdenas maintained contact with business interests and attempted to involve organized business groups in his administration through their formal participation in the official party. As in the case of the military, it seemed a good idea to incorporate potential enemies directly into the intraparty political process rather than simply sitting back to await their attempts to sabotage or overthrow the government. For its part, the business community responded favorably to Cárdenas' initiative. Business leaders perceived the growing concentration of power in the federal government, and they opted for a strategy of maintaining links with the national administration in order to obtain the contracts, concessions, and compromises that would favor the expansion of business and industry.[52]

Thus, when Cárdenas called for the formation of a "popular sector," a large assortment of professional, trade, civic, and business associations were formally incorporated into the official party. By virtue of their membership in these organizations, industrialists, landowners, businessmen, and a variety of middle class groups automatically became affiliated with the ruling party. Included in the "popular sector" are doctors, lawyers, teachers, and other professionals, as well as merchants, manufacturers, middle and large sized landowners, youth organizations, women's organizations, and a number of social associations. This sector is basically a federation of middle class and elite interests rather than the "popular" grouping implied by its name. Nevertheless, included in the same heterogeneous conglomeration are some skilled workers' unions and the union of government employees. Thus it is probably most accurate to say that the popular sector brings together not only middle and upper class groups, but also people whose objective interests are much closer to those of the labor sector but who, for reasons of social status, are not considered —or more significantly, do not consider themselves—to be laborers. Through their incorporation into the popular sector, skilled workers, white collar employees, managers, clerks, low level government functionaries, postal workers, and even municipal street sweepers are encouraged to identify with their employers, rather than with their own class interests.

In 1943 the groups that had been drawn into the popular sector were reorganized as the National Confederation of Popular Organizations (Confederación Nacional de Organizaciones Populares, or CNOP). The CNOP, like the peasants' CNC and the workers' CTM, operates at local, regional, state, and national levels. The secretary general of the CNOP sits on the party's Central Executive Committee, as do the secretaries general of the CNC and CTM. However, unlike the CNC and CTM, the CNOP has no legally prescribed relationship with the government. No special legislation such as the labor code or the agrarian code formally binds the CNOP to the machinery of government.[53] This lack of institutionalized restraint has left the CNOP relatively free to develop along the lines most convenient to its membership. Because membership in the CNOP and the official party is more a matter of choice for popular sector people than for peasants and labor, "its members must be continually courted and cajoled into allegiance. This gives a premium to the political skills of the CNOP leadership and creates pressures for efficiency and effectiveness that often are missing in the other sectors."[54]

The popular sector enjoys other political advantages over the peasant and labor sectors. Members of the popular sector have generally received specialized education or technical training far superior to that available to either peasants or workers. Their representatives are professional bureaucrats, technicians, lawyers, and entrepreneurs, people well equipped by background and training to lobby effectively for the sector's interests. Such people also command extensive corporate or personal fortunes which provide them with the financial means to work as vigorously and efficiently as possible to defend their political and economic interests. To the extent that crucial policy decisions are fought out within the official party, the popular sector clearly has the upper hand in terms of financial, educational, technical, and personal resources.

The result is that of the three sectors, the popular sector receives by far the greatest share of government benefits.[55] Since the creation of the CNOP in 1943, this sector has dominated the legislature. In the Chamber of Deputies the proportion of popular sector representatives has climbed steadily. The number of senators who belong to the CNOP has also increased over the years, while the number of peasant and labor sector representatives has declined proportionately.[56] Hence, the peasants and workers are underrepresented in the national governing bodies. They are also underrepresented throughout the official party apparatus. Popular sector members control the vast bulk of committee positions and political appointments at all levels of the party hierarchy. Through this numerical advantage on party committees and the preponderance of nominations and appointments it receives, the popular sector plays a role in the government which is disproportionate to its size, but not to its economic importance. Of the three party sectors, popular sector members have the greatest access to the president of the republic and the greatest influence over policy formation. Hence, party decisions on the allocation of scarce resources among the three sectors are generally highly favorable to this powerful sector.

Political Dominance of the Bourgeoisie

We know that one of Cárdenas' main purposes in organizing the various sectors of the official party was to provide the workers and peasants with some political clout to strengthen their political position with respect to the middle class and the bourgeoisie. But neither the CTM nor the CNC evolved into the vigorous representative organ that Cárdenas envisioned. To the extent that the CTM and CNC were organized to consolidate worker and peasant support for the governing party and its leaders, the two confederations have functioned with relative success. But insofar as their role is also that of representing the working class and peasantry, articulating the demands of these classes and pressuring effectively for their interests, the official party's labor and peasant sectors have been a failure. Within the official party itself, both the peasant and labor sectors have continually lost ground to the increasingly powerful popular sector. This process has accelerated since the official party was reorganized in 1946. In that year, the ruling party was renamed the Institutional Revolutionary Party (Partido Revolucionario Institucional, or PRI), and neither its name nor its basic structure has been altered since. The reorganization of the official party in 1946 did nothing to redress the imbalance among the three sectors. On the contrary, the PRI is structured in such a way that the preponderance of appointments, nominations, and patronage of all kinds continue to flow to the popular sector.

While the popular sector has come to dominate intraparty politics, the old landowners, the industrialists, the businessmen and bankers, in short, the bourgeoisie, has also strengthened and consolidated its political position outside the ruling party. The economic power of the bourgeoisie is so great that this group constitutes the most influential pressure group in Mexico. Although some crucial sectors of the Mexican economy are state owned or state controlled (petroleum, railroads, electricity), and while a variety of government credit banks play a key role in directing development, the entire public sector produces less than 10 percent of the gross national product.[57] The remaining 90.5 percent is produced by private enterprise. And among the largest enterprises, foreign-owned businesses, or those with strong foreign participation earn more than half of the total income.[58] Together, Mexican and foreign-owned enterprises wield enormous economic and political influence in the decision making process. The economic and political power of these entrepreneurs is further enhanced by the confederations, associations, chambers of commerce, and clubs which they have organized to protect their interests.[59] Giant umbrella organizations like the National Confederation of Industrial Chambers (CONCAMIN) and the National Confederation of Chambers of Commerce (CONCANACO) do not operate as members of the official party, yet they exercise great influence over PRI and government policy. In these confederations, member enterprises cooperate with one another and with their foreign colleagues to work out a unified strategy for the pressure group. The organized business community has virtually unlimited financial resources at its disposal, and is able to employ the full-time services of lawyers, technicians, and experts in every field, as well as paying full salaries to the representatives elected by the organizations to speak out for business interests. In this way the entrepreneurs' organizations have developed effective techniques for influencing legislation and administration and for modifying decisions made by the president.[60] CONCAMIN and CONCANACO "can censure the economic reports sent them by the government and, with the support of the major newspapers, propose modification of the government's economic and financial policy."[61] This high degree of organization and efficiency backed by big money gives the capitalists formidable influence above and beyond their participation in formal party politics.

In addition to the influence they exert through the popular sector of the PRI and through organized pressure groups like the CONCAMIN and CONCANACO, bourgeois interests make their influence felt in yet another critical way. Representatives of the bourgeoisie play a key role in a political elite called the "revolutionary coalition" or the "revolutionary family," which is an inner circle of extremely powerful men who have the ear of the President and advise him on all key questions of policy or succession. All other political organs in Mexico—the PRI itself, the Senate, the Chamber of Deputies, the federal and state government bureaucracies—are subordinate to the revolutionary family. So powerful is this small elite that it easily overrides the decisions of the official party and all the formal interest organizations that stand behind that hierarchy.

The exact membership of this inner circle is a matter of speculation. Probably only the members of the family themselves know for certain who belongs to the group and who among that number are the most influential members. But among those who have studied Mexican politics, there is general agreement that all living ex-presidents, the most powerful regional strongmen, the governors of the most important and richest states, the mayor of the federal district, the commander-in-chief of the army, the head of the Bank of Mexico and other important banks, the wealthiest foreign and domestic industrialists and those who control key industries, the

American ambassador, key cabinet ministers, the secretaries general of the CTM, CNC, and CNOP, the president of the Senate, the rector of the National University, and a few intellectuals of international repute may all enjoy partial or full access to the deliberations and decisions of this select policy making group. In general, the "family" consists of those men whom the president feels constrained to consult on major policy decisions.[62] The decision on who will succeed in the presidency, the choice of PRI nominees for state governors, the selection of federal senators and deputies, and the choice of party candidates for the most important political posts at national, state, and sometimes even the local level, are all decisions in which the revolutionary family plays a determining role.

Not every member of this elite is consulted on every issue, nor does each member's opinion carry equal weight.[63] Indeed it might be more accurate to speak of an "immediate family" of very influential men, and a larger "extended revolutionary family" which includes all members of this elite circle. But even the term "family" itself is somewhat misleading in that it tends to conjure up an image of a close-knit group of people who sit together around a table hammering out political decisions. In fact members of the revolutionary family may never see one another. The president does not arrive at his decisions by a show of hands or by counting votes, but rather by sounding out the opinions of family members and assuring that no particular policy or decision meets with the intractable opposition of a significant number of important family members.[64] The idea of the family conclave is to build consensus among the most important representatives of the most powerful or potentially powerful elements in Mexican society.

Members of the three party sectors, particularly members of the popular sector, participate in the revolutionary family as selected advisors to the president, but not as formal representatives of their sectors. In the deliberations of the revolutionary family, as in the decision making process in the official party, the interests of peasants and workers are underrepresented, or they are not represented at all. If and when they are consulted by the president, the secretaries general of the CNC and CTM may try to influence the selection of candidates, and particularly the choice of a presidential nominee acceptable to the peasantry and to labor.[65] However, although the president may consider the objections raised by a peasant or labor representative, in the end the preferences of these two groups are usually outweighed by the members of the revolutionary family who represent the interests of foreign capital and the national bourgeoisie.[66]

Mexican political mythology has it that the peasants and workers are the heirs of the Mexican Revolution. However, as discussed in chapter 1, the group that really emerged victorious from the Revolution was the rising middle class, the industrial and agricultural bourgeoisie, and members of the prerevolutionary elite who managed to preserve their former positions of power and privilege by declaring themselves to be "with the Revolution." During the five decades of relative political stability that have followed the Revolution, the power relationships that emerged at the end of that struggle have been institutionalized in the official party and in the extraparty pressure groups. The popular sector enjoys an advantaged position within the governing party, and bourgeois interests are preeminent in the Mexican political system as a whole. As a result, the development policies that have been promoted in Mexico over the last thirty years clearly reflect the interests of the national bourgeoisie and its foreign business partners.

3. La Vía Mexicana:
The Mexican Road to Development

The "Mexican Miracle"

Chapters 1 and 2 reviewed the process through which a bourgeoisie composed of industrialists, bankers, businessmen, and large landowners has come to rule in Mexico. This class has consolidated its power within the official party, it occupies the vast preponderance of power positions within the government apparatus, and, at the same time, exercises enormous influence through the interest associations it has formed and the direct access it enjoys to the president and top ranking government officials. Logically enough, the development policy pursued by the PRI and by successive administrations from 1940 onward have clearly promoted the interests of the dominant national bourgeoisie and their foreign business partners. This policy has brought about the rapid modernization and economic development of Mexico. So impressive has been Mexico's economic growth that Mexico is often regarded as one of the two or three outstanding models of economic and political modernization in a nonsocialist, Third World country. Indeed, it has become common to hear the development process which has unfolded since the forties described as the "Mexican miracle." In this section we will look at the indicators of growth to determine just how miraculous this phenomenon really is.

55

Although Mexico has one of the highest rates of population growth in the world (3.5 percent a year), and the total population has more than tripled from 16.6 million in 1930 to almost 52 million in 1973, during the last fifteen years the economy has grown steadily at an average annual rate of almost 6.5 percent.[1] In 1969-1970 the rate of growth reached 7.4 percent,[2] a figure so high that it was surpassed only by Japan and Finland among the nonsocialist developed nations, and a few especially advantaged countries (Libya, Korea, and Israel) in the developing world.[3] To put it another way, although the population tripled from the mid-1930s to the present, during this same period the per capita value of all goods and services produced in Mexico has nevertheless increased by more than 160 percent.[4] In 1971, production per person reached $700 per year, placing Mexico somewhere between Portugal and Spain in the economic hierarchy of nations.[5] Fifteen years ago Mexico still had to import food. But by the 1970s, Mexico had become a net exporter of food. It had also become self-sufficient in the production of petroleum products, steel, and most consumer goods.[6] In 1940, 65 percent of the population lived in the countryside. By the 1970s far more than half of all Mexicans were living in towns and cities of more than 2,500 inhabitants. The rural-urban migration has been prompted by a shift away from agricultural employment. While 65 percent of the 1940 work force labored in agriculture, by 1970 less than half were agricultural workers, and the majority of working Mexicans were employed in industry, commerce, finance, transport, communication, and services.[7] Throughout this period of rapid economic growth, population growth, and demographic shifts from the countryside to the cities and from agriculture to industry and services, the Mexican peso has remained relatively stable. Notwithstanding two periods of inflation and devaluation in the 1940s and '50s, it has been used by the International Monetary Fund and other international banking agencies to support shaky currencies in other countries. Economists who have studied the growth rate, the stable currency patterns, the rate of investment and other indicators have projected that per capita income in Mexico will reach $1,000 per year at the end of this decade.[8] Roger Hansen has noted that whether we measure Mexico's growth in aggregate or per capita terms, whether we compare the Mexican statistics with other Latin American countries or with the industrialized, developed countries of the world, whether we look only at the period from 1935 to the present or compare Mexican development with that which occurred during the period of most rapid industrial growth for each country concerned, the Mexican record is a singular achievement.[9]

The Mexican Strategy for Development: The "Trickle-Down" Theory

Mexico's outstanding rate of economic growth and steady expansion in the industrial sector is the result of a calculated strategy of development that has been pursued with considerable consistency since Cárdenas left office in 1940. This strategy is based on a "trickle-down" theory of development that focuses on the long-term aspects of economic growth.[10] The strategy presupposes that as a nation's economic output grows, some of the benefits of development ultimately reach people at all levels of society. But the distribution of the benefits of development takes place only *after* a period during which the profits of economic growth are reinvested to build an industrial base for future development.[11]

In order to sustain a rapid rate of growth, a developing nation like Mexico must raise its rate of domestic savings and investment.[12] That is, the profits that result from industrial growth must be poured back into industry. The trickle-down theory holds that if a country like Mexico is to maximize economic growth, these profits cannot be distributed to workers in the form of higher wages.

In line with this strategy, Mexican wages have risen very slowly during the post-1940 period of rapid industrialization. The slow rise in wages has not kept pace with a rapidly rising cost of living. As a result, Mexican workers have experienced a fall in real wages; that is, while their paychecks have been increased from time to time, rises in the price of food, clothing, housing, etc., have been even greater, and thus workers find that their peso buys less with each passing year.[13]

While workers' real wages have declined, the income of industrial entrepreneurs has climbed rapidly.[14] The government has placed almost no limits on profits nor on the expansion of industrialists' incomes. Naturally, government policy makers are aware that when a rise in entrepreneurial incomes accompanies a fall in real wages for workers, the gap between rich and poor grows wider. However, the growing inequality of income distribution in Mexican society has been viewed by those in power as a necessary, if unfortunate, short-term consequence of industrialization.

Taxation Policy

There are strategic reasons why the government does not step in to curb the accumulation of wealth in the hands of rich industrialists. In order to assure a supply of capital for private investment in industry, the Mexican development plan calls for a policy to provide strong incentives to both domestic and foreign entrepreneurs. Part of this policy is to maintain an extremely low rate of taxation on income received by industrialists. Taxes are low on both interest earned from investments, and the profits derived from production. Although taxation of high income groups is known to be one effective way of redistributing wealth throughout a society and narrowing the gap between rich and poor, it has not been utilized by the Mexican government. Indeed, a recent study of tax policy in Latin America revealed that Mexico imposes the lightest tax burden on her upper class of any of the eighteen countries studied.[15] And taxation on foreign-owned enterprises is so low that in foreign business circles Mexico enjoys the reputation of providing one of the most favorable investment climates in all the world.

Where the Mexican government has taxed the public, the taxes imposed tend to be regressive in that they fall with equal weight on rich and poor alike. In contrast, income tax is so light that it not only fails as a redistributive method, but it raises very little revenue for government spending. Tax evasion, a common enough practice in most countries, reaches truly impressive proportions in Mexico. One Mexican expert estimates that roughly 75 percent of the upper class manages to escape payment of the relatively light taxes levied on them.[16] They do so while those in charge of tax collection wink and look the other way. However, this and other aspects of the Mexican taxation policy are entirely consistent with the development strategy that has been applied since 1940; the government assures that entrepreneurs need not worry about heavy taxes biting into profits, and, as such, they are stimulated to make further investments in the industrial sector.

Other Incentives to Investment

Throughout the 1940s new Mexican industries were protected from foreign competition by high tariffs on imported manufactures. In the '50s import licensing, that is, government control over goods imported into the country, became the mainstay of the protectionist policy for Mexican industry.[17] This protectionist policy is part of a drive toward "import substitution." Under an import substitution program a government attempts to encourage the establishment and growth of manufacturing firms producing goods that have previously been imported from abroad. High tariffs and import licensing give Mexican entrepreneurs and their foreign business partners a strong competitive advantage over firms producing goods abroad. At the same time the government can also use licensing to restrict the amount of internal competition with which a new producer must contend.[18]

In addition to providing protection for Mexican manufactures, the government has devised other policies designed to encourage investment by private businessmen and to attract foreign capital. Since 1941 new enterprises have been granted tax exemptions for periods ranging up to ten years. Furthermore, duties paid by manufacturers on the machinery and materials they purchase abroad have been rebated to them.[19] The government has also provided credit to entrepreneurs at rock bottom rates of interest. Nacional Financiera, a government bank established in 1933, provides funds to private businessmen who would otherwise encounter serious difficulties in raising capital for investment in industry. With government backing, this credit bank has expanded into international credit markets and is able to channel foreign loans into private business. In this way low-cost capital from international sources is available to Mexican entrepreneurs through loans guaranteed by Nacional Financiera.[20]

Taken as a whole, these government policies have created a very favorable climate for both foreign and domestic private investors. "It is reported that profit rates in Mexico are among the highest in the world."[21] High returns on investment and economic stability have stimulated a steady flow of foreign capital into Mexico. One of the challenges facing policy makers is how this flow of foreign funds is to be regulated.

Foreign Investment and "Mexicanization"

Since 1940, Mexican policy on foreign investment has been a compromise between two conflicting tendencies or desires. The first is a desire to reduce or eliminate foreign economic control over the Mexican economy. Indeed, as noted in chapter 1, the elimination of foreign economic influence was a primary objective of the national bourgeoisie which led the Revolution and established the official party. At the turn of the century these people had found their own economic ambitions cramped by the dominance of American, British, and other foreign businessmen in virtually all key areas of the Mexican economy. Many representatives of the national bourgeoisie joined the Revolution in 1910 precisely to oust the foreign business-men who had gained such extensive control during the regime of the old dictator, Porfirio Díaz.

The sons of the old bourgeois revolutionaries are now the people who formulate policy in Mexico, through their role in the govern-ment, the official party, or the various influential businessmen's associations. Many of them still cherish the dream of a Mexican economy completely controlled by Mexican entrepreneurs, by men like themselves. As a group, these men share a repugnance toward the notion of foreigners, particularly Americans, holding economic power in their country.[22] Therefore, when they formulate the gov-ernment's economic policies, they are moved in part by strong desires to exclude foreign investors from a controlling role in the Mexican economy.

On the other hand, the Mexican leadership's commitment to the goal of rapid economic development has prevented them from indulging their desire to go it alone with no outside financing from the Americans or other foreign sources. Policy makers operate on the assumption that high rates of growth cannot be achieved without heavy foreign investment. Their chosen development strategy has forced them to lay aside their nationalist pride and to accept the inevitability of policies designed to attract foreign capital. In any event, American influence over policy making is so compelling and the role of American capital in the Mexican economy so crucial that the Mexican government would be obliged to make room for Ameri-can capitalists regardless of their own policy preferences.

Thus Mexican policy makers have worked out a compromise between their desire for economic independence and their need for foreign capital. Their compromise is a policy that encourages foreign investment at the same time that it subjects that investment to cer-tain nationalistic restrictions. It is a policy of so-called partnership through which foreign capital is obtained while control over its use supposedly remains in the hands of Mexican nationals. The name given to this policy is "mexicanization."

Mexicanization divides all industries into four categories: The first are fields reserved exclusively for the state. These include all key public services such as railroads, telegraph, postal service, and electricity. The oil industry and primary processing of petrochemicals all fall into this category, but concessions are granted by the government to private firms. The second category includes fields reserved for Mexican investors such as broadcasting, automotive transport, and gas. The third category covers fields in which foreign ownership is limited to 49 percent. Insurance, advertising, publishing, cinema, domestic transport, food processing and canning, soft drinks, basic chemicals, insecticide, fertilizer, mining, agriculture, and livestock all belong to this category. The fourth category covers all fields in which foreign capitalists are free to invest without restraint.[23]

Mexicanization policy requires that Mexican nationals hold majority ownership of enterprises in certain key sectors of the economy. The industries to which this restriction applies are defined by law. However, the interpretation and application of the legislation (i.e., which enterprises fall into which category) is left to the Mexican executive, and there is considerable leeway for the president to determine where and when mexicanization restrictions will be applied. It is precisely this flexibility that leaves foreign firms so much room for maneuver. The discretionary power allows the government to accept or reject foreign capitalists' contentions that they should be exempt from restrictions. The methods of persuasion used by foreign firms range from simple, straightforward payoffs, to diplomatic arm-twisting, to threats that they will withdraw their proposals for creating thousands of jobs unless they are permitted to create them on their own terms.[24] In 1972, for example, Chrysler Corporation threatened to pull out of Mexico completely unless it was given leave to acquire full ownership of the failing enterprise it had previously shared with Mexican capital.[25]

As a result of the pressure they exert and the loopholes that are left open, many favored foreign industries manage to escape mexicanization limitations entirely.[26] Several of the largest firms in Mexico—General Motors, Ford, General Electric, Anderson Clayton, Monsanto, and Admiral, to name a few—are entirely owned by American interests. In some cases these U.S. firms have made their investments in sectors where Mexican partnership is not required. In other cases, their continued activity in the Mexican economy has been considered so important that the government has simply chosen to look the other way and ignore violations of the mexicanization principles.[27]

Sometimes, despite their efforts to prevent it, foreign firms are forced to mexicanize, that is, to sell majority control of an enterprise to Mexican investors. When a foreign owned company is faced with the prospect of mexicanization, there are a number of ways in which it can comply with the law by selling a majority of its stock to Mexican citizens, and at the same time retain control of the enterprise. Thus many foreign firms have developed a variety of techniques to evade the mexicanization requirements. Some of the favorite methods include:

1. Spreading the stock among a group of Mexican investors so numerous that none of the Mexicans is able to challenge the foreign company's controlling block of stock.

2. Retaining control of the company's management through a special management contract.

3. Retaining control by becoming the main purchaser of the goods produced by the "mexicanized" firm (e.g., DuPont owns only 33 percent of Química Flúor, but is the major customer of the chemicals produced by Química Flúor).

4. "Selling" the Mexican stock to a trusted Mexican investor or issuing the stock to the public without issuing voting rights to the public.

5. Paying a Mexican businessman for the use of his name as a majority Mexican partner.[28]

Circumvention of the mexicanization requirements is facilitated by the fact that there is a great deal of money to be made by Mexican businessmen who are willing to lend their names and influential connections to help foreign firms gain or retain control over enterprises in Mexico. This is a symbiotic relationship: the foreign investors need the collaboration of their Mexican "partners" and stand to realize enormous profits with the help of a Mexican "front man," while the Mexican "name-lender," (*prestanombre*) is normally well paid for his cooperation. However, the relationship between the Mexican front man and his American partners can be as hostile as it is mutually profitable. In Carlos Fuentes' novel *The Death of Artemio Cruz,* the protagonist is engaged in such activities and has increased an already substantial fortune by fronting for American firms who wish to circumvent the restrictions on the foreign ownership of natural resources. We come upon Cruz as he meets in his Mexico City office with two American businessmen who seek his aid (and specifically the use of his name) in obtaining concessions to exploit sulfur deposits along the Mexican Gulf Coast.

Boiling water would be injected into the deposits, the North American explained, and would dissolve the sulfur which would be carried to the surface by compressed air. He explained the process again, while his compatriot said that they were quite satisfied with the exploration, . . . Cruz, at his desk, tapped his fingers on the glass and nodded, accustomed to the fact that when they spoke Spanish to him they believed he did not understand, not because they spoke it badly, but because he would not understand [the scientific details] in any language. . . . One North American spread the map on the desk as he removed his elbows, and the other explained that the zone was so rich that it could be exploited to the limit until well into the twenty-first century, to the limit, he repeated, until the deposits ran dry. . . .

The North American winked an eye and said that the timber cedar and mahogany, was also an enormous resource and in this, he, their Mexican partner, would have one hundred per cent of the profit; they, the North Americans would not meddle, except to advise continuous reforestation. . . .

Then [Cruz], behind the desk stood and smiled, hooked his thumbs in his belt and rolled his cigar between his lips waiting for one of them to cup a burning match and hold it to him. He demanded two million dollars immediately. They questioned him: to what account? For although they would cheerfully admit him as their Mexican partner for an investment of only three hundred thousand, he had to understand that no one could collect a cent until the sulfur domes began to produce. . . .

[Cruz] repeated quietly, those are my conditions, and let the North Americans not suppose that they would be paying him an advance or anything of that sort: it would merely be what they owed him for trying to gain the concession for them, and indeed, without that payment, there would be no concession: in time they would make back the present they were going to give him now, but without him, without their front man, their figurehead—and he begged them to excuse his frank choice of words—they would not be able to obtain the concession and exploit the domes.

He touched a bell and called in his secretary who read, rapidly, a page of concise figures, and the North Americans said okay a number of times, okay, okay, okay, and Cruz smiled and offered them whiskies and told them that although they might exploit the sulfur until well into the twenty-first century, they were not going to exploit him for even one minute in the twentieth century, and everyone exchanged toasts and the North Americans smiled while muttering "that s.o.b." under their breath.[29]

Cruz, like real-life Mexican businessmen, is willing, for a price, to use his influence in government circles to win his American partners the concessions they desire, and to protect their investment from nationalization by the government. It is a mutually beneficial arrangement, and part of what makes Mexico such an inviting field for foreign investors eager for both high profits and maximum stability. " 'Mexicanization' has its bright side for foreign companies: they become eligible for generous tax and import duty exemptions, are virtually assured of immunity from nationalization or expropriation, and have greatly increased opportunities for expansion."[30] American businessmen have long recognized the advantages offered by Mexico as a field for investment, and American investment in Mexico has expanded with each passing year.[31] Just in the period 1950 to 1966, direct American investment in Mexico grew from $286 million to almost $1.2 billion.[32]

The Emphasis on Capital Intensive Production

One consequence of the heavy flow of foreign investment into Mexico has been the importation of advanced technology along with foreign capital. The trend of government policy has been to encourage modern, highly mechanized means of production because this type of production is generally believed to result in higher rates of capital accumulation leading, in turn, to higher rates of growth. Stimulated by government loans, Mexican and foreign entrepreneurs have built modern factories outfitted with equipment imported from industrially advanced countries, particularly the United States. Indeed, 80 percent of the goods imported into Mexico are machinery, chemicals, or semiprocessed manufactures produced in the United States. Mexico has become the United States' leading customer in Latin America, and ranks sixth among all nations purchasing American-made goods. While the prices of the raw materials which Mexico exports to the United States have declined steadily over the last twenty years, the cost of machines and manufactures supplied to Mexico by the U.S. has risen. The result of this disparity has been an increasingly unfavorable balance of trade for Mexico with respect to the United States.[33] Thus, the Mexican government has gone heavily into debt to finance the purchase of the modern machinery with which Mexico's new factories are equipped.[34]

In addition to putting Mexico heavily in debt to American and international banking agencies, the import of modern industrial equipment has had disastrous consequences on an already serious problem of unemployment. The machinery purchased abroad is designed for economies in which the cost of labor is relatively high and labor-saving devices are at a premium.[35]

In a country like Mexico where there is a scarcity of capital and a plentiful supply of workers, it might seem logical that industrialists would search for production techniques that emphasize the use of manpower ("labor intensive" production) rather than machines ("capital intensive" production). But Mexican industry is so closely tied to foreign capital that Mexican factories tend to be designed as branch plants of North American, European, or Japanese firms. The same technology applied at the parent plant in Pittsburgh, Hamburg, or Osaka is applied in the Mexican plant. There has been very little experimentation in Mexico with labor intensive forms of production. Both Mexican and foreign capitalists find it more profitable to invest in machinery than to rely on the labor of human beings. It may be that some experimentation with labor intensive techniques would create more jobs in Mexican industry and ultimately improve the economic and social conditions of the Mexican working class. But the welfare of the working class does not concern either the foreign or the Mexican capitalists, except insofar as higher incomes for workers expand the internal market for the goods produced by modern industry. What concerns the capitalists, of course, is higher profits. And higher profits are realized with greater certainty and ease when sophisticated machinery is employed in place of people.

As we might expect, the result of a development policy that emphasizes capital rather than labor intensive production is that employment has not kept pace with industrial growth. As the industrial sector has expanded in Mexico, the number of laborers added to the work force each year has declined. That is, the industrial work force has grown at a slower rate than industrial output.[36] Each year about 650,000 new people enter the work force. But the number of jobs available in industry has not grown sufficiently to absorb even these people, much less the additional agricultural workers who would have to be absorbed into industry if overpopulation and unemployment in the countryside is to be reduced.[37] Estimates on unemployment vary, because the official statistics tend to disguise much of the problem. However, most reliable sources indicate that as much as 40 percent of the work force is chronically unemployed.

When unemployment is high and the supply of labor overabundant, the surplus of available workers tends to keep wage levels very low. Lower wages, of course, mean a lower standard of living for workers and higher profits for the industrial entrepreneurs. And higher profits for industrialists, as we have noted, is a key part of the Mexican government's strategy to stimulate private investment. In countries where labor unions are militant and independent of government control, it is difficult, if not impossible, for the political elite to pursue a development program in which wage increases are held to a minimum. But when the vast majority of labor unions are incorporated into a single labor federation like the CTM which is neither militant nor independent of government control, this type of development is quite feasible.

A relatively tiny proportion of the labor force is organized into certain unions which constitute an "elite" within the working class. These few unions (petroleum workers, electricians, railroad workers) have a long tradition of militancy, and have managed to win wages that are substantially higher than those earned by any other sector of the Mexican labor force. But the aggressive tradition of the petroleum workers, electricians, and railroad workers union stand out as the great exceptions within the labor movement. Virtually all other workers are forced to accept wage contracts negotiated for them by their leaders in close collaboration with the private owners of the enterprises involved. In contrast, the wage contracts of electricians, petroleum and railroad workers are negotiated directly with the government, because these are the industries that are government owned. The higher wages enjoyed by workers in the nationalized industries "appear to be the price the government is willing to pay for the loyalty and support of these groups of workers in the name of the whole working class."[38]

Government Spending

The last aspect of the Mexican industrialization policy that we must examine is the trend in government investment. If a government is determined to maximize economic growth, it must concentrate its expenditures in "bottleneck breaking" investments; that is, investments in road construction, hydraulic systems, electrification, communication lines, and so forth—investments that create the infrastructure underlying a modern industrialized economy.[39] Because private investors are generally unwilling or unable to undertake projects that yield low profits in the short run, the task of building an infrastructure usually falls to the government. Government spending on infrastructure, like other aspects of the Mexican development policy, is specifically designed to create the optimum conditions for productive private investment.[40] Large government investments are made for improvements in transportation, electric power, the distribution network for petroleum and gas products, and so forth. These public outlays are aimed at creating an environment in which industrialists find it easy to establish new firms and to build productive facilities.[41]

If a government pours revenue into the construction of a modern infrastructure, subsidies to business, and credit concessions to nascent industry, it may have very little money left over to spend on essential public welfare services. It is difficult for a government to undertake the expansion of education, medical facilities, rural electrification, and public housing when the bulk of its revenue is tied up in bottleneck breaking investments to increase industrial output. For example, throughout the 1940s and 1950s while investing heavily in industrialization, less than 15 percent of Mexico's total government investment was allocated to social welfare expenditures.[42] Since 1960, just over 20 percent of all government investment has been channeled into welfare services.[43] As late as 1950, government spending on education was averaging only 1.4 percent of Mexico's gross national product. In 1967 only 6.1 percent of the total population and 19 percent of the working class was covered by Mexico's much praised social security system.[44]

Priorities

There are limits on the financial resources that any government has at its disposal. Consequently policy makers must choose among a variety of development patterns or strategies, some of which emphasize rapid economic growth, others which stress more equal income distribution and more immediate social benefits for the population. No government can spend its money in a way that *maximizes* industrial development and, at the same time, make the needs of a population of desperately poor people its top priority. A choice must be made. And in Mexico, official party leaders have consistently opted for those development policies which give highest priority to the growth of the industrial and commercial agricultural sector. Other national goals such as full employment, higher wages, more equitable income distribution, and social welfare have been given low priority as Mexico's ruling elite has pushed the economy toward ever higher levels of productivity.

The government's policy on agriculture has been consistent with its policy for the industrial sector. Let us look now at agrarian policy and examine the relationship between the development of the agricultural sector and the commitment of the PRI to a program of land reform.

Agricultural Policy

Land reform under Cárdenas.   As we know, land reform was one of the central goals of the Mexican Revolution. The incorporation of agrarian reform legislation into the Constitution of 1917 represented a great victory for peasants and peasant leaders, and paved the way for a series of agrarian laws promulgated during the 1920s and '30s. We also recall, however, that agrarian reform was carried out on only a token basis during the '20s and early '30s, and it was not until Lázaro Cárdenas came to power in 1934 that large-scale land distribution began in earnest. During Cárdenas' administration it appeared that the Mexican peasant would finally realize the great *agrarista* dream: the day when the government would provide each peasant family with a plot of land sufficient to guarantee an income adequate to meet their family needs.

Cárdenas' land reform was spectacular, not only because he distributed close to 45 million acres in five years, but also because of the type, quality, and location of the land he distributed. In the twenty years that had elapsed since the Revolution, Cárdenas' predecessors had distributed less than 19 million acres of mostly marginal land. The earlier land distributions consisted almost entirely of arid, unirrigated, steep, rocky, and unfertile land lying far from roads and markets. Large productive estates were not touched. The holdings of powerful landowners were left intact, and their economic and political power was not diminished by any of the half-hearted agrarian reform gestures made during the 1920s and early '30s.

Cárdenas' approach to land reform was far more radical. Rather than handing out marginal lands that no one had ever been able to work profitably, Cárdenas expropriated and distributed highly productive, choice lands. Almost all of the land distributed by Cárdenas was already under cultivation in modern, economically efficient plantations.

The Laguna region in north-central Mexico was the setting of Cárdenas' largest and most dramatic land reform effort. It was here, in one of the most modern agricultural areas of Mexico, that well over a million acres of efficiently organized and highly profitable cotton plantations were seized by the government under the provisions of the Agrarian Code, and distributed to 38,000 peasant families. With the assistance of three hundred government engineers and agronomists, Cárdenas carried out most of the Laguna reform in just forty days. The speed of the Laguna distribution was typical of Cárdenas' approach during his administration. When attempting to effect radical change, Cárdenas favored the swift, irreversible, political act. As in the case of the expropriation of the petroleum industry, Cárdenas made up his mind to act, and then implemented his decision with such speed that he was able to expropriate hundreds of large *haciendas* before the opposition had time to rally its forces to obstruct the sweeping changes. The extraordinary rapidity with which land reform was carried out meant that the old order was swept away while the large landowners were still reeling under the shock and could offer no concerted opposition to Cárdenas' program. [45]

The goals of land reform. Cárdenas understood the far-reaching implications of land reform in a society such as Mexico. Agrarian reform is an instrument through which land, as a productive resource, can be transferred from one part of society to another; generally speaking, from certain individuals in a society (a small number of large landowners), to other members of that society (a mass of landless peasants). But in addition to the transfer of land as a *productive* resource, land reform can operate to redistribute wealth, status, and political power within a society. In a traditional agricultural society, where land is the basis of most socioeconomic status and political power, the implementation of a thoroughgoing land reform has profound social and political as well as economic consequences. [46] Cárdenas understood this fact well enough. He was aware that in expropriating and redistributing large landholdings, he would do more than break up some large estates and divide these holdings among thousands of hitherto landless peasants. He understood that in so doing, he would transfer to the peasants new economic and political power as well as a new social status. He would lay the basis for a redistribution of economic and political power within Mexican society.

Given that Cárdenas needed the political support of the peasantry, he was anxious to assure that social and political power would in fact be transferred to the landless peasants. Therefore he was determined to promote the *economic* success of the land reform he had set into motion. In order to establish a firm economic base for the ejidal program, he (1) organized the ejidal holdings into farming collectives, and (2) set up government institutions to support the land reform program and to aid the new land recipients in their struggle to break the old patterns of dependency on large landowners.[47]

Collective agriculture.   As we have already noted, most of the land distributed by Cárdenas had previously been organized into large, modern agricultural enterprises. The basic rationale for the collective *ejido* was the desire to distribute the land of the few to the many, without destroying the productive capacity of what had been highly productive estates. Therefore, some way had to be found to break up the large estates and distribute their land in the form of small holdings, and at the same time to preserve the economies of scale that go along with large-scale enterprises. The answer to this problem was the collective *ejido*. Under this system each peasant in a peasant community was given a specific piece of land on what had been a neighboring *hacienda*. Each peasant, then, had the right to farm his small plot, but agricultural machinery, wells, fertilizers, insecticides, and other equipment were owned or purchased on a collective basis. A variety of different, more and less collectivized forms evolved to meet the needs of the *ejidatarios*. In some *ejido* communities, all the individual plots were merged into a single large agricultural unit and worked on a collective basis from sowing to harvest. At harvest time the profits from the sale of the crop would be divided according to a formula which allotted each member of the *ejido* some measure of profit corresponding to his contribution to the joint effort. On other collectivized *ejidos, ejidatarios* farmed only the plot they had been assigned, but shared in the use of the expensive agricultural equipment.

The collectivized form of agriculture featured a number of advantages. It maximized the economic use of scarce irrigation waters. It facilitated the use of heavy, expensive agricultural equipment, as well as the harvesting and marketing of the crop. And finally, it permitted the peasants—long used to executing fairly specialized tasks on the *hacienda*—to continue to work in specialized teams. As one observer explained it, the system of collectivized agriculture helped "to smooth the transition from *hacienda* to *ejido* agriculture by maintaining the existing labor organization as far as possible."[48]

Under the land reform program of 1937, a variety of supporting institutions were established to aid the newly landed peasantry. The National Ejidal Credit Bank was set up to provide credit, technical assistance, and supervision to the collective *ejidos* and to guide the *ejidatarios* in establishing their own internal administrative structures. In addition to the bank, Cárdenas oversaw the creation of schools of agricultural technology designed to train *ejidatarios* and their sons. Furthermore, the new land recipients were encouraged by the Cárdenas administration to form their own unions, councils, and associations. These organizations were specifically designed to arbitrate disputes arising within or between *ejido* communities, to protect and promote the interests of the *ejidatarios* in their dealings with the Ejidal Bank and other government agencies, and to consolidate the political support of the *ejidatarios* for the government that had given them land.

There is a considerable body of statistics recorded in the first few years of the collective ejidal experiment in Mexico.[49] These data indicate substantial economic progress for the new *ejidatarios*. After a brief period of economic disorganization immediately following the land distribution, the *ejidos* soon began to function with an efficiency that permitted them to repay the credit loans initially extended by the Ejidal Credit Bank and, in some cases, to realize substantial profits. For example, in one area of the Laguna region, the purchasing power of the peasants increased more than 400 percent during the first three years following the land reform.[50]

The downfall of the collective ejido. Unfortunately, the honeymoon period of the collective *ejidos* was all too brief. Serious troubles began for the collectives as soon as the Cárdenas administration came to an end in 1940. Some of the problems that developed were inevitable, in the sense in that they arose from shortcomings built into the ejidal system at the time that the land reform was carried out. Some of the difficulties confronted by the *ejidos* grew out of the contradictions inherent in an attempt to establish an island of socialism in a sea of capitalism. Other problems which have plagued the *ejidos* over the last thirty-five years spring from limitations on their success imposed by government policies inamicable or even hostile to their development. We will look at each of these limitations in turn.[51]

Shortcomings built into the ejidal system. Many of the problems that were to plague the ejidal system in Mexico were built into the system from the beginning. In the Laguna region, where the first large-scale land reform was undertaken, many problems arose simply from the haste with which the program was carried out. For example, the engineers and agronomists who surveyed the region miscalculated the amount of irrigated land available for distribution. Much of the land originally classified as irrigable subsequently received water only in the years when the Rio Nazas, the region's principal water source, reached its maximum height. Likewise, the boundary lines established for the new *ejidos* were only vaguely determined, and often boundaries drawn between two *ejidos* or an *ejido* and a private property overlapped, creating a situation ripe for conflict. Finally, the census carried out in 1937 to determine the number of peasants eligible for land grants included not only 18,000 peasants native to the region, but about 10,000 seasonal laborers and 10,000 strikebreakers who had moved into the Laguna during a general strike that immediately preceded the reform. Thus, once the ejidal grants were distributed, the number of people to be supported by the land had more than doubled. [52]

Other problems that developed in the Laguna reform, as well as in the land reform programs which followed, grew from deficiencies in the Agrarian Code that provided the legislative basis for the program. Several provisions in the Agrarian Code created confusion and economic waste when applied to the concrete situation of a land distribution. In addition, the Code was riddled with loopholes that permitted the large landowners to retain a substantial part of their old estates, and with these estates, much of the political and economic power they had monopolized in the prereform era. For example, the Agrarian Code permitted landowners to choose the 150 hectares he was allowed to retain as a "small private property" (*pequeño propiedad*). Naturally, he chose the part of the *hacienda* that included his house, stables, barns, warehouses, wells, irrigation canals, and the network of roads and communication lines connecting the estate with the outside world. [53]

> Sometimes [the landowner] chose irregularly shaped, narrow strips, extending outward from his buildings in order to retain what he considered to be the most productive lands. . . . In other words, the heart or hub of the *hacienda* was detached, and the remaining parts were given to the *ejidatarios*. The *ejido* was thus formed from fractionated appendages detached from the central core. [54]

During the process of land reform the unity and logic of well-organized and efficient agricultural properties were often destroyed.

The agrarian law emphasized that the unity of agricultural production should not be disrupted.[55] This was the rationale for distributing land in the form of collectives rather than autonomous individual plots. But when it came time to put this theory into practice, it was the poorest land that was distributed to peasants in disjointed blocks, while the landowning class was permitted to retain the most fertile, best-irrigated land, and virtually all of the capital equipment.

Under the agrarian law, in addition to retaining 150 hectares of his own choice land, the landowner was permitted to subdivide and sell any land that was not required for distribution to neighboring peasant communities. As a result, the *hacienda* was often "broken up" into 150 hectare parcels and "sold" to various members of the same family. This system of "parceling out" a huge estate which is then worked as a single *hacienda* unit is a common phenomenon in all regions of Mexico. It has come to be known as "neolatifundism," the creation of new *latifundia* (large landholdings). In addition to the "sale" of 150 hectare parcels to family members (including minors), it is not uncommon for neolatifundists to employ a lawyer or some other trusted person, who for a fee, lends his name to be used for a land title. As in the case of Mexican businessmen who front for foreign investors in order to circumvent mexicanization laws, an individual who lends his name to cover illegal land concentration is called a *prestenombre*, or name lender.

Where a *hacienda* was located in an area of particularly dense peasant population, it would be unlikely that the old landowner would find himself in possession of land that was not required for the agrarian reform. In such cases, the old landowner would retain only the 150 hectares guaranteed him under the Agrarian Code. But even those whose property was genuinely reduced to 150 hectares enjoyed the advantages of working a capital intensive enterprise. And in many such cases, the old landowner used his newly acquired capital resources to set himself up in a variety of agriculture-related businesses in the main cities and towns of the principal agricultural regions. In this way many of the old *hacienda* owners came to control the supply of credit, machinery, fertilizer, insecticides, and other products essential to the *ejidatarios* of the region. Hence the *hacienda* owners whose wealth had formerly been based on land ownership, entered into a powerful modern commercial class with strong ties to the industrialists. In this way many members of the old landowning class became even more closely integrated into the national bourgeoisie.

An island of socialism. The Mexican land reform, even in its most dramatic instances, did not produce a total change in land tenure patterns. Indeed, in no region of Mexico, not even during the Cárdenas years, did the land reform program bring about a thorough-going transformation. Nowhere did private landholdings disappear. On the contrary, the Mexican government was quick to reassure Mexicans and foreigners alike that the right of private ownership would continue to be respected. Wherever private property, be it land or petroleum holdings, was expropriated, some form of compensation was provided.[56] In theory, the huge estate, the *hacienda,* was reduced to a number of so-called small private properties. But, in practice, the large estate continued to be a prominent feature of the rural Mexican scene.

In the regions where agrarian reform was implemented, the Mexican countryside became a crazy quilt of agricultural collectives scattered among *haciendas.* The collective *ejidos,* with their communal labor, profit sharing, cooperative credit system, and marketing system were islands of socialism floating in a sea of capitalism. The peasants involved in this experiment were socially isolated from the surrounding environment in which the values of capitalism prevailed. Although Cárdenas attempted to carry forward a series of reforms in rural Mexico, the country was then and remains today an economy dominated by capitalist enterprise. Thus, from the very start, the collective *ejidos* were an aberrant form, struggling for survival in a capitalist society. Obviously this situation was full of contradictions that were difficult if not impossible for the collectives to resolve.

One contradiction inherent in this situation was that the goods produced on the collective *ejidos* had to compete on the market with goods produced by capitalist enterprises. While a private commercial farmer can cut production costs by laying off workers and replacing them with machinery, the numbers of workers involved in ejidal production necessarily remains constant. The collective *ejido* cannot reduce its labor force because labor is provided by the members of the collective itself.

A second contradiction between the collective *ejidos* and the larger society quickly developed as ejidal leaders sought to increase the self-sufficiency of the collectives. The early years of the agrarian reform witnessed the birth of collective credit societies, mutual crop insurance companies, marketing co-ops, collective agricultural machine stations, and a host of other cooperative enterprises. But to the extent that these cooperative and collective institutions were successful, they directly threatened the interests of the old land-owners who had converted themselves into agricultural entrepreneurs dealing in agricultural equipment, supplying agricultural credit, and marketing cotton, wheat, and sugar. Any growth of the economic independence of the *ejidatarios* automatically conflicted with the interests of this new agribusiness sector which was dominated by the old landowners and by American capital. Therefore, it is not surprising that almost all the peasant-run projects aimed at increased economic independence for the collective *ejidos* were eventually quashed by the withdrawal of government approval or government funds.

The shift in government policy on land reform. The collective ejidal system, for all its technical problems implanted at the time of the land distribution, and for all the contradictions inherent in the establishment of an isolated socialist experiment, might still have survived as a viable system were it not for the conservative swing in agrarian policy following the selection of Manuel Avila Camacho as official party candidate in 1940.

The international politics of the World War II period provided the rationale for the dramatic shift in agricultural policy away from the *agrarista* priorities of the Cárdenas years. During the 1940s, government support for the peasants' struggle against the large landowner was brought to a close. As the Mexican historian Jesús Silva Herzog explained, "Revolutionary language was toned down and substituted by new terminology. Very seldom did one hear of revolutionaries and reactionaries, but of the unity of all Mexicans."[57] With fascist forces gaining strength in Mexico (as occurred in several Latin American countries),[58] communist and socialist leaders as well as official party spokesmen expressed the belief that the national security of the country required all leftist elements to close ranks behind the constitutional government. Led by the socialist Lombardo Toledano, the CTM, for example, virtually prohibited its affiliated members from exercising their right to strike lest they jeopardize the national security and the allied war effort.[59] Tremendous stress was laid upon the need to increase production of raw materials to supply the allied forces. Avila Camacho and the ranking officials of his government seldom missed the opportunity to develop this theme in their public addresses:

> The soldier will fight until death to preserve our national territory, but together with him we will all fight, each person in accordance with his own resources and within the range of his special activities. The worker, by producing more and sensing—during all his working hours—that our survival will depend in great part upon the number and quality of what he produces. The peasant by multiplying his effort and his crops so that in these great years of trial, the plow and the spade will prove as indispensable as the gun or airplane. . . .[60]

Not only were workers and peasants urged to defend democracy in the field or in the factory, but in the name of both national unity and the need for higher production of raw materials, the expropriation and distribution of land slowed from 2,934,856 hectares per year during the Cárdenas administration to 559,262 hectares per year under Avila Camacho.[61]

Under President Miguel Alemán (1946-1952), land distribution slowed to a trickle, and the situation of peasants grew worse. Supported by the national bourgeoisie, Alemán placed overriding priority on rapid industrialization and the emergence of Mexico as an economically stable, developed country. Unfortunately these goals were pursued only at a high price.

> Rapid industrialization, an Alemán fetish, required low wages and the sacrifice of the labor force to capital accumulation. . . . Continuous protests from organized labor made no perceptible change in Alemán's philosophy or conduct. . . . For Alemán, the sacrifice of a generation of workers and peasants was a small price for making his nation materially strong, industrialized, modernized, advanced.[62]

The correlate of Alemán's emphasis on industrialization was the frankly anti-agrarian character of his regime. Alemán, like Avila Camacho before him, was obliged by his position at the head of the "Revolutionary" party to concern himself with the welfare of rural Mexico. He had to pay lip service to the "goals of the agrarian revolution," and he had to continue the pattern of heavy government investment in agriculture.[63] But for Alemán, government investment in agriculture meant investment in huge dams and other public works near the U.S. border; projects that increased the economic productivity of privately held lands.[64]

Alemán's very first legislative initiative, sent to Congress only two days after his inauguration, was a proposal for the revision of Article 27 of the Constitution. Alemán's revision of the agrarian law redefined the amount of land classified as "non-affectable"; it enlarged the size of estates that could be legally owned by single individuals.[65]

The changes in policy under Alemán were typical of the overall trend in agrarian policy in the post-Cárdenas years. Each new administration continued to repeat the rhetoric of the past, asserting the government's commitment to land reform as a "major goal" of the Mexican Revolution. At the same time, each of these administrations pursued specific policies which, logically enough, reflected the interests of the dominant bourgeoisie. Taken as a while, these policies undercut peasant gains of the past, and brought land reform to a premature end. The shift in agrarian policy over the last thirty-five years can be summarized as follows:

(1) The size of landholdings defined by agrarian law as "unaffectable" (unavailable for expropriation) has been increased.[66] At the same time, the government has ignored "neolatifundism," the illegal ownership of land in excess of the established maximum acreage. The result has been increased concentration of landholdings.

(2) As a consequence of the above, the number of acres of land distributed annually to peasants under the agrarian reform program has been drastically reduced.[67] Equally important, the quality of the land that has been distributed is markedly inferior to the land distributed during the Cárdenas land reform.[68]

(3) Militant peasant organizations, which under Cárdenas had received official sanction and had been encouraged to organize peasants to agitate for land distribution, have generally been repressed since 1940.[69]

(4) While *ejidatarios* had been encouraged by Cárdenas to work their land in collective form, later policy actively favored the breakup of the farming collectives and the formation of innumerable little groups within each *ejido*. In this way much of the political and economic potential of the collective *ejidos* has been reduced.[70]

(5) Perhaps most damaging to the future of all Mexican peasants was the fact that government spending on agriculture since 1940 has been channeled into the support of private commercial agriculture at the expense of the *ejidos* and the tiny subsistence farms (*minifundios*).

The planning of irrigation projects is typical of the government bias in favor of private commercial agriculture.

> Most [of Mexico's major irrigation projects] have been developed in the rather sparsely populated north and northwest, where large private holdings predominated over ejidal lands. In fact much of the land directly benefited by the new hydraulic systems is owned, directly or indirectly, by prominent Mexican politicians and their friends and relatives. . . . In contrast, little has been done to bring water to the heavily populated central mesa region where most of the land is held by *ejidatarios* and the owners of small private plots.[71]

Government spending on agricultural research reflects the same bias in favor of the large, commercial landholding. Over the last thirty years, government sponsored experiments have concentrated on raising the productivity of grain and cotton cultivated on large commercial estates. Techniques developed in the so-called green revolution have dramatically raised the productivity of wheat and cotton crops. But such increases are produced only with the heavy use of chemical inputs, mechanized equipment, and well irrigated land. The vast majority of *ejidatarios* have no access to these inputs and, as such, the "dramatic discoveries" of this sort of agricultural experimentation do not help them in any way.[72] Indeed, *ejidatarios* have suffered very directly as a result of the technological innovations developed in Mexico for the large commercial farm. As green revolution technology has raised the production of large commercial farmers, the market prices for these crops have dropped. When market prices decline, the commercial farmer can continue to increase his profits because the new technology permits him to increase his output. But the small peasant is unable to apply this technology to increase his production, so he must live with lower prices for the crops he produces. To make matters worse, as the government has poured funds into green revolution research, relatively little research money has been granted to study methods for increasing production on small subsistence plots.

The government policy on credit is also typical of this shift in priority. Agrarian law prohibits peasants from using their ejidal holdings as collateral for crop loans. As a result they are dependent on the government's Ejidal Bank as the only source of credit at normal interest rates.[73] "Statistics on government credit to the ejidal sector reveal just how limited the government commitment to *ejido* agriculture has been."[74] The proportion of government credit earmarked for support to the *ejidos* declined steadily after 1940. "Furthermore, even those funds available to ejidal agriculture have been channeled to the few highly productive, commercially oriented *ejidos*."[75] The cutback in credit supplied by the government bank has forced *ejidatarios* to borrow money at usurious rates from private banks and money lenders. The giant American owned corporation, Anderson-Clayton, has been particularly active in the field of loans to peasant farmers. The exorbitant interest rates paid by *ejidatarios* who have been denied government loans make it extremely difficult for them to realize profits at the end of the agricultural cycle. "In many cases half or three-quarters of the crop serves to repay such loans."[76]

Evaluation. In evaluating the results of the Mexican agrarian reform program, it is crucial to remember that any successful land reform program necessarily requires a great deal of initial and continued input on the part of government. Government input may take the form of investment in infrastructure (dams, irrigation canals, roads, rural electrification), provision of credit to peasant farmers, and/or government aid to a number of important supporting institutions (agricultural extension services, marketing facilities, agricultural schools). When this government input was made during the Cárdenas administration, ejidal agriculture showed great promise and potential as an economically viable and even highly productive form of agricultural exploitation. However, when this crucial government input was in large part withdrawn after 1940, the entire Mexican land reform faltered and sank into a morass from which it has yet to emerge.

In opting for a policy that gives large-scale private agriculture priority over land reform, official party policy makers have argued that the level of food production required by a modernizing nation can *only* be obtained by concentrating government funds in the development of the "more efficient" private agricultural sector. The following assumptions are behind this policy: (1) To promote overall economic development Mexico needs to increase her agricultural production. (2) The private sector is "more productive" than the *ejidos* or the small private farms. (3) Therefore, government spending must be directed to the private commercial sector.

But are these assumptions true? Rodolfo Stavenhagen, a Mexican expert on land reform, has explained that "the idea of the inefficient *ejido* is one of those myths which are propagated without scientific basis. There is no serious study of Mexican agriculture which does not show that the *ejidatario* and the private owners can make the soil produce with equal efficiency."[77] One study has demonstrated that if we measure agricultural productivity in terms of all units of input *except* the owner's labor (that is, if we look at the productivity per unit of capital invested, irrigation water, seed, fertilizer, etc.) we find that the tiny private plots (*minifundia*) are the most efficient of all types of farming in Mexico. The *ejidos* are the second most productive. And measured in these same terms, the large-scale landholdings turn out to be the least efficient producers.[78] In short, the small farmers, both *ejidatarios* and *minifundistas,* do more with what little resources they have than do the large landowners. The Mexican peasant farmers take the small amount of capital available to them, the few tractors and other agricultural equipment at their disposal, the piddling amount of irrigation water that they have for their fields, and grow more with these few resources than do the so-called efficient commercial farmers with similar inputs.

Although this same data has been available to government economists, the ruling elite has continued to cite the argument of "higher productivity" to justify a policy that favors private commercial agriculture at the expense of land reform and the social welfare of small peasant farmers. The outcome of this decision on allocation of resources has been the increased concentration of land and wealth in the hands of a few, and the stagnation of the land reform process.[79]

There is a widely held belief, particularly among foreigners who have studied the Mexican land reform, that the agrarian reform made by Cárdenas was "irreversible and final."[80] Those who hold this view are correct in that the land distributed to the peasants was never snatched away by the government and restored to the old *hacendados.* However, the post-1940 official attitude and legislation has gone a long way toward undoing the progress of the *ejidos* and undercutting their future success. Land was never officially returned to the old landowners, but the lack of government support to the *ejidatarios,* particularly the lack of government credit for ejidal agriculture, made their existence as farmers so difficult that many *ejidatarios* have sought a solution that is a total throwback to pre-revolutionary days: they secretly and illegally arrange to rent their ejidal parcel to a large commercial farmer who possesses the necessary capital to make a profit from the land. Then the *ejidatario* works for the commercial farmer as a peon on the land parcel that is, on paper at least, his own.[81]

It is important to note that no Mexican president has ever taken any measure against the *ejido* as an institution.[82] All the post-1940 presidents have defended the *ejido* as the primary *symbol* of the Revolution. Indeed, all the speeches and statistics are designed to suggest that the reform which culminated under Cárdenas is actually still in progress and still being carried to new heights.[83]

In line with this effort, much official concern is expressed about the future of the land reform program. A great deal of official party rhetoric flies back and forth, all of it underlining the government's preoccupation with the plight of the *ejidatarios, minifundistas,* and ever-growing population of landless peasants. At the same time, however, policies are implemented which condemn these same peasants to a continued state of deprivation and economic insecurity. One Mexican agrarian specialist described the official attitude in this way:

> For a long time there has been an unwillingness on the part of the government to recognize or acknowledge the sheer dimensions of the problems faced by peasants in rural Mexico. Anyone who looks at the official statistics can see, among other things, that there are more than three million landless peasants in Mexico today. Yet, when one writes an article about this situation, there is great excitement and surprise, as if one had made a startling new discovery.

There is an apparent conflict between the government's expressed concern for the landless peasant and governmental policies that favor large private commercial agriculture. Yet, this same agrarian policy is entirely consistent with the government's overall program for development. Mexican development policy, as we have noted, is geared toward rapid economic growth at any price. The type of industrial growth that has been promoted in Mexico depends upon modern technology imported from advanced industrialized countries, plus the services of a steady supply of cheap labor ready to work for any wage offered. Thus, if the agricultural policy makes life increasingly untenable for the small peasant farmer, if it leads to the growth of a huge mass of landless peasants, if it ultimately forces people off the land and into the urban slums, at the same time it provides the pool of cheap labor that is seen as one of the preconditions for rapid industrialization. Were peasants able to make a go of it in the countryside, it is unlikely that they would be anxious to leave their villages and make their way to the cities to sell their labor for low wages. As it is, the agrarian policies favoring large-scale commercial agriculture over small peasant farming contribute to and perpetuate the hopeless situation of the rural poor. The result is that peasants do abandon their villages for the urban slums, and ultimately the needs of the industrial bourgeoisie are served, as both Mexican and foreign capitalists exploit cheap labor for higher profits.

The Human Costs

The development strategy chosen by those in power in Mexico has led to a high rate of economic growth accompanied by social neglect and economic inequality. Per capita income may have reached $700 in 1971, but this figure is more a reflection of the enormous wealth acquired by a small group of industrialists than an improvement in the overall standard of living in Mexico.[84] The income of upper class and upper middle class groups has grown steadily over the last thirty years. Their increased affluence is reflected in the construction of palatial homes, private country clubs, golf courses, stables, exclusive new resort areas, modern shopping plazas, and similarly extravagant projects.

However, at the same time that the growth of national income has produced greater luxury and ease for a small sector of Mexicans at the top of the economic ladder, the cost of living has risen steadily for all Mexicans.[85] But as inflation has driven prices up, workers and peasants have not experienced a corresponding increase in wages or income from the land they work.[86] In terms of what their money will buy, peasants and workers find that they are poorer with each passing year. For this reason, the data on national income and overall production reveal only a part of the picture. For a fuller understanding of what development means in Mexico, we will focus on those statistics that indicate what lies behind the impressive figures on gross national product and national income. In the remainder of this chapter we will look at statistics that provide a picture of the way the great majority of Mexicans live while their country is undergoing rapid modernization.

Rural Mexico

Unemployment and underemployment.   Unemployment and under-employment is a very serious problem for rural Mexicans. On any given day, in villages throughout the countryside, hundreds of thousands of able-bodied men can be found sitting in front of their houses or in the center of a dusty little plaza waiting for work. These are the people who either have no land of their own or who own a *minifundio*, a plot of land so small that it does not require the labor of all family members who might contribute their manpower. To survive, these peasants rely on work offered by large landowners in the region or by more fortunate peasants who have small plots of their own which occasionally require the labor of extra farm hands. Perhaps a truck will be sent from a neighboring estate to cart the landless peasants off for a day of work in a landowner's fields. If the truck should come, the agricultural workers are in no position to haggle over wages. More likely, no truck will come at all. On the average, agricultural day laborers find work only 135 days out of the year.[87] As a result, their income level is very low—the lowest in Mexico.[88]

The average income of all people engaged in agricultural work is $64 per month. Almost 30 percent of the people working in agriculture have a family income of less than $24 per month.[89] The most critical situation is that of the families of agricultural day workers, or *jornaleros*. This group includes families who have never received a parcel of land under the agrarian reform program. It includes *minifundistas* whose parcel is too small to sustain a single family. It also includes the families of younger sons of *ejidatarios* who, in accordance with agrarian reform law, have passed along their ejidal land grants intact to their oldest son. In 1970, of the 1.5 million families headed by an agricultural wage worker, one-third earned an average of only $18 per month. Another 43 percent earned between $24 and $48 per month, while only 5 percent managed to bring home more than $80.[90] These figures refer to the combined income of all wage earners in the *jornalero* family, which, on the average is comprised of at least five potential wage earners. Although five people may be prepared to contribute their labor, the family income remains so low because the *jornaleros* are unable to find steady employment and when they get work, they often receive far less than the legal minimum wage.[91]

The minimum wage is established by a National Commission according to the type of work performed, local conditions, the cost of living index in the region, availability of work, and a series of other economic factors. Increases in the minimum wage over the last

ten years have run approximately 7 percent per annum, which is
often less than the increase in the cost of living from year to year.
The minimum wage presently works out to an average of approximately $1.25 (U.S.) per day for all of rural Mexico. However, the
President of the National Commission on Minimum Salaries, Gilberto
Loyo, recently acknowledged in an interview that 80 percent of the
employers in some rural areas (Chiapas, Guerrero, and Oaxaca) do
not pay their employees the minimum wage established by law.
Evasion of the minimum wage law by employers appears to be far
more widespread than Loyo indicated. Apparently the National
Commission was powerless to do anything about this situation.[92]

Social and economic conditions.   The daily life of peasants, whether
they are *ejidatarios,* agricultural wage workers or the owners of tiny
private plots (*minifundistas*) is full of hardship. In general, the
income they receive from their work on the land is insufficient to
sustain themselves and their families. Their land is mostly rocky,
infertile, and either too arid or too wet to be cultivated profitably.
The vast majority of peasants farm without the help of work animals,
tractors, or machinery more sophisticated than a machete, wooden
plough, or hoe.[93] In the mountains and in the tropical regions where
the bulk of the peasantry are *minifundistas,* the peasant is likely to
leave his house at four or five in the morning to walk for hours just
to reach his plot of land. The land may lie five or ten miles away from
his village, and the peasant must reach his plot before the midday sun
makes heavy work in the fields impossible. On this small parcel of
land, the peasant is likely to raise subsistence crops for his family's
consumption: corn, beans, chile peppers, and calabash. The more
fortunate peasant may own a cow, a few pigs, a mule, or a donkey. If
he has no work animals he may have to walk for miles carrying as
much as eighty or a hundred pounds of firewood on his back.[94]

When we look at the peasant population as a whole (including
ejidatarios as well as landless peasants and *minifundistas*), we find
that peasants throughout Mexico occupy the lowest position on all
the different scales used to measure standard of living. For example,
there is greater illiteracy among the peasants than among any other
group in Mexico. More than two-thirds of all Mexicans who can
neither read nor write live in the countryside. Even among the economically active portion of the rural population, 83 percent are considered to be functionally illiterate, having had less than two years of
schooling. Almost half of all rural dwellings consist of no more than

one room. Only a third of peasant homes are supplied with electricity. More than a third of the rural population cannot afford to buy shoes, and roughly the same proportion cannot afford to eat bread.

Nutrition in Mexico is poor in general. It has been estimated that one-half to three-quarters of the population do not receive the minimum daily nutritional requirement established by the World Health Organization. In terms of diet, again peasants as a group are worse off than urban Mexicans: less than half the peasant population regularly eat either meat, fish, milk, or eggs.[95] The figures in Table 1, taken from the 1970 census, show the contrast between urban and rural standards of living and life style.

Table 1
Urban and Rural Life Styles

	Urban Population	Rural Population
	(Percentages)	
Live in dwellings of only one room	30.6	48.1
Live in homes supplied with electricity	84.5	34.5
Cannot read or write (persons over the age of six)	17.8	39
Go barefoot	1.6	12
Wear *huaraches* (sandals)	3.8	22
Wear shoes	94.4	65.6
Eat only *tortillas* (i.e., no bread)	12.8	34
Do not eat meat even once a week	11	30
Do not eat eggs even once week	15.8	30

Source: Secretaria de Industria y Comercio, Dirección General de Estadística, *IX Censo General de Población, 1970,* (México, D.F.: 1972), pp. 135, 273, 1081-1082.

Marginality. Taken together, these statistics can be used to construct an "index of marginality."[96] When we analyze the data on housing, literacy, diet, and education we find that the people who do not eat meat are often the same people who do not drink milk. Those who do not drink milk are often the same people who do not wear shoes, who cannot read or write, who live in one-room dwellings, and so on.[97]

There is a close correspondence among all these factors. The population that is marginal in terms of one variable is also likely to be marginal in terms of all the others.[98] Therefore, not only are there great numbers of Mexicans who have little of anything, but, as the Mexican sociologist González Casanova has observed, "there is an immense number of Mexicans who have nothing of nothing. . . ."

> Despite the fact that the percent of marginal population has decreased in the past 50 years . . . the marginal population has increased in absolute numbers, and should present trends continue, it will increase in the future. . . . And although marginality is found in the city slums, it is a phenomenon which is most closely associated with rural life.[99]

Not only are the peasants the poorest sector of the population, but the gap between the rich and poor is far wider in the countryside than in the towns and cities of the Republic.[100] The accumulation of wealth in the hands of a few and the poverty of the vast majority of rural people is a direct result of the governmental policies examined in the first part of this chapter. If there remains any doubt concerning the decline and ultimate failure of the land reform program in Mexico, the persistence of economic and social inequalities in the countryside gives silent testimony to the demise of agrarian reform since 1940.

Rural exodus. The rise in the number of marginal people in rural Mexico is due in part to the increased pressure of population on the land. Only 12 percent of the land surface of Mexico is suitable for agriculture without irrigation. Under the existing agrarian reform program, utilizing the technology presently applied in Mexico, this amount of land is insufficient to support the current rural population, not to speak of the generations to come.[101] Even if official projections on new irrigation water to be produced by future hydraulic projects are correct, the amount of farm land that could be made available with the additional irrigation waters would still be inadequate to feed and employ the rural population. Those peasants who have received ejidal grants are prohibited by law from subdividing their land among several sons and daughters. Thus, for each peasant who inherits an ejidal plot from his father, there may be five or six brothers and sisters who take their place in the ranks of the landless peasantry. For this reason the number of landless peasants increases each year.

From the Second World War through the early 1960s, the pressure of overpopulation in the countryside was somewhat relieved by the opportunity for temporary immigration and employment offered by the *bracero* program in the United States. The *bracero* program was conceived in 1942 as a way to cope with the severe wartime labor shortage in the United States. The *braceros* (hired hands, or in Spanish "arms") were workers—mostly agricultural workers—who contracted to work in the United States for a specific period of time, usually three to four months, at a wage determined in advance. During the next two decades Mexican *braceros* sweated in the fields of the southwestern United States and in the factories of the North, often under highly exploitative conditions and at wages well below those established for American workers. In the United States the *braceros* faced both racial prejudice and the hostility of the American agricultural work force whose own wage level—low as it was—was further undercut by the *bracero* program. The Mexican migrants often worked, ate, and slept in substandard conditions while the official program inspectors, under pressure from the American employers, ignored violations of the safeguards built into the *bracero* contract. In the end, some *braceros* were cheated out of the wages that were due them after months of labor in the field or factory. [102] But in spite of the often grim situation encountered by *bracero* laborers in the United States, the conditions in rural Mexico were such that each year hundreds of thousands of workers sought to enter the *bracero* program. At times northern Mexican cities witnessed the outbreak of riots as hundreds of hungry peasants were turned away from the *bracero* induction centers once the quotas were filled. [103]

In 1964, under pressure from the American labor movement, the *bracero* program was terminated by joint Mexican-U.S. agreement. But between 1942 and 1964 an estimated twelve million men had worked as *braceros,* some of them returning to the U.S. for a few months each year over a period of ten to fifteen years. [104] The money earned by the *braceros* in the last six years of the program alone brought an estimated one billion dollars into Mexico. [105] Once the *bracero* program ended, legal migration to the U.S. by agricultural workers was reduced to 100,000 seasonal workers, [106] and the Mexican government lost not only an important source of revenue, but an important safety valve for the reduction of unrest in the countryside. [107]

With the steam valve provided by the *bracero* program shut tight in the mid-sixties, the only apparent alternative open to rural people is migration to the cities. Sensing that their life in the countryside is a vicious circle of poverty, rural people pour into the cities hoping to improve their economic and social situation. Rural migrants enter Mexico City at a rate of more than half a million each year. This means an average of about 1,370 people arrive in the Capital *each day* to seek their fortunes in the big city.[108] And, although the population of the Capital is swelled by these migrants, Mexico City is only eighth among Mexican urban centers in its rate of population growth.[109]

Unfortunately, the jobs sought by the migrants are seldom available. As we noted earlier, 650,000 new people enter the Mexican work force each year. And if there are few job opportunities for people in the countryside, jobs in industry have certainly not expanded to absorb this rural surplus. In 1970 the National Chamber of Manufacturing Industries estimated that 400,000 new jobs would have to be created each year just to keep pace with new entries into the job market in a country where 55 percent of the population is under the age of twenty and 80 percent under the age of thirty-four.[110] Unfortunately, because industrial development in Mexico has moved steadily in the direction of increased reliance on advanced technology, as industry expands, the number of jobs has not increased proportionately.[111] The rural migrant makes his way to the city, full of hope, only to discover that the city is already full of urban unemployed. According to the estimate made in a study of social conditions in the Federal District, there are more than three million unemployed workers in Mexico City alone.[112]

Urban Mexico

Life in the slums.   Generally unable to find the jobs they seek in the city, the rural migrants are forced to squat on the outskirts of the large urban centers. Here, on the periphery of the cities, squalid slums spring up like mushrooms as migrants construct makeshift dwellings out of mud, corrugated paper, hammered-out tin cans and scrap lumber. There are 452 such slums or "lost cities" (*ciudades perdidas*) in and around Mexico City which house 1.5 million people, 70 percent of them rural migrants. In addition to the lost cities, poor neighborhoods (*vecindades* or *barrios*) in the Capital house another two to three million people. Some of the lost cities are perched at the very edge of deep ravines on the Mexico City-Toluca road, while others sit rotting in the heart of downtown Mexico City, stashed away in the streets behind the National Palace.[113] The slums on the main route between downtown Mexico City and the international airport are carefully concealed from the eyes of tourists and other foreign visitors by high walls, constructed by the municipal government and decorated with slogans praising the PRI and its candidates of the day.

Hidden away behind the municipal walls, the lost cities grow and fester. In many of these communities the birthrate is even higher than in the countryside, but the infant mortality rate is also tragically high. Manuel Mejido, muckraking reporter for the Mexican daily *Excelsior,* found that in the slum called Colonia Juan Polainas 60 percent of all babies die before their first birthday. In Juan Polainas 2,032 people live in 441 one-room dwellings. Together the 2,032 residents share 27 water taps, 51 open toilets, and 77 wash basins. Often more than one family will occupy a 10-foot square windowless room, and sometimes pigs, goats, and chickens, and other domestic animals live indoors as well. [114]

El Capulín, a slum that sits precariously under a web of high tension wires is typical of thousands of poor neighborhoods and lost cities in the capital. El Capulín lacks the most rudimentary public services. The people light their homes by pirating electric current from the heavy electric lines that run directly overhead. There are no schools or medical services, no paved roads, no drinking water, no garbage collection, and no sewage system. Drainage is so poor that one torrential rainfall can wash away hundreds of houses. In May 1972, for example, 50,000 people in Mexico City were left homeless after an unusually heavy rain and hailstorm. Even when the weather is clear, the unpaved streets run with black, brackish water that is full of human and animal wastes. Poverty is the common denominator among the residents of El Capulín. Although the general census for 1970 indicated that only 36,559 people in the capital go barefoot, in El Capulín, where 90 percent of the people have migrated from rural areas, no one wears shoes. [115]

Nativitas, a community of 2,500 people who share only 236 houses, suffers much the same conditions as Juan Polainas and El Capulín. In these and other squatter communities, *caciquillos* ("little strongmen") who have no legal title to the property, lay claim to the land beneath the squatters' huts. The *caciquillos* force the squatters to pay rents up to $15 per month for the privilege of occupying the little squares of land on which their huts sit. The slum dwellers may be forcibly thrown out at any time. Although they may have been paying rent to the self-appointed "landlord" for a period of years, the squatters have no legal recourse if they are turned out of their makeshift homes. For the most part the police are conspicuously absent from the slums and lost cities, and the crime rate in these places is so high that, by 1970, Mexico had attained the sad distinction of numbering among the five countries with the highest rate of homicide in the world. [116]

When the police do appear, it is often to extort money from the owners of the tiny general stores that serve the residents of the lost cities. However, the uniformed police and the small payoff they demand seem benign in comparison with the secret police who are well known for their extortion of large sums from those whom they discover have a previous criminal record. [117] In order to produce the forty or fifty dollars demanded by the secret agents for their monthly payoff, those with past criminal records tend to fall back on the tricks of their former trade: armed robbery, mugging, and picking pockets.

One high crime area is Netzahualcoyotl, the city that has become infamous as the largest slum in the Western Hemisphere. This lost city of 700,000 sprawls just to the east of Mexico City's modern international airport. Netzahualcoyotl developed in the 1940s as a refuge for the poor who could not find housing of any sort inside the Capital. During the 1950s and 1960s the slum grew rapidly as thousands of migrants joined the initial squatters on the public lands they had made their home. In 1970, conditions in Netzahualcoyotl were little changed from its spontaneous, makeshift beginnings a quarter of a century earlier. Although the giant slum had received an official city status, [118] and electric power had been extended into its main streets, municipal "improvements" never kept pace with Netzahualcoyotl's growth. In 1970 only 2 percent of the roads were paved, and the streets still ran with putrid garbage in the rainy season, and became thick with dust in the dry season. [119]

Lacking drinking water, sewers, or garbage collection, disease ravages the overcrowded population of Netzahualcoyotl, as it does slum dwellers throughout the Republic. The big killers are gastroenteritis and amoebic dysentery. Diseases like polio, rabies, and typhoid fever still occur in Mexico with alarming frequency. In the first half of 1972, the Pan American Health Organization reported 1,400 cases of typhoid, "the world's worst typhoid epidemic since World War II and possibly the worst of this century." [120] Reliable observers feared that "the total case count is much higher, perhaps measured in tens of thousands." [121]

Occupation and income. The vast majority of slum dwellers, whether they have migrated from the countryside or were born in the city, are unable to find steady employment. In some of the slums and lost cities like Colonia Juan Polainas, the proportion of adults who cannot find regular work runs as high as 97 percent. How do these people manage to survive and provide for their families?

Most of the people who cannot find steady work engage in such work as selling chewing gum, pencils, plastic toys, or national lottery tickets. Normally they have no fixed stall from which they vend their wares. Rather, they wander the streets, looking for customers for their handicrafts, candy, ice cream, pops, hairpins (sold in 5-pin bunches), and plaster statues. They jump on and off city buses hawking plastic combs, comic books, movie magazines, hair tonic, ballpoint pens, and glossy postcards.[122] From tiny little boys to stooped old men, they bend low to shine the shoes of passersby. Some manage to live on what they earn singing on crowded buses, playing musical instruments on street corners, or improvising dances for the benefit of tourists strolling in Chapultepec Park. Others clean windshields, wash, and "guard" cars in the hope that when the owner returns to his auto, he will reward this attention with a few pesos. The early morning edition of newspapers are often sold in the streets at 4 A.M. by children sometimes no older than eight or nine. To beat out their competitors, the newspaper vendors rush up to the windows of cars stopped temporarily at crowded intersections.

Some of the unemployed who live at the outskirts of the city wait at the roadside for the trucks that pass carrying produce destined for the city markets. These people gather the fruits and vegetables that fall off the back of the trucks, wash them in the polluted water of their slum community, and travel on into the city where they set up little pyramids of guavas, papayas, tomatoes, peanuts, etc., on the sidewalks of the main plazas and shopping districts. Here, unfortunately, they must compete with peasants who have left their villages in the middle of the night to make it to the city in time to set up their own little pyramids of fruit, vegetables, and nuts.

Another occupation is the age-old standby of the poor: prostitution. And thousands of women who will not or cannot sell their bodies gather up their children each day and travel downtown where they ask directly for alms or beg indirectly, pretending to have lost their busfare home. Those who ask for alms are known as *pordioseros,* from the words *por Dios,* "for God's sake" or "for love of God."

Finally, there are approximately 4,000 families in Mexico City totaling more than 20,000 people, who live by scrounging the garbage dumps for saleable waste.[123] These people have a long-standing grudge against the municipal garbage collectors whom they accuse of skimming off the most desirable waste items such as paper, cartons, glass bottles, and metal cans, which represent the more highly prized merchandise on the rubbish market.[124] In the city of Monterrey, where there are an estimated 90,000 ownerless dogs,[125] garbage scroungers compete with dogs and rats as well as municipal garbage collectors for access to the garbage dumps.

Whatever the job that a desperate slum dweller creates for himself, the going is usually rough. Obviously there is no social security for those who perform the kind of work described above. In addition, these people are often victimized by policemen and other authority figures who demand kickbacks from the poor to allow them to sell whatever it is they are trying to sell. Finally, the urban sprawl of Mexico City, Guadalajara, or Monterrey is such that simply reaching his place of work may cost the peripheral slum dweller as much as two hours on one of the rickety old buses that crawl downtown through the city streets. In the nation's capital, more than 1,000 miles of streets remain unpaved.[126] Even with the construction of an ultra-modern twenty-five mile subway line, public transport in most poor neighborhoods remains woefully inadequate. In many cases the poor cannot afford the price of a subway ticket, which, at one peso (U.S. $.08) costs twice as much as the first class bus and more than three times as much as the fare for the old second class buses. Only about half of the buses registered for service are in operation at any one time. In grave need of repair, the buses lurch back and forth, belching out the heavy black diesel exhaust that helps make Mexico's large cities among the most dangerously polluted in the world.

The average family income for poor neighborhoods and lost cities in the Capital is less than $72 per month. Of all slum families 35.6 percent[127] earn less than $80 each month.[128]

The working class. Urban poor people who are fortunate enough to find steady employment generally live in conditions that are only slightly better than those of the rural migrants and the urban subproletariat. Like their unemployed neighbors, workers find that housing and social services are in short supply. Most working class districts suffer from inadequate schools, medical facilities, drainage, refuse collection, and other services. Indeed the line between a working class *barrio* and a full fledged slum is often difficult to establish.

As we have noted, the abundant supply of unskilled labor tends to depress the wages of those who are already employed. Minimum wage laws are often disregarded, and the basic labor guarantees provided by the Constitution of 1917 have yet to be applied. Only 19 percent of the working class is covered by social security. [129] Inflation bites into the worker's paycheck, and the cost of living has risen so rapidly over the past ten years that workers are forced to labor longer and longer hours simply to maintain their families at the same standard of living. After basic food and rent are paid, these people rarely have any money left to put aside as savings. As a result, an illness or an unforeseen expense normally precipitates an economic crisis for the working class family. Even salaried workers who are somewhat better off have great difficulty accumulating savings. Salaried workers bear a particularly heavy tax burden because the unemployed have no reported income to tax, while the bourgeoisie is taxed lightly or manages to evade taxation altogether. [130]

Naturally many workers dream of a better future for their children, if not for themselves. Accordingly, they struggle to send their children on to higher education. However, the number of working class students attending secondary school in Mexico is disproportionately small, and we find that among all the students enrolled in the public National University, only 14.7 percent are sons or daughters of workers. [131]

Conclusion

In this chapter we have examined the rapid process of economic development, which those in power like to call the Mexican Miracle. We have also surveyed the conditions in which the bulk of the population lives as the ruling elite struggles to push Mexico into the ranks of the advanced, modernized, industrial nations. The data presented in this chapter should give some notion of the real life experiences that are often lumped together under such seemingly neutral terms as "foregone consumption," "the social costs of development," and "social dislocation." While Mexico has shown remarkable progress on a number of economic scales, the majority of its people continue to live in a condition most accurately described as wretchedness or squalor. And most live this way with very little hope of ever escaping

these conditions. For people whose social welfare has been sacrificed
to the goal of capital accumulation, the term "Mexican miracle"
must have a very bitter ring. One group of Mexican intellectuals
described the miracle in this way:

> If there is something "miraculous" in Mexico, it is that the people tolerate
> a situation of backwardness and dependency in which millions of Mexicans
> barely manage to survive, and justice and democracy are conspicuous by
> their absence or exist only in the rhetoric of the PRI.[132]

4. Opposition, Co-optation, and Repression

> "The people want their rights respected. They want to be paid attention to and listened to."
>
> Emiliano Zapata

Mexican peasants and workers are well aware that their country has undergone rapid economic development in recent decades. Indeed they are frequently reminded of this achievement by the government that has fostered this growth. But they are also aware that they have not shared equally in the fruits of the development process. And this realization has led to great frustration and unrest in both the countryside and the cities. Those who have been the victims rather than the beneficiaries of economic development look for some way to demand changes in government policies that condemn them to a continued life of poverty. But, as we know from our earlier discussion, the CTM and CNC, the official party sectors originally designed to give voice to workers' and peasants' demands, do not, in practice, operate as militant champions of the two groups they ostensibly represent. Even less do they pressure to see peasant and working class interests incorporated into national policy. Despite elaborately constructed appearances to the contrary, neither the CTM nor the CNC is a popular organization in the sense in which we normally think of a peasant or labor union movement. As we have noted, the main work of these two organizations is to modify or suppress the demands of its members and to contain potential unrest among peasants and workers. It is their job to deliver peasant and worker support for the PRI (particularly at election time) and to gain popular acceptance for government policies which, in most instances, run counter to the interests of both peasants and workers.

CNC and CTM politicians often organize mass rallies at which banner-waving peasants and workers, carted to the scene by the truckful, shout and cheer for official party candidates and for government representatives. But these carefully orchestrated displays should not be confused with genuine support for the PRI or its program. When peasants and workers are interviewed privately, there is a striking unanimity of disaffection and disenchantment with the official party. As one peasant told me in 1970:

> I have only two years of schooling. But you do not need to read and write to understand that the program of the PRI is made to benefit rich and powerful people like the PRI politicians themselves. For people like us, things grow worse year by year. But I go to the demonstrations and shout "vivas" along with everyone else, because they give you five, sometimes ten pesos and a meal. Besides, if you refuse to go when the truck comes to the *ejido* to pick you up, you only make enemies in the CNC and trouble for yourself.

Similar expressions of disillusionment with the organs of the PRI can be heard in private conversations in any city, town or village in Mexico. These feelings of discontent are voiced not only by the peasants, workers, and the chronically unemployed who bear the heaviest brunt of the official development policy, but also by students, intellectuals, and a sizable sector of middle class people who feel the bite of taxes and inflation and the stultifying effects of one-party rule. The fact that so much discontent is expressed, albeit privately, suggests that Mexicans enjoy a certain freedom to vent their dissatisfaction, so long as their criticism remains incoherent. It is when the discontented attempt to organize and act in unison to give impact to their criticism and demands for change that they run into trouble. For the official organizations linked to the PRI provide no hope for those who want to push for a reordering of the priorities of

Mexican development. And the forms of political expression available to people who want to modify the Mexican system and the policies it produces are severely limited. In this chapter we will look at those limitations and at the various alternatives open to Mexicans who are unhappy with four and a half decades of official party management.

A Hegemonic System

If it is not totalitarian, Mexico's government is a far cry from what we understand to be a liberal democracy in spite of the rhetoric and the laws on the books. The Mexican Constitution provides for the separation of power among three branches of government, legal opposition parties, independent organized interest groups—in short, most of the features characteristic of a liberal democratic system. This appearance is utterly deceptive. For in reality, the Mexican system is marked by a nearly complete centralization of power and authority in the hands of the President and his party.

The president heads both the PRI and the national government and enjoys a wide range of constitutionally invested and *de facto* authority. His word is rarely challenged publicly. A ban on direct criticism of the president in the Mexican press is enforced by the government monopoly on the supply of newsprint paper. Neither the judicial nor the legislative branches are independent of his control. The decisions of the Supreme Court of Justice generally follow the policy of the executive, and the preponderance of citizens who do make use of the judicial process are businessmen, large landowners, and members of the middle class seeking relief from taxation and land expropriation orders.[1] Because the process is complicated and expensive, workers and peasants who appeal to the Court constitute a small minority.[2]

The legislative branch displays even less independence than the judicial. The Chamber of Senators is composed entirely of members of the president's party, and both the Chamber of Deputies and the Chamber of Senators are frankly regarded in Mexico as a rubber stamp for presidential policy. Bills passed to the legislature by the president are normally approved by acclaim. Those few pieces of legislation which are not passed unanimously never meet with more than 5 percent opposition.[3] Furthermore all essential legislation passed on to the chambers of Senators and Deputies by the president is immediately approved by unanimous decision.

Opposition Parties

The power of the president and the PRI is not checked by a vigorous opposition party or parties. The Mexican political system does feature a number of so-called opposition parties, the most prominent of which are the occasionally left wing Popular Socialist Party (Partido Popular Socialista, or PPS) and the right wing National Action Party (Partido de Acción Nacional, or PAN). But these parties do not play the role normally associated with opposition parties in most democratic systems. Although they occupy an established place in the political arena, Mexican opposition parties have no chance whatsoever of taking power through electoral means. Over the last fifty years the electoral process has taken root in Mexico and contests for the presidency, the Senate, the Chamber of Deputies, and other offices have all proceeded in an orderly sequence, if not without frequent outbreaks of violence, particularly at the local level.[4] But when we look at that orderly procession of electoral contests, one fact stands out: the winner is inevitably the candidate of the official party. Although many political groups have been successful in gaining registration as legally recognized parties, none has won even 20 percent of the vote in any presidential election. Ballot stealing, strong-arm pressure at the polls and electoral fraud of every description contribute to the official party's electoral preeminence. On occasions when opposition candidates have polled a substantial majority over their PRI competition for the governorship or a seat in the Senate, the election results have been nullified by the government for one technicality or another. The corruption of the electoral process in Mexico is so well known and well documented that few people take the final statistics without a large serving of salt. But the fact remains that when the final votes are tallied, by whatever process they are tallied, the official party has never lost a presidential, gubernatorial, or senatorial contest, and opposition parties have never achieved more than the status of pressure groups.[5]

Table 2
Presidential Elections 1924-1970

Year	Candidate	Percentage of Vote
1924	Calles	84
	Flores	16
1928	Obregón	100
1929	Ortiz Rubio	94
	Vasconcelos	5
	Others	1
1934	Cárdenas	98
	Villaneal	1
	Tejeda } Laborde }	1
1940	Avila Camacho	94
	Almazán	6
1946	Alemán	78
	Padilla	19
	Castro } Calderon }	3
1952	Ruíz Cortines	74
	Henríquez	16
	González Luna	8
	Toledano	2
1958	López Mateos	90
	Álvarez	9
1964	Díaz Ordaz	89
	González Torres	11
1970	Echeverría	84
	González Morfín	14
	Others	2

The relationship between the PRI and its official opposition is so close that these parties are often referred to as a "kept" opposition. Indeed, in some cases opposition parties have been financed by the government itself.[6] At election time the opposition parties either throw their support to the official party candidate from the outset, or they provisionally oppose PRI candidates as a means of bargaining with the government for patronage positions, loans, contracts, and other favors for the most prominent opposition party members.[7] Obviously this situation detracts from the independence of the opposition parties and their capacity to serve as an avenue of protest for those Mexicans who are discontent with the rule of the PRI.

The PPS, PAN, and lesser opposition parties play a crucial role in maintaining the political status quo. Their presence in the political arena promotes the myth that orderly democratic procedures operate in Mexico. As such they contribute to the legitimacy of one-party rule, and in so doing they reinforce the centralization of power in the hands of the president and his party.

Organized opposition parties are not the only political groupings that tend to be drawn into the center of gravity occupied by the PRI. So complete is the concentration of power and authority in the hands of the ruling party that a range of political activity outside the PRI is tolerated simply because the political leaders involved have no chance of success. In short, the PRI system tends to absorb all opposition: organized and unorganized, institutional and spontaneous, urban and rural, individuals as well as groups. The PRI manages to neutralize potential opposition and retain political control by *co-opting* all serious rivals for power.

The Co-optation Process

"Co-optation" is a term used to describe the process by which individuals or groups independent enough to threaten the ongoing domination of a single group or party (in this case, the PRI) are traded small concessions or favors in exchange for moderating their demands and reducing their challenge to the dominant group's control over the system.[8] This process takes place to some extent in almost every political system. But in Mexico, the process has been refined by the PRI to the point that it has paralyzed almost all potential opposition.

The key to the co-optation process lies in the centralization of power in the hands of a very few people who sit in Mexico City. There is only one way to get things done in Mexico. Whether one is a functionary of the PRI, a government bureaucrat, or the leader of an "independent" peasant or labor union, one is forced to go to the center, to the government offices in Mexico City to get action. There is no alternative source of authority. Bureaucratic institutions exist at the local, regional, and state levels, but decision making of all kinds takes place in Mexico City and nearly all policy directives emanate from the government offices in the capital. In many cases politicians find they must go directly to the president himself for the favors or governmental decisions they seek. Peasant leaders, for example, note that they spend as much as one-third of the year in government offices in Mexico City because, although these government agencies all have branch offices at the regional or state level, it is more efficient to travel a thousand kilometers to Mexico City than labor long hours in the state capital to win a favorable decision from, say, the regional Secretary of Water Resources, only to have that decision overturned in Mexico City.[9]

With all decision making in the hands of the president, his close advisors, and his party, how can would-be independent peasant or labor unions win the concessions they need to retain the support of their membership? How can they win these concessions without compromising too much, without being absorbed by the centralized system they are attempting to challenge or change? As we will see, in most cases they do not retain their independence. In most cases they are co-opted or bought off. They receive policy concessions for their followers only in return for moderating their militancy.

Most would-be independent popular movements in Mexico are sooner or later absorbed into the system they originally set out to change. Co-optation of this sort occurs because cooperation or collaboration with the PRI is one of the few avenues of social and economic mobility open to many people in Mexico. More important, it is practically the only way organizations can win the concessions from government that they need to fulfill their role as peasants' or workers' representatives.

Co-optation for Personal Mobility

Intellectuals

There are some fortunate individuals who manage to achieve prestige, power, or wealth without scrambling for a prominent position in the PRI-government structure. In some cases a person is so rich that the wealth and status available through politics will not substantially enhance his position. Another obvious category of people who do not need to play at PRI politics are Catholic priests, who have their own hierarchy of prestige and whose participation in politics, in any event, is strictly prohibited by the Mexican Constitution. Finally, people who are talented or educated enough to gain an international reputation need not depend on the place they could make for themselves in the official party or government bureaucracies. Opposition scholars and intellectuals, for example, enjoy an obvious advantage. Many of these people retain some degree of political independence and personal integrity by finding work with an international organization like the United Nations, by taking positions as visiting professors at European and North American universities, by publishing abroad, and so on. But when and if these appointments come to an end, even the most independent intellectual comes face to face with a sad fact: private universities in Mexico tend to be traditional, conservative, and, for the most part, Catholic. For intellectuals who choose to live in Mexico, some direct or indirect association with the government is virtually impossible to avoid, whether they are employed at the National University, work in a government sponsored research center, or work for the government or party itself.[10] Obviously, not every intellectual in Mexico can earn a living on the staff of the handful of opposition publishing houses and periodicals. Sooner or later all intellectuals who are not independently wealthy must deal with this dilemma: how to earn a living in Mexico and still retain political independence.

Once an intellectual is on the government payroll, he normally finds it difficult to change the system from within. For example, most leftists who enter the government or the PRI with the hope of "burrowing from within" are deeply frustrated after a relatively brief association with the inner workings of the government and party. Some leftists find themselves undergoing a rapid change in attitudes and even in vocabulary. One left wing economist described the process in this way:

> When I returned to Mexico from my studies abroad, the only job offering open to me was on a special commission on agrarian problems in the Ministry of the Presidency. I reluctantly took the job, because by that time I had a wife and two children to support and could not afford to fool around launching left wing study groups and magazines. Naturally, I promised myself that I would do everything in my power to remain consistent with my ideals, and to work for change from my position within the government.

But very soon, I found that I was changing. Even my vocabulary and my way of expressing myself was altered. Rather than call the president "Díaz Ordaz," I soon picked up the exaggeratedly respectful "El Señor Presidente" that all my colleagues used. My vocabulary soon filled with classic PRI rhetoric, with talk of "the ideals of the Mexican Revolution" and "devoted service and self-sacrifice for the fatherland." I had the greatest difficulty in dropping this language even when I came home at night.

I believe that nothing I was able to accomplish in two years at the Ministry of the Presidency changed government policy in any way at all. To pretend otherwise would be sheer self-deception.

Although the experience can be deeply frustrating, a large proportion of self-defined leftists end up working either in the government or in the PRI bureaucracy. A graphic illustration of this tendency is provided by the story of one group of young graduates from the National University.

In the early 1960s the graduating class of the School of Political Science of the National University was comprised of a majority of leftist students. It is the custom for each graduating class to choose some person to stand as their *padrino de graduación*, a godfather for the graduating class. Normally a relatively rich and influential person is chosen because the honor carries with it certain obligations. The *padrino* generally provides a banquet for the graduating group and presents each student with a class ring.

In this case, the left wing students prevailed over their more conservative classmates, and rather than choose a rich businessman or a PRI *politico* to serve as the class' *padrino*, a left wing publisher was honored. Instead of receiving class rings, each student received a book from their godfather's publishing house, and a set of volumes was raffled off to provide funds for a banquet. The students were proud and happy to have honored someone whose political views they respected, and the graduating banquet turned out to be a most festive occasion.

Two years later, according to custom, the group was to meet with their *padrino* for a class reunion. Only a handful of students showed up. Everyone else in this once largely left wing group of young political scientists was employed by either the PRI or the government. Of the few who were not, two had become housewives and two were unemployed. Only one member of the class had managed to find a job outside the government or party.

We can infer from this and other tales that recruitment of university graduates directly into government or official party jobs is a direct and often irresistible process even for students with a history of left wing politics. Indeed, one of the best ways for a student to assure himself an attractive job offer after graduation is to build himself a reputation as a militant leftist student leader. Many of the choicest plums in the government and party hierarchy are reserved for buying off the most articulate, charismatic, and hence, politically dangerous leftist students. The routine co-optation of militant student leadership has become so institutionalized in Mexico that personally ambitious students have been known to form radical student movements and initiate student strikes specifically to draw the government's attention to themselves so that they might reap the rewards which accrue to a co-opted militant.

Nevertheless, as we will see, there are students and intellectuals who are totally committed to challenging the government and the PRI. To maintain their integrity and independence from government control, they move within the small, constricted range of job alternatives open to educated people who do not wish to work directly or indirectly for the PRI. These people are fortunate because this range of possibilities, though narrowly limited, does exist. But what, we might ask, happens to peasants and workers whose educational preparation is such that these options are unavailable to them?

Peasant Leaders

In chapter 2, we noted that official party politics is one of the few avenues of upward mobility open to people of peasant origin. Working with the CNC, a peasant who is ambitious and anxious to raise his socioeconomic status may overcome his disadvantaged background and rise through the ranks to occupy positions that provide considerable power and wealth.

Peasants who rise through their affiliation with the CNC normally begin their career as the representative of their own *ejido*'s administration. The job carries with it a daily salary equal to the minimum wage in the countryside and the opportunity for frequent interaction with men influentially placed in the regional CNC hierarchy. If he displays the proper mixture of deference and assertiveness, the ejidal representative will eventually be recognized and placed in one of the CNC's lower level patronage positions.

The peasant who wins such a position generally improves his economic situation because service as the CNC representative to a government agency normally carries with it a salary that is substantial by rural Mexican standards.[11] For example, in the Laguna region in 1968 some of the posts offered to peasant representatives by the government were (1) twelve representatives to the Ejidal Bank at a salary of $7.20 (U.S.) per week; (2) ten representatives to the Medical Services Committee at a salary of $7.20 per week; and (3) twelve representatives to the Government Insurance Bank at weekly salaries ranging from $7.20 to $20.00 per week.

If we bear in mind that the 1965 mean yearly income for *ejidatarios* in the Laguna region was between $112.00 and $128.00, while the smallest yearly income received by men serving in the official party as peasant representatives was $336.00, it is easy to understand the economic value of these patronage positions.[12]

Once a peasant's "loyalty" to the CNC and the party is recognized and rewarded in this way, tighter bonds of "mutual aid and trust" may develop between him and stronger figures in the CNC-PRI machine. One of the advantages of admission to the circle of low level patronage recipients is precisely this opportunity to interact and develop political alliances with key men in the CNC structure at the regional or even the state level. The quick and ambitious peasant should be able to trade his current post for ever more prestigious and lucrative positions in the CNC hierarchy. With every step up the CNC ladder, the salary grows and so do the opportunities for kickbacks, payoffs, and other illicit gains. Some particularly adept peasants have parlayed their positions as professional peasant representatives into sizable personal fortunes. Some have even acquired enough money and land to take their place in the ranks of large landowners.

Because the CNC provides stepping-stones for socioeconomic advancement on an individual basis, some peasants are drawn into the official peasant organization precisely because it offers opportunities for the extraction of wealth and prestige that are otherwise absent in the world of an uneducated or poorly educated rural Mexican. For peasants who refuse either to join the CNC or to cooperate with the government and the official party, life is very difficult indeed. Obviously, then, the temptation to work within the system is very great for potential peasant leaders.

Labor Leaders

The same temptations that lure peasant leaders into the official party machine also draw many potential labor leaders into the CTM.

Affiliation with the CTM opens to an ambitious worker a wide range of patronage positions and sinecures at salaries well above a laborer's pay. The top leaders of the CTM are regularly assigned seats in the federal legislature, and, at lower levels, salaried positions in local and state government, on regional committees, as labor representatives to government agencies, arbitration boards and the like are available to the tried and true CTM man.

If we compare the opportunities for upward mobility that exist in Mexican society for ordinary peasants and workers with the range of economic and social possibilities that open to peasants and workers who are co-opted into the official party family, we must wonder not that so many people are co-opted, but rather that many peasants and workers actually choose the rough rocky course of independent political action.

The Co-optation of Organizations

Thus far we have looked primarily at the process of co-optation on the personal level. What stands out is the nearly irresistible pull of the PRI as the major avenue to personal success for peasants, workers, and even for intellectuals. But, part of this same process, and even more significant than the co-optation of individuals, is the co-optation of whole organizations.[13]

There is a wide range of Mexican peasant and labor organizations that are not affiliated with either the CNC or CTM. Most of them have developed in response to specific dissatisfaction with the two PRI sectors in terms of their performance as representative organs. Some of these peasant and labor unions are locally or regionally based, while some, at least nominally, blanket the entire republic. Some are affiliated with the Mexican Communist Party; some are independent of affiliation with any political party. But all face a common dilemma.

Generally speaking, the leadership of independent organizations is not imposed from above as with CTM and CNC officials. Independent leaders need popular support to stay in office. Indeed, they need popular support if the organizations themselves are to survive. Obviously the leaders of independent organizations cannot maintain the loyalty of their membership if they cannot effectively represent these members' interests. Peasants and workers who choose to affiliate with an independent organization have normally taken a bold step. In most cases the easy road is to register with the appropriate affiliate of the PRI. Opting for membership in an independent union is often a very committed act. But regardless of how committed a peasant or worker may be to certain ideals, he still needs to be represented by an organization that can effectively advance his interests; an organization that can win labor contracts, represent him before an arbitration board, petition the Ejidal Bank in his behalf, or market his cotton crop at a decent price. Peasant and labor unions that cannot provide these services for their members have great difficulty in surviving as viable organizations.

Unfortunately, independent labor and peasant unions operate at a serious disadvantage. The bureaucracy that administers the land reform program, for example, is complex, enormous, and totally in the hands of official party politicians. A variety of federal banks, agencies, ministries, and departments exercise a determining control over land distribution, agricultural production, sales, and the rural economy as a whole. Together these federal banks and agencies decide which and how much land will be distributed to landless petitioners, which peasants (and which private owners) will receive irrigation water from national hydraulic projects, and how much technical aid, agricultural equipment, fertilizer, and insecticide will be made available to peasant landholders. In addition, they determine when and where new lands will be opened to cultivation, when credit will be supplied for crop diversification, and when processing plants such as cotton gins and cane mills can be set up by peasants in the countryside. The Department of Agrarian Affairs (after 1971 the Ministry for Agrarian Reform), for example, investigates the cases of lands held in violation of the limits set by agrarian law or maximum holdings. This same agency determines when and if these lands should be expropriated, and which peasants will become the beneficiaries of the distribution. In many cases independent peasant groups struggle for years to draw official attention to illegal holdings only to find that when the land is expropriated, it is distributed to CNC-affiliated peasants.[14] In other cases, independent peasant groups have lobbied vigorously for crop diversification or large-scale irrigation projects. But when the project becomes a reality, the independent peasant organization members are excluded from the program.

In short, the administrative bureaucracy that directs almost every aspect of the agricultural economy is firmly controlled by the ruling party. As a result, the more militant the peasant organizations are, or the more serious the challenge they present to PRI control, the greater are the difficulties they face in winning concessions for their members or in consolidating the concessions they have won in the past.

Independent labor organizations are likewise in a disadvantaged position with respect to the government bureaucracies with which they deal. In many cases they are denied legal recognition from the Ministry of Labor. If they are not formally registered as labor representatives, the leaders of such independent unions cannot enter arbitration proceedings on behalf of their members, nor negotiate labor contracts, nor hold positions on the government commissions on wages. About the only thing these unions can do is call a wildcat strike that is not authorized by the CTM. So restricted is the role independent labor federations can legally play that most workers who join these organizations are forced to hold dual union membership; they retain their CTM union cards so that they will be included in the collective work contracts negotiated by the CTM, and, at the same time, they attend union meetings at the independent federation and bring their grievances to the attention of the independent labor leaders. For their part, all that the independent union leaders can do is to make extralegal representations to the Ministry of Labor or to the owners of the factory involved in the grievance. Yet, often even this extralegal representation yields more satisfactory results for the worker than he gets when he brings his complaint to his CTM representative, who is likely to be in the pay of the factory owner and who, in any event, has nothing to gain from stirring up trouble for the factory owner.

Independent labor unions typically grow directly from workers' dissatisfaction with the CTM. As the leader of one such organization explained,

> In 1954 a group of us could stand it no longer. The *charros*[15] of the CTM were accepting money from the owners. When the CTM leaders started signing labor agreements behind the back of the workers, we began to meet as a group to see what we could do. It was then that we formed the Sindicato Independiente de ___, but we had to fight another three years to win registration from the Ministry of the Interior. Even today the CTM controls all the Juntas de Conciliación y Arbitraje and we have no representation on those committees. We have great difficulty getting work contracts for our members. But the men stay with our Union because we are the only ones who fight. And the owners are afraid of us because they

know we are the only ones who fight, who make demands for the working man.

With so many factors working to the disadvantage of independent organizations, the pressure is great to conform, to assume a conciliatory position toward the government and even to bring the organization into alliance with the CTM or CNC. Careful study of those independent peasant and labor organizations that have survived for a decade or more generally shows a trend away from militant, oppositionist positions in favor of conformity, collaboration, and cooperation with the government.

The Politics of Tamales: A Case Study [16]

One way to study the process of co-optation and the trend away from opposition politics is to look at the political evolution of a specific opposition organization. An interesting organization to study is the Central Union,[17] a communist-led peasant union that has played an important role in the politics of the Laguna region for more than three and a half decades. In the preceding chapters we have made frequent reference to the cotton growing Laguna region of north-central Mexico. This area is interesting not only because it was the site of the first truly large-scale land reform effort in all Latin America, but also because, historically, it has been the major, and at times the only, area of Communist Party strength in the Mexican countryside.

The Central Union: The Early Years of Political and Economic Strength

The original leadership of the Central Union was drawn from the ranks of the militant *agraristas* who led the fight for agrarian reform in the years before Cárdenas carried out his land distribution in the region. Some of the older Central Union leaders had histories of radical agrarianism dating back to the Revolution. But the bulk of the leadership received political training in the communist youth organizations active in the Laguna region throughout the 1920s and early '30s. These youth cadres, encouraged by the Cárdenas administration's benign attitude toward the Mexican Communist Party, brought together young peasants and workers, and sped the formation of political consciousness and political ties between industrial workers in Torreón and the surrounding population of landless, agricultural day laborers.

During the most active period of agrarian conflict (1934-1937), the young men who were later to become Central Union officers gained valuable experience and region-wide contacts organizing their families, friends, and neighbors in support of the *agrarista* cause. Most of the Central Union officers played leading roles in the great general strike that paralyzed the Laguna from August to October 1936, the strike used by Cárdenas to justify a massive land distribution in the region. Thus, in the years following the land reform, the original strike leaders, many of them formally affiliated with the Mexican Communist Party (the PCM), enjoyed widespread prestige among the new *ejidatarios.* Many of the strike leaders were elected by their fellow *ejidatarios* to fill positions requiring some leadership experience, a good general knowledge of the region, and contacts with emerging peasant leaders in neighboring *ejidos.*

In 1939 a "Central Union" of representatives of the newly created *ejidos* was founded by peasants and given legal recognition by the Cárdenas administration. It was authorized by the government to carry out banking operations, administer warehouses, dams, and wells, and to establish commercial and industrial enterprises on behalf of the *ejidatarios* in the Laguna region. Most important, the Central Union was authorized to represent peasants in their dealings with local, state, and national governments and their agencies.[18] Given the early influence of the Communist Party organizers in the Laguna region, and the role of communist affiliated peasants in organizing and sustaining the general strike of 1936, it is not surprising that the leadership of the newly established Central Union was supplied in great part by peasants formally affiliated with the Communist Party.

As long as Cárdenas was in power, the communist peasant leaders pursued a policy of amicable cooperation with the government. This policy reflected the affinity of the communist peasant leaders for the government responsible for the agrarian reform, and at the same time corresponded to the formal policy adopted by the Communist International of fostering a popular front with all "progressive forces" on the political scene.

During the late thirties the Central Union fared well under its communist leadership. It expanded its membership and activities and by 1940 was directing the operation of collective, peasant-owned cotton gins, electric power stations, mule-drawn railways, ware-houses, Russian-style machine stations, and a mutual crop insurance company. The Union was also in the process of launching a program of cooperative health services, educational and cultural centers, cooperative ejidal food stores, and agricultural experimentation and demonstration centers—all run by and for peasant members. Perhaps the most important activity of the Central Union during this period was its effort to gain complete peasant control over the selection, packing, marketing, and processing of the ejidal crop, as well as control over the distribution of credit funds to *ejidatarios*.

At this point in its development, the Central Union was the most powerful peasant organization in the Laguna region, more influential even than the regional committees of the CNC. The Union's membership of some 30,000 highly politicized peasants formed the basis of its political strength. The Central Union also enjoyed significant economic power because the financial success of its economic enterprises gave the organization increasing independence from government support or control. Cooperative enterprises further provided Central Union members a certain measure of independence from the commercial network of money lenders, cotton merchants, and agricultural equipment suppliers, all controlled by the old landholding class and by foreign capital. Accordingly, as the growing strength of the peasants organized in the Central Union gradually came to threaten the advantages of the bourgeoisie and other vested interests, strenuous efforts were made to curb this peasant organization.

Political Repression

When the conservative Manuel Avila Camacho succeeded Cárdenas in the presidency, a series of new policies drastically altered the political climate that had permitted a peasant organization like the Central Union to thrive and accumulate political and economic clout. The inauguration of Avila Camacho ushered in a new period of anticommunism in Mexico, which was immediately expressed in a governmental effort to remove from office all Communist Party members holding important positions in peasant and labor organizations. This policy forced upon Central Union leaders the difficult choice of aligning themselves with the official party, turning over their posts to CNC delegated peasants, or accepting a drastic reduction in the activities their organization would be allowed to pursue.

The Central Union officers chose to fight it out and to remain at the head of their organization. They neither joined the official party nor renounced their Communist Party membership. The government responded to this decision with an effort to break the power of the Central Union. Almost all of the cooperative enterprises directed by the Central Union were taken out of the control of this organization and placed under the administration of the Ejidal Bank and other government agencies.

This attack on the Central Union was effective inasmuch as it deprived the communist-led union of its economic power base, at the same time forcing it to curtail much of its political activity. Without the financial resources to move about rapidly and extensively in the region, much less between the Laguna and Mexico City, it became increasingly difficult for the Central Union to attend effectively to the problems of its members, or to act as a spokesman for peasant interests.

Over the next twenty-five years the communist-led union survived in an atmosphere of official hostility which gave way at times to outright political repression. During the forties, Central Union officers were imprisoned, members were physically ousted from their desks at the State Agrarian Leagues, and Central Union meetings, rallies, and demonstrations were broken up by police or paid provocateurs. Central Union members lost their seats as peasant representatives on Ejidal Bank, water resource, and other committees, and were replaced in these positions by faithful CNC peasant appointees. Economic blackmail was used to force Central Union members to affiliate with the CNC on pain of losing their credit payments from the Ejidal Bank. In 1947, a rival "Central Union" (CNC affiliated) was established by the Alemán administration to channel off what remained of the official authorities originally delegated to the communist-led Central Union.

Central Union Achievements

Largely as a result of these efforts at political sabotage, Central Union membership declined from 30,000 in 1940 to roughly 3,500 members in the late sixties. Notwithstanding the decline in membership, the Central Union survived as a significant political force in the Laguna region. Not only did it survive, but it realized some substantial political and economic achievements. Without renouncing its communist affiliation or joining the official party family, it managed to establish a relatively permanent place for itself in the agrarian politics of the region, and it was recognized by successive regimes as the most articulate spokesman for peasant interests in the Laguna.

The Central Union's achievements would hardly be described as "revolutionary victories." Rather, those peasants who stuck with the Central Union were rewarded for their loyalty by a number of concrete economic benefits. For example, the communist peasant leaders won the right to bargain and to sell their members' cotton with no intervention on the part of the Ejidal Bank.[19] Along the same lines, the Central Union has trained or hired technicians to provide members with expert advice, so that they would not have to depend on the unreliable and sometimes corrupt technical services of the Ejidal Bank. These concessions, won after years of politicking by Central Union leaders at both the regional and national level, have meant a few more pesos in the pockets of Central Union members. The 1 percent commission on the sale of members' produce has also provided the organization with a substantial part of its operating budget. But, obviously, these achievements are not radical in any sense of the word. These efforts in no way altered the basic social, political, or even the economic structure of the Laguna region.

Somewhat more significant in terms of its implications for socioeconomic change have been the efforts of the Central Union to win credit concessions for the diversification of ejidal agriculture. By moving away from cotton to a variety of new agricultural activities (dairy farming, cultivation of grapes, walnuts, alfalfa, wheat), Central Union leaders hoped to break the vicious circle of region-wide dependency on a single crop with a declining price on the world market. The Central Union expended years of effort, thousands of pesos, called meeting after meeting, issued report after report in its efforts to persuade not only Union members but peasants throughout the Laguna of the need to switch from monoculture to a variety of crops. And once the demonstration experiments and educational program mounted by the organization had effectively persuaded most peasants that their increasingly precarious economic situation was intimately linked to dependency on cotton, great effort was still needed to convince the government to make funds available for crop diversification in the Laguna.

Thus most of the Central Union's political battles of the last three decades have not involved efforts to transform the economic system, much less to overthrow the existing form of government. Rather, the communist-led peasant union has struggled simply to salvage the ejidal system as it was originally created in the Laguna region. As we have noted, the economic viability of the ejidal system has not enjoyed a very high priority in the development plans of those who have held power in Mexico since 1940. Since that time, investment funds that might have been made available for credit, research, hydraulic projects, and other benefits to the ejidal sector have instead been channeled into private commercial agriculture. However, the Laguna ejidal community represents a partial exception to this overall trend. The government has poured more money and attention into the Laguna *ejidos* than almost any other region in the country (with the significant exception of the large, commercially oriented *ejidos* of the Northwest). And if the Laguna *ejidos* have received a slightly bigger slice of the investment pie, this is largely due to the steady agitation of the Central Union. Both in the region and in Mexico City, Central Union leaders have been the most active, militant, and vocal advocates of a better deal for the Laguna.

Even during the forties and fifties, a period marked by increasing governmental neglect of land reform and hostility toward agrarian movements and demands, the Central Union regularly mounted mass demonstrations, brought pressure to bear on the Department of Agrarian Affairs, and sent a steady stream of delegates to Mexico City to demand audiences with incumbent presidents. The Union ran candidates for public office who had no chance of electoral victory, simply to use the campaign period to raise important issues. On several occasions huge "caravans" made up of hundreds of men, women, and children were organized by the Central Union and sent more than a thousand kilometers to Mexico City to march through the streets of the Capital, dramatizing the economic difficulties of the Laguna *ejidatarios,* capturing the attention of the press and the government, and forcing the latter to give way, at least in part, to some of the demands of the Laguneros.

The agitation of the Central Union has been conspicuous in contrast to the inaction and quiescence of the Laguna CNC. The Central Union fight against corruption in the administration of the Ejidal Bank and other government agencies has been untiring. The Union is the only organization to effectively organize to defend ejidal land and water rights from encroachment by the large landowners, and has been the main spokesman in the fight for improved medical, educational, technical, and credit facilities for all peasants in the region. Finally, this communist-led peasant union was directly responsible for bringing to the Laguna an agricultural rehabilitation plan which doubled the surface of irrigated land in the region.

Obviously these achievements, if not revolutionary, are at least substantial and indicate a good deal more political capacity than is normally displayed by CNC affiliated peasant organizations. We might ask how it was possible for a group in no way connected with the official party to accomplish so much.

Playing by the Rules of the Game

The Central Union accomplished what it did by playing strictly by the rules of the Mexican power game. Success in this game calls for special skills and, above all, flexibility and a superb sense of balance. It requires that opposition leaders know when to strike hard and when to ease off on political pressure; when to make militant, threatening gestures, and when to give in; when to hold out, and when to accept considerably less than the concessions demanded.

To play this game successfully, politicians who work outside the PRI must build a reputation for strength, flexing their political muscles often enough to remind the government that they represent a political force to be reckoned with. This is what the business of mass demonstrations, caravans, and running electoral candidates is all about. They all serve to remind those in power that a particular opposition group is strong, well organized, and can, if ignored too long, threaten the control of the ruling party in a given region. When a peasant organization like the Central Union loads five hundred *ejidatarios* onto trucks and sends them off to Mexico City to march through the streets or to make a nuisance of themselves sitting in the antechambers of the National Palace, the leadership is effectively telling the government: "These five hundred peasants are only a fraction of the people whose loyalty we command. If we can send this group to Mexico City, we have the organizational skills to bring together the discontented and transport them anywhere in the Republic. We are a political group of significance, an organization to be taken seriously. Our demands must be met at least in part if we are not to create serious trouble for those in power."

The Central Union traditionally enjoyed the leadership of individuals astute and flexible enough to understand these rules and to play the game with great skill. These leaders were able to read the direction of the political winds and respond quickly to changes in the political climate. For example, in the early forties, every meeting of the Central Union opened with a demand for the expropriation of all holdings in excess of fifty acres. However, in response to a new era of intense anticommunism and antiagrarianism, these demands were dropped in favor of appeals for compliance with existing agrarian legislation; demands that the peasants receive the land and water that they already had coming to them under the Agrarian Code. Central Union pressure for total peasant control over all the economic affairs of the *ejidos* was reduced to calls for the recognition of the Union as a bargaining agent for *ejidatarios* in a number of key transactions. When interviewed in 1968, Central Union leaders explained that these reduced demands were "more realistic, given the difficult conditions faced by peasant and labor organizations in that period."

Again in the fifties, Central Union leaders responded to a new set of political conditions. When Adolfo Ruíz Cortines assumed the presidency in 1952, the prestige of the government and the official party was at one of its lowest ebbs. The antiagrarian and antilabor policies of Ruíz Cortines' predecessor, Alemán, had alienated peasants and workers, while the flagrantly corrupt activities of *alemanistas* at all levels of government had become distressing to even the least idealistic of Mexicans.[20] Disaffection was so great that Ruíz Cortines came into office with the smallest majority of the vote ever recorded by an official party candidate for the presidency.[21]

Accordingly, the new President at once began the fence-mending process. In addition to a large scale "cleanup of corruption," this administration sought reconciliation with those who had suffered most severely the effects of Alemán's program of rapid industrialization. In virtually all his public addresses Ruíz Cortines indicated that he would try to mollify peasant groups throughout Mexico. Central Union leaders seized on this evidence to sharpen their pressure and demands on the government. Indeed, the Ruíz Cortines years were a relatively successful period for the Central Union which, among other substantial concessions, received a 200 million peso credit to launch its long-ignored plan for crop diversification.

Ruíz Cortines' successor, Adolfo López Mateos, likewise projected his regime as a period of "renovation" in the countryside. Central Union leaders once more stepped up their activities and pressure, and once again received some significant economic concessions for their members.

During the 50s and 60s the Central Union seemed to be more "successful" in its dealings with each new regime: opposing the government less, but winning more in the way of economic benefits for its constituency. This process culminated under the administration of Gustavo Díaz Ordaz, who came to power in 1964.

As early as 1947 a special political friendship developed between Díaz Ordaz and Arturo Orona, the principal leader of the Central Union. Díaz Ordaz, then a senator and an official party regular, came to the Laguna to attend the regional congress of the CNC. During the day, Díaz Ordaz met with PRI and CNC regulars and denounced the communist-led Central Union at an assembly of CNC delegates saying, ". . . for the CNC there exists no group of enemy peasants except those who provoke disunity to satisfy personal appetites, and those who live off the sweat of the peasants. . . ."[22] But that night he accepted an invitation for dinner at the home of Orona, where, over a plate of *tamales*, the two men established a relationship that would subsequently prove very valuable to both of them.

On successive visits to Mexico City, above all in moments of crisis for the Central Union, Orona could count on the support of Díaz Ordaz, among other key politicians, for the help he needed to keep his organization alive. Not all members of the directorate of the Central Union agreed with this approach to the problem of political survival, but, in general, cultivation of some important politicians on the national level, combined with displays of political strength on the local level, helped to keep the Central Union afloat during the bleak years.

Once Díaz Ordaz came to power in 1964, the political and economic fortunes of the Central Union improved markedly. When Díaz made his much heralded official visit to the Laguna in 1966, the Chief Executive openly snubbed the entire range of local, regional, and state CNC representatives when, stepping from his helicopter, he walked directly over to Orona, embraced the old communist warmly and, taking his arm, led him into the presidential touring bus. During the Díaz Ordaz years, Orona could count on a sympathetic hearing and prompt action from the president when the Central Union was unable to · resolve problems through the ordinary government channels.

However, the political friendship between Orona and Díaz Ordaz placed the Central Union in a very awkward position when the Díaz Ordaz regime was rocked by the student movement of 1968. The student crisis brought into the open a deep internal conflict within the peasant union. The dominant faction, led by Orona, insisted that the organization declare its support for Díaz Ordaz, even in the face of the atrocities committed by his government. The minority faction, composed in general of younger, more militant peasants, came out in favor of an antigovernment demonstration. Orona's view prevailed, and in mid-October of 1968, the Union took an advertisement in the regional daily, *La Opinión,* proclaiming the Central Union's support for the Díaz Ordaz regime.[23]

This gesture of solidarity with the regime in its weakest hour bore very tangible fruit in the form of a 3.5 million peso credit given to the Central Union for the purchase of walnut seedlings and the development of a dairy industry. And in November of that same year Orona received the following letter from the president of the Republic:

> Los Pinos
> México, D.F.
> November 5, 1968

Sr. Arturo Orona
Torreón, Coahuila

Esteemed friend,

Sr. Norberto Aguirre [Secretary of the Department of Agrarian Affairs] was kind enough to transmit your message to me. Your thoughts moved me deeply, and when I said as much to Sr. Aguirre, he told me that you, too, had expressed them with great emotion.

Your words of profound human warmth and encouragement in such difficult hours of injustice and misunderstanding constituted one of the best offerings I could have received.

I also received the *tamales* that you so kindly sent me, and we ate them at home with complete confidence and pleasure. They were very delicious.

Thanking you for your courtesy, I salute you affectionately,

> Gustavo Díaz Ordaz

In January of 1972, Arturo Orona was expelled from the Mexican Communist Party in which he had sat as a member of the Central Committee off and on for many years.[24] At the same time he was dropped from the ranks of the Independent Peasant Central and other communist affiliates that had once been proud to associate his name with their organization. Orona had gone too far in his policy of collaborating with the government in return for concrete economic gains. In the eyes of many of his comrades, Orona's policy

Porfirio Díaz seized power in 1876 by military coup and ruled Mexico as a dictator for more than thirty years.

Under the pretext of gathering to play music, peasants would meet on the weekends to drink *pulque* and secretly discuss their discontent with the porfirian regime. ca. 1907.

Under the banner of "Effective Suffrage and No Re election," Francisco I. Madero, a politically progres sive landowner from northern Mexico, touched off the struggle to overthrow the porfirian dictatorship and went on to become the Revolution's first president.

Venustiano Carranza, the most conservative of the principal revolutionary leaders of the North, emerged by 1914 as the dominant force among the armies of the Revolution.

In 1915, a *soldadera,* Ana María Fernández, posed for the camera with an unidentified comrade-in-arms.

General Francisco "Pancho" Villa, the bandit-turned-revolutionary, was a Robin Hood figure who led the famous Division del Norte, an army comprised of cowboys, miners, gamblers, bandits, and drifters.

Their homes destroyed, their lives uprooted, women joined the revolutionary armies as combatants as well as camp followers. This woman is Valentina Ramírez, a *soldadera* who took part in the seige of Culiacán.

The *zapatistas* enter Mexico City under the banner of the Virgin of Guadalupe.

The *zapatistas* and *villistas* marched on Mexico City and took the capital. The two leaders celebrated their alliance in the National Palace, but neither felt prepared for national leadership.

The various armies of the North split and reunited along new lines. Soldiers surrendered to an enemy force one day and, as a condition of their release, took up arms the next day to fight under a new general.

A *huertista* soldier and his sweetheart say farewell.

Throughout the years of struggle, Emiliano Zapata was able to count upon the adhesion and collaboration of a group of urban and rural radical intellectuals as well as the intense loyalty of his peasant troops.

April 1926. President Alvaro Obregón (fourth from the left) with his protégé, Plutarco Elías Calles (fifth from left) and the increasingly powerful labor boss, Luís Morones (next to Calles).

President Plutarco Elías Calles (1924-1928) oversaw the postrevolutionary period of physical reconstruction and industrial and commercial expansion at the same time that he consolidated national power through the formation of an official party. Here he steps from the first commercial Mexican aircraft, as he inaugurates the national airline.

The candidacy of Lázaro Cárdenas was supported by progressives in 1933 because the Governor of Michoacán had built a reputation as an honest and popular leader who had promoted land reform and other social transformations in his home state.

During his electoral campaign and throughout his administration (1934-1940), Lázaro Cárdenas expressed his concern for social justice by traveling to remote corners of the Republic to meet face to face with his peasant and working class supporters.

Manuél Avila Camacho (1940-1946), the wartime president who oversaw the shift away from the populist priorities of Cárdenas, played host to Mexico's ally, Franklin Delano Roosevelt and first lady Eleanor Roosevelt.

Four Mexican presidents (left to right) Luís Echeverría (1970-1976), Emilio Portes Gil (1928-1929), Miguel Alemán (1946-1952), and Gustavo Díaz Ordaz (1964-1970) leave the Chamber of Deputies after attending a homage to President Adolfo Ruíz Cortines (1952-1958).

The cover of *Siempre* takes a jibe at the expectations raised by the campaign promises made by incoming President Adolfo López Mateos (1958-1964).

Although his victory was assured from the time he was named official party candidate in 1969, Echeverría traveled 350,000 miles and visited more than 900 villages, towns, and cities in a seven-month tour designed to build popular support for his regime.

Carrying over his campaign techniques to his administration, Echeverría became the most visible and accessible president since Lázaro Cárdenas.

Presidential candidate José López Portillo receives the official support of CTM and CNOP affiliated unions.

Not only are peasants the poorest sector of the population, but the gap between rich and poor is wider in the countryside than in the towns and cities of Mexico.

Despite the modernization of agriculture in key regions of Mexico, technology remains crude in many marginal areas of the country.

The backward technology of the poor agricultural regions contrasts with an area like the Laguna in northern Mexico where the cultivation of an important commercial crop and the existence of highly politicized and well organized peasant unions has given peasants a means to pressure the national government to provide credit for the purchase of tractors and other sophisticated agricultural equipment.

Throughout Mexico, landless peasants have abandoned the countryside to migrate to the cities in hope of improving their lot. But jobs in the cities have not increased at a rate adequate to absorb this rural surplus.

On the periphery of the cities squalid slums spring up like mushrooms as migrants construct makeshift dwellings out of mud, corrugated paper, hammered-out tin cans, and scrap lumber.

The squatters build wherever they find space: in deep ravines, under electric power lines, along the railroad right of way. In some "lost cities" unemployment runs as high as 95 percent.

The student movement of 1968 expressed young Mexicans' anger at the hunger and misery produced by the distorted priorities of Mexican development.

The government's response to the student movement was a brutal, sweeping repression in which hundreds of Mexicans were killed and wounded and hundreds more imprisoned.

Despite widespread discontent with PRI rule, this political machine is still capable of mobilizing support as in this demonstration in the Constitutional Plaza, March 20, 1976.

tú, ¿que has hecho por defender las conquistas por las que nosotros dimos la vida?

A poster carried by student protestors in the Corpus Christi day demonstration June 1971, read, "You—What have you done to defend the achievements for which we gave our lives?"

of playing along with the government in exchange for benefits to constituents had gradually become outright opportunism. In their opinion Orona had sold out; he had become thoroughly co-opted, and he had brought his organization right along with him. They reasoned that the Central Union had traded its independence and integrity in return for economic concessions, and that the long-term welfare of the peasants had been forgotten or sacrificed in the rush for short-term, bread and butter gains.

It is our intention to analyze these political developments rather than to judge them. Therefore it is important to note that Central Union leaders started out in the 1930s as Marxists committed to the struggle for a thoroughgoing transformation in the countryside, a complete land reform that would have left no individual with more than fifty acres. The realities of the political world in which they found themselves forced them to accept much less. It forced them to struggle with all their energy simply to win what amounted to compliance with long-existing legislation, with agrarian goals that were already well articulated back in 1910. They were like men on a treadmill, obliged to run at full speed simply to remain in the same place. In time they found it more useful to collaborate with what they like to call the "progressive elements" within the government "rather than permit the administration to come under the domination of reactionary forces."[25]

The experience of the Central Union illustrates that opposition movements can and do wrest concessions from the government. However, they do so, generally speaking, only at the cost of altering if not totally subverting the original goals of their movement.

Some Guidelines for Political Survival

The gradual moderation or co-optation of the Central Union is best understood in light of what we know about the hegemonic nature of the Mexican political system. As we noted earlier, independent organizations, however pure or true to their goals they may wish to remain, exist within a one-party system. If such organizations refuse to compromise or make some kind of accommodation with the government, they may find it impossible to survive, and they certainly will find it impossible to win for their members the concessions which give the organization reason to exist in the first place. To win concessions for their political supporters, many, if not most,

opposition organizations eventually accept certain limitations or restrictions on their political activities and tacitly agree to play politics
within certain guidelines.

To grasp the rules of the game, it is essential to understand the
central role of the president of the Republic as a symbol of the
legitimacy of the Mexican political system. As head of the revolutionary family, the government, and the official party, he enjoys a
kind of immunity from criticism that borders on sacrosanctity.
Regardless of the nature of his pre-presidential career, despite the
fact that everyone knows his "popular election" has been engineered
by his party, once in the presidential palace he becomes the principal
representative and symbol of the Mexican nation. Thus, a direct
public attack on the president constitutes an attack on the legitimacy
of the political system and even on the nation as a whole. Such an
attack on the president is widely acknowledged to be politically
dangerous if not suicidal. The most notable instance when the ban on
criticism of the president was ignored occurred during the student
strike in 1968. At that time President Gustavo Díaz Ordaz was
attacked directly by the student movement in slogans chanted in the
streets ("Díaz Ordaz, Incapaz!"), in epithets painted on streetcars,
buses and public buildings ("Díaz Ordaz, Asesino!"), and in posters
that superimposed the profile of the president over that of a gorilla.
But movement participants paid heavily for their break with tradition when, on the night of October 2, 1968, hundreds of demonstrators, disbanding after a peaceful rally, were gunned down by
federal troops in the now infamous Plaza of the Three Cultures in
Mexico City. If it was unprecedented in modern Mexican history that
the army be ordered to turn its guns on great masses of *urban* population, it was also unprecedented that any identifiable group of
people walk through the streets bearing placards that insult the president of the Republic. The ruling party has manipulated political
symbols so that an insult to the president becomes an insult to the
Mexican nation.

Even when a group's interests are severely injured by presidential
policies, group spokesmen normally continue to maintain that the
president is a man of good will and generous spirit—a "great Mexican" and a true friend of the group in question, be it the *ejidatarios*
of the Laguna, the electricians of Puebla, or the small merchants of
Ciudad Juárez. The president himself is publicly portrayed as sin-
cerely committed to promoting the interests of people like *ejidatarios*

or electricians or small merchants. The fault, it is said, lies with others. Foreign capitalists are fair game. So are vaguely defined "reactionaries who attempt to undo the achievements of the Mexican Revolution."[26] Very frequently the blame falls on "insidious" individuals who surround the president and who, in their capacities as ministers, secretaries, and agency heads, misinform, misdirect, and misadvise the president. Policy injurious to the interests of a group can then be attributed to the nefarious machinations of unnamed advisors who have taken it upon themselves to reinterpret or ignore directives given by the president in good faith. But damaging policy must not be attributed directly to the president.

There are other rules. It is safe enough to talk vaguely about the "nefarious machinations of people who have somehow gained the ear of the president," but it is a very bad idea to directly name or attack an individual who is very close to the president—unless, of course, that individual's power is on the wane. Along this line, it may be necessary for opposition organizations to do some careful investigation to determine who in fact is close to the president at any given moment. They must determine who enjoys the president's confidence and who has fallen into disfavor. Because the real lines of power in the PRI or the government may bear very little correspondence to the formal hierarchy of power in those institutions, it requires alert observation simply to know who is "in" and who is "out" in official circles. These relationships often shift frequently and dramatically. And the benefits of reading them correctly—or the costs of misreading them—may also be quite dramatic.

Another requirement for opposition groups who mean to play by the rules is that they claim that everything they demand and all their political activities are "well within the traditions of the Mexican Revolution." A favorite smear tactic used against leftist organizations is the assertion that the PRI is "the party of the Mexican Revolution," while the activities of left-wing opposition groups represent an effort to foist the Russian or Chinese revolutions on the Mexican people who already have their own proud tradition of revolution. Hence, groups must struggle to steer clear of any close association with the Russian, Chinese, or Cuban revolution, or, by extension, association with any foreign models.[27] The safest thing for opposition groups is to identify themselves with some of the major heroes of the Mexican Revolution. For example, peasant organizations generally claim to be inspired by the militant tradition of Emiliano

Zapata,[28] while opposition labor groups look to revolutionary heroes like the anarcho-syndicalist brothers, Enrique and Ricardo Flores Magón, who gave radical intellectual inspiration to the Mexican Revolution.

It is clear that rules such as these were observed by Central Union leaders. We might well ask if the Union's leadership had to compromise as much or as often as they did. We might also question whether the benefits won for the Union's constituency were worth the loss of political independence. But questions like these are almost impossible to answer. For one thing, it is risky for outsiders to attempt to measure the importance to peasant members of the economic benefits won for them by their organization. Secondly, it is very difficult for any organization to find that middle ground between a principled, independent stance and co-optation. Most organizations are unable to establish themselves on that middle ground, and the best they can do is to play the political game skillfully and hope they can build a strong enough power base to give them some space in which to maneuver.

The political history of the Central Union illustrates the point that co-optation is not a black-and-white process. We cannot readily identify specific moments in time when an organization is "militant" or "principled" and then mark another moment when it "sells out." Rather, we are looking at a subtle, complex process in which, according to the political climate and the amount of opposition activity a given regime will tolerate, organizations move back and forth between positions of close collaboration with the government and positions of greater independence.[29]

Naturally not all opposition organizations succumb to the pressure to collaborate with the government. And among those organizations that we might identify as having been co-opted, not all have been compromised to the same degree. The line between partial and total co-optation is hazy, but, roughly speaking, we could say that those individuals or organizations that give up an independent political identity to affiliate directly with the official party or consistently support official party candidates in electoral contests, have been completely co-opted. Those people and organizations who remain outside the PRI but cooperate off and on with the government, occasionally supporting PRI candidates at election time and playing the political game for concessions according to the established rules, could be called partially co-opted.

Co-optation vs. Repression

When oppositionists refuse to modify their demands or to accommodate themselves or their organization to the system, they are repressed. Repression, like co-optation, differs in degree. Like co-optation, it may be more or less complete.

One form of repression is constant harassment. Meetings and demonstrations are broken up, printing presses are destroyed by hired thugs, armed provocateurs are sent in to menace students in their classrooms, and so forth. Individuals may be followed by police agents, and they or their families may be implicitly or explicitly threatened with violence. One particularly chilling example of harassment is the case of a student leader from Nuevo León who was seized by secret police agents, blindfolded and tied to an unused railroad track immediately adjacent to a track carrying heavy rail traffic. The crucial point about all these forms of harassment is that they are likely to make it difficult, if not impossible, for an organization or an individual to act politically. In such cases so much energy must be devoted to self-defense and, in the case of organizations, to internal security that the harassed person or organization may become politically paralyzed.

An even more serious stage of repression is reached when movement leaders are summarily arrested and clapped into prison, frequently at the most crucial moment in the development of their political struggle. The leaders may be held for a year or longer, with or without a trial. But even if their imprisonment is relatively short-term, they may find upon their release that their movement has lost a momentum that is nearly impossible to recover. Some organizations have been repeatedly subject to the short-term imprisonment of their leadership, a tactic of repression both intimidating and politically debilitating.

Further along the scale of repression is the long-term imprisonment of a movement's key leaders. During long-term imprisonment the health and at times even the spirit of leaders may be broken while, without its leadership, the movement may lose momentum and, in the long run, disintegrate completely. After their lengthy term behind bars, the leaders may be released only to find that they have neither the physical strength nor the remaining political support to resume their activities or rebuild their movement.

Lastly, the most serious and final form of repression is the

assassination of principal leaders and slaying of supporters.[30] It is difficult to know how often the Mexican government has recourse to this
extreme measure, but if we consider only the well known, well documented incidents of assassination, we must conclude that it is not
infrequently employed. The names of some of the leaders who were
killed because they would not compromise are well known. The
peasant leaders, Rubén Jaramillo, Jénaro Vázquez, and Lucio
Cabañas are three that come immediately to mind.[31] But in most
cases we will never know the names or numbers of people who
refused to moderate their political behavior, because these people
were eliminated before they reached national or international prominence. Rural people are most often killed in their local areas and
word seldom gets beyond the region, while urban oppositionists "disappear" in a variety of mysterious ways, one being the practice of
dropping people out of airplanes into the Gulf of Mexico. For this
reason we cannot make an accurate count of these people. However,
extensive interviews in the countryside and cities together with a
careful between-the-lines reading of the "agrarian affairs" page of
El Día or *Excelsior*, suggest that they are numerous.[32] Indeed, it
would be no exaggeration to say that probably every day in some
part of Mexico, a dissident peasant, a radical labor leader, or a militant student is killed either by the army, the police, or by political
opponents on the local scene.

Thus, while we have some idea how many organizations make an
accommodation with the government, we can only guess at the number of people and groups that refuse to be co-opted. Accordingly, we
can only speculate whether as many people resist co-optation (and
are eliminated from the political scene as a result) as choose the path
of collaboration with their government.

It is difficult to give specific examples of opposition groups that
fall into these different categories, because a group that is harassed
today may be more severely repressed tomorrow, while another
organization that presently has a shaky hold on its political independence may be partially co-opted in the near future. However, we
could say that the Mexican Communist Party is an organization subject to constant harassment. The communist-affiliated Independent
Peasant Central (Central Campesino Independiente, or CCI) whose
leaders have been in and out of prison numerous times in the last
twenty years, provides an example of an organization repressed by
frequent short-term imprisonment of leaders. The railroad workers'

movement, broken in 1958 by severe physical repression and the jailing of its two principal leaders, Demetrio Vallejo (twelve years in prison) and Valentín Campa (eleven years), exemplifies a militant movement suppressed by long-term imprisonment.

Finally, the list of opposition movements decapitated by the assassination of leaders would have to include not only the movements of militants like Jaramillo and Vázquez, but also a group of moderates who represented the left wing of the PRI. Led by an ambitious lawyer, Carlos A. Madrazo, who had served as head of the official party from 1964 to 1965, this group was pushing for structural reforms within the PRI and greater popular participation in the nomination process. In the spring of 1969, Madrazo, together with a group of his most influential supporters, was killed in a suspicious plane crash near the city of Monterrey.

Table 3 shows the range of possibilities between total co-optation and political annihilation.

The Guerrilla "Alternative"

Guerrilla movements in Mexico have been subject to the same forms of control used by the government to suppress other types of opposition movements. As in other Latin American countries, the success of Fidel Castro's guerrilla forces in Cuba has inspired many dissident Mexicans to try the route of armed struggle. And, as in other parts of Latin America, the Mexican government has developed increasingly sophisticated techniques designed to combat the threat of guerrilla insurgence. Throughout the sixties, small guerrilla bands appeared in the Mexican countryside but were usually repressed before they could gain a foothold. In the mountainous state of Chihuahua, for example, a small guerrilla troop composed of young students, teachers, and doctors was wiped out in its very first action, an attack on a military garrison in Madera City.[33] Three years later, a student group calling itself the 23rd of September Movement launched a new guerrilla front in Chihuahua. This movement, too, was quickly eradicated.[34] In the South of Mexico, where extreme poverty and an untracked, mountainous jungle terrain create more favorable conditions for guerrilla struggle, a series of armed movements have been launched. The National Revolutionary Civic Association, led by Jénaro Vázquez in Guerrero, the Mexican Insurgent Army in Campeche, Tobasco, Veracruz, and Chiapas, and the Partido de los

Table 3

CO-OPTATION		Middle Ground	REPRESSION			
Total Sell Out	Partial Sell Out		Constant Harassment	Short-Term Imprisonment (1-2 yrs.)	Long-Term Imprisonment (more than 2 yrs.)	Elimination
(a) Dissident individuals accept positions in the PRI or in certain govt. jobs. (b) Opposition organizations affiliate with the PRI.	(a) Dissident individuals preserve some of their personal political integrity. Take jobs in the government, but in special areas of government (typically in newly created committees, agencies, etc.; in special task forces, in new clean-up campaigns and in semi-autonomous agencies, research institutes, etc. (b) Organizations maintain their name, do not affiliate with the PRI, make shows of independence but "play the game" strictly by the rules, expressing loyalty to the government, never attacking the president directly, moderating their opposition in return for concrete concessions for their membership.	Varies in size according to the political climate; the amount of opposition activity a regime will tolerate.	Political Paralysis (a) Personal paranoia, sapping of political energy, due to threat to self and family. (b) Organization may spend so much time countering harassment tactics that it cannot act politically.	(a) Leaders snatched from their organization at a crucial moment in the development of a political action. (b) Organization unable to carry through on a crucial political initiative because leadership has been imprisoned.	(a) Leaders will and health broken, political following may be dispersed. (b) Organization may disintegrate due to long absence of leadership.	(a) Leaders are assassinated. (b) Organizations completely wiped out either by "decapitation" (i.e., they are left without leadership when all their leaders have been assassinated) or the membership itself is wiped out by police, army action, or landowners' private forces.

Pobres, led by Lucio Cabañas in Guerrero, were some of the better known movements active in the late sixties and early seventies.

To eliminate guerrilla movements, the Mexican government has drawn upon its standard repertory of control techniques. Generally speaking, those people who have chosen the path of armed struggle are not susceptible to co-optation. Nonetheless, the co-optive approach is tried from time to time, even when dealing with committed guerrilla leaders. For example, shortly before Genaro Vázquez was killed in 1972, high government officials offered to be "kidnapped" by the Vázquez force so that they might "engage the guerrilla leader in a dialogue." But Vázquez would have none of it. He ignored the government's overtures and was killed a short time later.

Since co-optation is generally ineffective in the case of guerrilla movements, the government normally applies repressive measures. To repress armed struggle, the government uses its standard tactic of imprisonment and assassination of leaders, but also can count on an arsenal of counterinsurgency techniques developed in the United States.

The United States has used Vietnam as a testing ground to improve counterinsurgency methods designed for application in dense forest or jungle.[35] Special arms, radio equipment, and highly acute sensor devices have all been used with American assistance in the suppression of armed struggle all over Latin America. The United States has been most anxious to share this technology with the Mexican government. Between 1950 and 1968, U.S. military assistance expenditures in Mexico amounted to $1.7 million.[36] Under this American-funded program, 546 Mexicans were trained in counterinsurgency methods at Fort Benning, Georgia.[37] In addition to military training, the United States sent Mexico $745,000 in police assistance between 1961 and 1969 to cover "in-country training" by U.S. Public Safety Advisors and materials including radios, small arms, gas, and riot equipment.[38]

When compared with U.S. military assistance elsewhere in Latin America, American military aid to Mexico constitutes a very modest program.[39] However, what is significant about the training and equipment funneled into Mexico by the Pentagon is that a variety of other forms of American aid received by other Latin American countries (Food for Peace, the Peace Corps, the United States Agency for International Development, and others) have been firmly rejected by the Mexican government. This official rejection of other

types of American aid grows in part from Mexican nationalist senti-
ment, and in part from the fear that the introduction of aid programs
would establish sources of funds, power and prestige outside of the
PRI controlled system. Thus it is noteworthy that when it comes to
the suppression of guerrilla insurgency, the Mexican government has
been willing to set aside its usual policy and has accepted both
American arms and American advisors.

Well supplied with U.S. training, advisors, and equipment, the
main thrust of the Mexican counterinsurgency effort is to isolate the
guerrillas in a small area and prevent them from expanding their
operations beyond this restricted zone. The army takes severe repressive measures against the peasants who live in the area to dis-
courage their support of the guerrilla forces. Peasants are tortured to
reveal the location of guerrilla camps, and those who have coop-
erated with the insurgents are executed as an example to their neighbors. Terms such as "strategic hamlet" and "pacification program,"
made familiar by the war in Vietnam, are now part of the working
vocabulary of the Mexican soldier.

Up to the present time, the Mexican government has been largely
successful in wiping out those who have attempted to overturn the
system by armed force. The government has been able to respond
quickly and effectively because the methods involved—while techno-
logically more sophisticated—operate on the same theory as those
used to neutralize unarmed political opposition. The leaders are
eliminated—either imprisoned or killed—and the movement is decapitated and left without direction.

Conclusion

In this chapter we have examined the way that the government and
the official party manage to monopolize political power by neutral-
izing potential opposition. The pattern of control is clear enough:
some groups are co-opted by the government, while those that refuse
to cooperate are harassed, repressed, or decapitated through the
imprisonment or assassination of their leaders. And so the party that
came to power in the 1920s, emerging from a decade of revolutionary struggle, continues to perpetuate itself in power. It is not
that opposition movements do not develop to challenge the dominance of the ruling party. It is rather that such movements are
demobilized by the PRI before they can grow powerful enough to

make their impact felt, because the very monolithic qualities of the PRI prevent potential opposition from developing the requisite strength to wrest power from the ruling party.

5. The Student Movement of 1968

> The student movement was only the drop
> of water that made the glass overflow.
>
> Miguel Eduardo del Valle Espinosa,
> Lecumberi Prison, September 1970

We have focused thus far on co-optation and repression and the role of these interrelated mechanisms in the maintenance of political stability. In modern Mexican history these techniques have been employed by the ruling party in a consistent fashion. For the most part they have proved effective in curtailing opposition and suppressing dissent. However, to round out our discussion of political control, we must also look at an important instance when these devices proved inadequate. We must consider what occurs when those in power are threatened by a large militant movement that they can neither buy off nor decapitate.

The student movement of 1968 is the outstanding example of an occasion when the standard techniques of co-optation and repression were not equal to the task. The movement began late in July of 1968 when students from two rival secondary schools clashed in a brief encounter in the center of Mexico City. The police intervened, arresting several students and injuring a good many others. Weeks of violence followed as riot police and plainclothes shock troops moved against the students wherever they gathered to discuss their grievances against the police and the government. From late July through

131

August the police repeatedly attacked student gatherings and invaded secondary schools, on one occasion using a bazooka to blow down the seventeenth-century carved doors of a school. Secondary students from both the vocational (technical) and preparatory (liberal arts) schools as well as university students from the National Autonomous University (UNAM) and the National Politechnic Institute (IPN) organized daily demonstrations to protest these acts of brutality, in particular the army and police occupation of academic facilities.[1]

Participants in these rallies were repeatedly ambushed, beaten by riot police, and the first student deaths were registered. The force used to repress the movement became heavier every day: paratroop riflemen, military police armed with bayonetted rifles, and high-caliber machine guns backed by tanks, helicopters, and armored cars, were brought into play. By the end of July, hundreds of students had been killed, hospitalized, or arrested and imprisoned, while many others simply "disappeared," never to be heard from again.

A New Kind of Movement

The experience of Mexican students with the techniques of mass mobilization was limited. Until 1968 the Mexican universities differed from campuses in other Latin American countries where the presence of "youth sectors" of major political parties often turned universities into centers of intense political conflict that reflected political cleavages on the national level. In Mexico, the predominant student organization was the official student federation of the PRI, a highly bureaucratized organization serving chiefly as a training ground for future PRI politicians. Apart from this federation, "there existed only a multiplicity of small political organizations, mostly concerned with internal squabbling."[2] Historically, the Mexican universities were peripheral to the Revolution of 1917 and to the other important events in the political development of the country. The two major student strikes that shook the university in 1929 and 1966 both concerned internal academic issues related to conditions of admission, study, and examinations.[3]

In the summer of 1968, the escalating brutality directed against the students provided them with a cause, with a sense of group identity, and with a clearly defined enemy: the riot police acting as the agents of the government and the official party. The violence unified students and brought them into the center of the political stage. As repressive measures grew, many who were initially apathetic or unmoved by the events left their classrooms and joined the movement with firm conviction that the time had come for all students to present a united front. The students began to prepare themselves to stand up to the repression. They commandeered buses and built barricades. They occupied school buildings and laid in supplies of food, medical equipment, rags, bottles, and gasoline. They began to set up communications networks to contact the parents and friends of students who were taken prisoner or to military hospitals.

Finally, as the feeling grew that 1968 would be a decisive moment of confrontation with the government, steps were taken to give some organized form to the protest. Normally hostile political organizations and tendencies of the left began to collaborate within the framework of the new movement.[4] The wide diversity of groups was further unified when students from the UNAM and the IPN laid aside traditional differences to unite their movements, and vocational and preparatory students quickly followed suit.[5] In August a general student strike was called, and a National Strike Council was formed. Comprised of 250 representatives from 128 schools, the National Strike Council included both private and public universities and secondary schools. In each school *comités de lucha* (struggle committees) organized the local protest demonstrations and directed the activities of political brigades. The brigades, each composed of roughly ten students, carried out a variety of tasks. Publicity brigades handled the distribution of leaflets, the design and printing of posters, and the painting of walls, buses, and other likely spots for political slogans, communicating to the public through all these means and by simple street-corner speeches, the grievances, demands, and goals of the movement. Medical brigades made up of students from the faculties of medicine and dentistry were responsible for medical supplies and first aid to movement participants. Supply brigades provided food, water, and materiel. A variety of other brigades carried out a series of political chores, including the collection of funds for the movement on street corners, buses, and trams. These brigades would appear in the streets for quick, spontaneous meetings and demonstrations and then disappear just as fast, before the police could pinpoint their meeting place.

The structure of the movement reflected the students' concern for the principles of direct democracy as well as their rejection of the hierarchical and bureaucratized student organizations of the past. The struggle committees operated with virtual autonomy under the loose coordination of the National Strike Council.[6] The emphasis was on direct personal participation in collective political activities. There was a corresponding rejection of complex forms of organization, particularly those involving the delegation of power and the establishment of intermediary authorities.[7] The position of the movement was hammered out in daily seminars, meetings, permanent assemblies, teach-ins, and rallies. Here principles of free speech and participatory democracy were observed despite the awkwardness of such forms in a movement that brings together people of so many political tendencies.[8]

The most significant fact about the organization of the student movement was that the National Strike Council, which coordinated the activities of these various political units and at the same time formulated the strategy for the movement, was headed by a *rotating directorate* of representatives from the 128 participating schools. Strictly speaking, the movement had no identifiable "student leaders," but rather a rotating committee of representatives whose composition changed weekly. In this respect the Mexican movement was similar to other contemporary student movements, because the participants made a concerted effort to move away from "personalities" and the identification of the struggle with specific leaders toward more democratic forms emphasizing shared responsibilities and power.[9]

Thus in 1968 the Mexican government faced a peculiar situation that defied the standard, well-tried techniques of repression. All government methods of control had been based on the assumption that a radical opposition movement must have leaders. By definition, leaders are only human beings, and human beings are susceptible. They can be put out of action: co-opted, imprisoned, or killed.

But the students also understood this fundamental weakness of radical movements; the frailty of human beings in their role as leaders. They knew that most serious movements in the past had disintegrated when the leadership was bought off or eliminated. So, fully conscious of this problem, they determined to build an organization in which the leadership would rotate so frequently among so many different people that the government could not eliminate a handful of organizers and, in so doing, decapitate the movement. They designed their National Strike Council so that a rotating directorate would take responsibility for organizational and political activities. In this way the government would be unable to identify a few "troublemakers" and earmark them for co-optation or destruction, and the students could build a reservoir of leaders to replace those who might be lost in the process of struggle.

Throughout the summer the government continued to arrest and torture individuals it identified as the principal agitators. In some cases police intelligence was accurate enough to pinpoint and seize people who had histories of radical political leadership and who were, in fact, playing leading roles in the movement. In many other cases, however, individuals with no history of political involvement were caught in the wide-flung net and paraded before news cameras as "apprehended student leaders." For a time the government made a weak effort to portray the "disturbances" as the work of foreign agitators, mostly veterans of the May Revolution in France. To that end, several young foreign tourists were snatched by the police as they walked through the streets, Mexicans with foreign-sounding last names were featured prominently in press releases on the arrests, and the police went so far as to record Mexican names like Emilio, Antonio, or Maria Antonieta as Emile, Antoine, and Marie Antoinette, with duly gallicized last names. Later the "foreign devil" tactic was dropped when the government realized that the question of responsibility for the "disturbances" could be used to destroy the credibility of a wide variety of domestic opposition figures. Under torture a number of "confessions" were extracted from imprisoned students and a bewildering assortment of opposition figures was named as the source of arms, aid, and directives to the student movement. In addition, the Mexican Communist Party, the CIA, the Cubans, and—most significantly—political enemies of Díaz Ordaz within the official party itself were all accused at one point or another of employing politically naive students to do their destructive work.[10]

But in spite of these smear tactics and the large number of students arrested, bribed, tortured, and killed, the movement persisted and grew. It persisted because its survival was not contingent upon the survival of a few identifiable leaders. And it grew because the movement demands had struck a responsive chord among other sectors of the population who shared the students' intense feelings of discontent with the status quo.[11]

The Movement Grows

When the National University was invaded by the army, moderate professors and university administrators were drawn into the movement.[12] Led by the rector of the National University and a group of prominent professors, some 80,000 students and teachers marched solemnly through downtown Mexico City in what was to be the first of several extremely well organized and effective mass demonstrations. By mid-August the National School of Agriculture, the teachers' colleges, and several other educational institutions had voted to join the strike. On August 13 the Teachers Coalition for Democratic Freedom marched 200,000 strong in front of the National Palace.

The strike spread to schools, colleges, and universities throughout the Republic as teachers and students in the provinces undertook political activities in solidarity with the Mexico City movement. Each day brought fresh arrests, yet the movement grew as more and more people saw in the student protests the long-awaited opportunity to give voice to their own discontent.

The well-publicized "official" position of peasants and workers toward the movement was conveyed by a CTM statement.

> The discontent of some disoriented students has been exploited by sub-versive agents of the left and right in order to sow discontent and create an atmosphere of chaos in the country.[13]

But while the official sectors of the PRI pursued this line, the independent railroad workers and electricians unions and the Independent Peasant Central expressed their support. In addition, a number of CTM affiliated locals, acting in defiance of their own leadership, published statements of solidarity with the students.[14]

Although the students had great faith in the mass demonstration as a means of awakening consciousness, it was the brigades that carried out the work of building links with other sectors of the Mexican population. Political brigades sought direct contact with workers in the factory. Law and medical students established legal and medical clinics to serve the poor. Radio Universidad broadcast the message of the movement. By the end of August, the students were able to mobilize a crowd of half a million to march through the center of the Capital to the Constitutional Plaza. In addition to the students and large delegations of their parents and relatives, the demonstrators at this August 27 rally included contingents of railroad, petroleum, and factory workers, electricians, taxi drivers, and push-cart peddlers, as well as small groups of peasants from outlying regions of Mexico. Middle class people, shop workers, small merchants, professionals, and clerks left their offices and stores to cheer the demonstrators as they marched by, or to fall in behind the students who called out to them, *unite pueblo*! (people unite!).[15]

The movement did not grow simply in numbers, it also began to gain a measure of ideological cohesion. Initially the stance assumed by the participants was a defensive one. The students and their allies were intent on denying the charge that they were organized by outside agitators and inspired by foreign ideologies. As a matter of policy, portraits of Mexican heroes—Emiliano Zapata, Pancho Villa, Benito Juárez—were carried in preference to those of Che, Mao, or Ho Chi Minh. The march organizers wished to make clear that these were not demonstrations inspired by "foreign revolutionary doctrine," but a call for the fulfillment of Mexico's own Revolution. Clearly expressing the position of the movement was the slogan, "We are not the agitators. Hunger and misery are the agitators."

Gradually movement participants began to exchange this defensive posture for a more assertive stance. The forthcoming celebration of the Olympic Games and the repressive measures applied by the Mexican government to assure that the Games would be staged without disruption provided immediate focus for the movement. The movement's symbols and slogans centered on the Olympiad and highlighted the irony of claiming 1968 as the "Year of Peace" in Mexico. The placards they carried expressed the students' deeply felt disgust at the expenditure of millions of pesos on sports arenas, publicity, and apartments for foreign athletes by a government that could not find the resources to provide housing, medical services, and primary education for a vast sector of its population. The signs underscored the brutality of the regime that was playing host to the world's athletes: "Mexico will win the gold medal for repression"—"Welcome to Mexico, site of the Olympic Butchery, 1968." Others depicted the Olympic dove of peace with a knife in its breast, the five-ring Olympic symbol as five smoking grenades, and a riot policeman racing along with his club held aloft like a flaming Olympic torch.

The Student Demands

The demands that were formulated by the National Strike Council reflected both the fluid nature of that body and its fear of provoking ideological confrontation among the various political groups involved in the movement.[16] The demands necessarily dealt with government abuses so flagrant that every movement participant could support the points of protest as justified grievances. Thus, the demands focused on the agents and mechanisms of repression employed by those who hold power in Mexico, and they called for relief for the victims of this repressive process. Perhaps the most sweeping was the demand for the release of all political prisoners, both those arrested during the summer of 1968, and those serving long terms for radical activities in the past. The popular Demitrio Vallejo and Valentín Campa, radical railroad union leaders, had been held in prison since the government smashed their movement ten years earlier in 1958. Although the official line held that no Mexicans were ever jailed because of their political beliefs, Vallejo and Campa, together with other radical leaders, were clearly the victims of political persecution. Accordingly, the movement called not only for the release of these political victims, but for the repeal of Articles 145 and 145[b] of the Penal Code, the wide-ranging sedition acts under which they were held.[17]

Another demand called for the abolition of the special riot police (*granaderos*) and the resignation of their chief, General Frías. The students pointed out that the very existence of such a squad was illegal because the Constitution provides only for the maintenance of police forces under the jurisdiction of the Judicial Department, while the *granaderos* were independent of such control. The role played by the *granaderos* since 1944 (strike-breaking, suppression of demonstrations, etc.) made the riot police a particularly conspicuous agent of repression and a widespread object of popular antipathy.[18]

Along the same lines, the students also demanded the resignation of the chief of police, General Luis Cueto, and his deputy, General Mendiola. By focusing on these two men and demanding their dismissal, the students hoped to force the government to acknowledge publicly its responsibility for the repressive acts of the various police agencies. At the same time the students called for a full public investigation to determine the responsibility for police and army vandalism and brutality. For example, late in July in broad daylight, close to one hundred men in plain clothes, face masks, and unmarked cars machine-gunned the façade of Vocational School Number 5 in the Plaza of the Three Cultures. Later that night they returned with doubled strength to enter the school and beat those students they found within. These terrorists were members of a government-sponsored, paramilitary shock troop receiving training, salaries, and orders from the Department of the Federal District, the governing body of Mexico City. The students insisted that the President explain the existence of government-trained shock troops operating with no publicly acknowledged authorization.[19]

Finally, the students demanded that the military occupation of all schools be lifted, and that the government compensate the students wounded in conflicts with the police and army, as well as the families of those students who had been killed.

These demands were neither radical nor revolutionary. We should note that the students were still directing their grievances to the government, and that the very nature of their demands underlined the authority of that government. The student movement was essentially calling for the recognition of constitutional guarantees and the protection of civil liberties provided by the Constitution. When interviewed in 1968, the National Strike Council representatives who had drawn up the list of demands explained that they had settled upon these particular grievances because they dealt with highly visible, well-known government abuses of power. It was felt at the time that the unity of the movement could only be sustained and a widespread base of support could only be built if the students set as their goals a series of moderate, reformist objectives with which a majority of middle class people, peasants, and workers could identify. They reasoned that the people they potentially hoped to draw into their movement were not sufficiently politicized at that point in time to participate in a movement that questioned and challenged the fundamental institutions of the nation.[20]

The Underlying Causes

But underlying these fairly moderate demands were grievances far more serious. Although the spark that ignited the conflict of 1968 was a series of brutal police interventions, participation in the movement was an expression of political feelings far more complex and long-term. Behind the students' involvement lay a sense of outrage so profound that no slogan or demand could give it full expression. The students were angry at the distorted priorities that had been set for Mexico by its ruling elite. The expenditure of millions of pesos on the Olympic Games was only symptomatic of what the students regarded as a criminal mismanagement of the nation's resources by those in power. To the students, the Olympics and the years of excited preparation that preceded the staging of the spectacle were nothing more than an orgy of self-indulgence on the part of a national bourgeoisie that was determined to prove to the world (and to itself) that Mexico, where so many millions live in conditions of extreme poverty, was in fact a progressive, democratic, and modern nation. In short, the students were disgusted by the farce played out by those in power. They were tired of the speeches about "progress" and "development" and wished to put an end to the demagogical rhetoric used to camouflage the greed and corruption of the ruling elite. The movement, therefore, was born of a desire to strip away the mask and destroy forever the myth of the "institutionalized Revolution," the "democratically elected President," and his "revolutionary party."

The students were also angered by the inflexibility of the system and the lack of alternative avenues for upward mobility. They understood how the co-optation process works, and they were profoundly disheartened to realize that young Mexicans like themselves have little chance of holding a job or advancing economically or socially without seriously compromising their principles and accepting the rules of the PRI. It was difficult for these young people to accept the fact that they would be obliged to demean themselves, compromise their integrity, and run around back-slapping and hand-pumping in the corridors of the official party if they hoped to get or keep a decent job.

Finally, the students were outraged by the repressive nature of the system. They could no longer bear to see the most principled and courageous of their countrymen cut down by government assassins. They chose to take a stand rather than quietly watch the betrayal and assassination of Zapata played out again and again in their own time.

The sentiments that propelled students out of their classrooms and into the streets had begun to move other sectors of the population. Over the course of four months, the 1968 student movement evolved into the most articulate and threatening outburst of public disaffection that a modern Mexican government had ever faced. Not only had the standard techniques of control, co-optation, and decapitation failed to break the movement, but the students' courage and commitment had begun to inspire other Mexicans. The government was particularly worried that worker and peasant support for the student movement, which, up to this point, was only limited and inarticulate, might strengthen and spread to other parts of the Republic. Furthermore, the government was pressured to act quickly because the Olympic Games were scheduled to begin on October 12. And so, the government conceived a "final solution" to the problem it faced: a crushing blow calculated to obliterate the student movement.

The "Final Solution": Tlatelolco

Late on the afternoon of October 2, about 6,000 people gathered for a demonstration in the Plaza of the Three Cultures at the center of a modern Mexico City housing development in an area called Tlatelolco.[21] The original plan called for a mass march from the Plaza to the National Polytechnic Institute. But word had come that the parade route was blocked by armored cars and troop transports. So, rather than create a situation where a clash with the armed forces was inevitable, the National Strike Council decided that the demonstrators should stay put, hear a number of speakers, and then disperse quietly.

Around five o'clock in the evening, demonstrators began to converge on the Plaza. For roughly one hour they stood in a light rain listening to a series of speeches. At six, the Plaza was suddenly surrounded by a force of 10,000 soldiers armed with high-caliber weapons and expansion bullets. Before the demonstrators could react, the soldiers assumed prone firing positions and trained their rifles and machine guns down into the crowd below. Overhead an army helicopter circled. At exactly 6:10 P.M., the helicopter dropped two green flares into the crowd, giving the signal to attack. As the soldiers opened fire, secret police who had infiltrated the crowd moved toward the speakers' platform. The infiltrators were known to one another by the white handkerchiefs tied around their right hands. Students who had identified themselves as leaders by addressing the meeting were picked off in the first round, even as they counseled the crowd to leave quickly and quietly. Machine guns strafed the speakers' platform and a number of journalists, as well as National Strike Council members, were hit.[22] Those National Strike Council members who were taken alive were stripped naked and herded into an archeological excavation near the Aztec ruins, converted for the evening into a makeshift dungeon. Several were put against the wall and shot.[23]

The remaining casualties included disproportionate numbers of children and old people who had been unable to flee the Plaza, and people shot in their own living rooms as they rushed to take cover when the armored cars turned from the Plaza to train their cannons on the glass façades of the high-rise buildings. Probably as many as 50 people were killed outright in the Plaza and another 500 wounded (many critically), while some 1,500 others were arrested.[24] Many of those wounded later perished because doctors in the emergency wards of the city hospitals were not allowed to attend these victims until they had been placed under guard and interrogated. Eight soldiers caught in the crossfire of their own troops also died that night.[25]

The Aftermath

Where more subtle techniques of co-optation and decapitation had failed, the indiscriminate use of brute force worked. The level of violence used by the government at Tlatelolco terrorized the general public and staggered the student movement. The ruling elite had been unable to pinpoint the leaders of the movement. Therefore it struck at the movement as a whole, calculating that when a sufficiently large mass of people had been arrested or killed, somewhere amid that huge number the effective leaders of the movement would have been taken. In this way, by randomly seizing masses of active students, the leadership of the movement was captured and silenced and the movement participants were terrorized. No one knew who would be seized next, and the very lack of rational pattern to the arrests increased the fear among the students. New leaders did not step forward to replace those who had been killed or imprisoned, because they were justifiably afraid that they would share the same fate as their martyred comrades. The National Strike Council was in disarray and seemed to have lost its capacity to take initiatives or give direction to the movement. Rival factions began to emerge within the Strike Council, some favoring an end to the student strike, while others pushed for the escalation of demands. Its inability to reformulate a clear position and strategy for the movement became evident when, on November 19, the National Strike Council announced that the strike would continue until all political prisoners had been freed, and then, only days later, gave the official call for students to return to classes, though none of the six demands had been fulfilled.

In the months that followed, the student movement lost momentum and largely disintegrated. Those activities that were pursued in the next two years were organized around the demand for the release of movement activists held in federal and state prisons across the country. Protests were also registered against the countless abuses to which the political prisoners were subjected.[26] And when October 2 rolled around each year, there were small demonstrations to mark the anniversary of the Tlatelolco massacre. But what remained of the 1968 movement was a *reactive* rather than an active movement, responding to moves by the government rather than initiating its own line of activity. There was little agreement among the students as to what the next step should be.[27] There was a good deal of talk about building a genuinely *national* student federation, but the unity and consensus that would have made such a federation viable was lacking, particularly because the very idea of a national student federation was quickly taken up and pushed by the new President, Luís Echeverría, and, as such, the idea lost its appeal for genuinely radical students.

Even after the prisoners began to be released in small groups in 1971, they found it difficult to reunify the movement and push ahead with new political initiatives. A number of serious obstacles prevented a resurgence of the spirit of '68. On the one hand much ill feeling remained between the former prisoners and those whom they felt had done a poor job of maintaining the struggle in their absence. On the other side, the ex-prisoners came in for a good deal of suspicion and criticism: some for the "admissions of guilt" they had made as a precondition to the release, and others for accepting the "friendly" overtures of Echeverría. These feelings of bitterness and distrust exacerbated the differences between the old National Strike Council members and the new leadership, mostly members of the Communist Party Youth sector, who had gradually emerged in 1970-1971 at the head of the Comités Coordinadores, the new coordinating committees of the student movement. Perhaps the most serious problem was the difficulty the students had in formulating a new strategy for action. The problem, as one student explained, "was that people were only able to think in terms of mounting larger and larger street demonstrations. Everyone wanted to do something;

something dramatic. But no one was sure how to best express our feelings of unrest. Thus, there was a tendency to fall back on the old formulas: rallies and mass marches—even though 1968 had demonstrated the weakness of those forms."

Finally, it was extremely difficult to rebuild the student movement because, from 1968 on, the schools and universities were heavily infiltrated by armed provocateurs. Some of these terrorists were trained, equipped, and paid by powerful men within the government and the official party. Other bands of infiltrators were in the pay of political groups of the extreme right. Chapter 6 will look more closely at the actions and effect of these provocateurs. At this point it is sufficient to say that the presence in the schools of armed thugs disguised as students contributed to the political confusion and distrust that has made effective student action so difficult since 1968. In a sense the paramilitary terrorists, or *porras*,[28] are the current answer to the old problem of suppression of opposition movements.

Conclusion

The events of 1968 indicated to the government that the old techniques of co-optation, repression, and decapitation were no longer entirely satisfactory. The ruling elite could not rely on these methods alone to control and suppress the development of opposition movements. And what made the situation all the more explosive and dangerous to those in power was that none of the problems that gave birth to the 1968 movement had been resolved. Indeed the problems were all the more obvious. The discontent of young people with the distorted priorities of Mexican development, their disenchantment with the rhetoric of the PRI, their disgust with the rigidity of the system, and their outrage at the repressive measures taken against them in '68—none of these feelings had diminished in any way. At the same time, the number of landless peasants had grown. Unemployment was up. The cost of living in the cities continued to rise faster than the wages of working people. And the urban slums continued to grow and fester while the small sector of privileged Mexicans followed their normal pattern of conspicuous consumption. The influence of foreign capital was in no way reduced.

The resolution of these problems clearly called for radical measures. But when the new president took office in 1970 his talk of "open dialogue," "renovation of the PRI," and "new economic reforms" was received, to say the least, skeptically. All over Mexico people wondered if the new policies proposed by Echeverría would come to grips with the economic, social, and political crisis and if the initiatives of this new regime could resolve the most serious contradictions of Mexican development. It seemed clear that if this new administration could not find ways to deal with these problems, it was going to have to devise ever more imaginative and sophisticated ways to repress unrest.

6. Prospects for Reform and Prospects for Revolution

> If they come looking for me
> To make another Revolution,
> I'll tell them, "Sorry, I'm busy,
> Planting the fields of the landlord."
>
> "Juan Sin Tierra," popular *corrido*

When Luís Echeverría Alvarez assumed the presidency in 1970 he appeared to be well aware that the political situation in Mexico had reached a crisis point. This awareness was reflected in the vigor with which he conducted his political campaign. Although his victory was assured from the time he was named official party candidate in 1969, Echeverría traveled 35,000 miles and visited more than nine hundred villages, towns, and cities during a seven-month tour designed to build popular support for his administration. During this exceptionally strenuous and carefully choreographed campaign, Echeverría barnstormed the Republic, kissing babies, ceremoniously accepting an estimated 5,000 petitions from the poor, parading arm in arm with women colorfully dressed in regional costumes, and proclaiming that the work of the Revolution was indeed incomplete, and that the improved welfare of peasants and workers would be his first priority in office.

147

Notwithstanding Echeverría's efforts to convince Mexicans that his administration would open a new epoch in Mexican history—a period in which the inequalities and imbalances of Mexican development would be redressed—most Mexicans seemed to doubt that the Echeverría regime would do other than to continue the policies pursued by his predecessors since 1940. Thus, at election time in 1970, most observers of the Mexican scene anticipated six more years of official party rule featuring the same emphasis on high rates of industrial growth, heavy investment in the private commercial sector, fat concessions to foreign capital, and continued concentration of land, wealth, and power in the hands of the national bourgeoisie and foreign investors.

There was little in Echeverría's background to suggest otherwise. In 1945 at the age of twenty-three Luís Echeverría married the daughter of Guadalupe Zuno Hernández, a powerful political boss from Jalisco state, and the young lawyer's career was launched. Echeverría rose fairly rapidly through the ranks of the PRI, serving in the Ministry of Education where in 1956 he helped to arrange the army occupation of the National Polytechnic Institute. Serving in the Ministry of the Interior, he played an active role in the suppression of the 1958 railroad workers strike and gathered intelligence on Castroist left wing movements.[1] In 1963, when Díaz Ordaz, then Minister of the Interior, moved up to the presidency, Echeverría was named head of the Interior Ministry, a key position for political control. In this role, Echeverría became responsible for engineering PRI victories at the local, state, and national level, and he won a certain notoriety for himself for his tireless pursuit and persecution of communist organizations, the destruction of several left wing publications, the imposition of an official script in TV and radio newscasts, and the reversal of electoral results in two contests lost by the PRI.[2] Finally, with the exception of Díaz Ordaz himself, Echeverría was the nonmilitary national official most closely associated in the public mind with the policy of student repression in 1968. Indeed Echeverría was widely *believed* to have taken—in the face of an indecisive Díaz Ordaz—the fatal decision to move on the unarmed crowd at the Plaza of the Three Cultures and to put a rapid end to the movement with a public bloodbath of unprecedented proportions.

In light of his background, political record, his close association with Díaz Ordaz, and his overall reputation as a "hard liner," Echeverría's promises of "new and unprecedented democratic overtures" were greeted with a good deal of suspicion. There was, of course, an anticipation that the first two years of the new President's term would bring a general reduction in the most repressive aspects of the political control unleashed by Díaz Ordaz, a slight easing off in the persecution of left wing organizations, and some token attempt at rapprochement with dissident students. For this kind of moderation was part of the standard pattern of a President's six-year term. It is expected that each new President will attempt to mend fences and restore some measure of the political prestige of the PRI and the government if they have been badly damaged by his predecessor.[3] And certainly Echeverría was acknowledged to be intelligent and skillful enough to play this conciliatory role. Indeed many Mexicans who expected to see no meaningful change in the political climate under Echeverría nevertheless hoped that the fence-mending process alone would lead him to extend a mass amnesty to the political prisoners arrested in 1968, and they were greatly dismayed when this did not occur.

Some Changes in the Political Climate

Although Echeverría's conciliatory overtures were initially dismissed on many sides as electoral rhetoric, tokenism, or unabashed demagoguery, by 1971 Echeverría had succeeded in cultivating a new style in national government, and he had begun to give substance to some of his promises.

Carrying over his campaign techniques to his administration, Echeverría became the most visible and accessible President since Lázaro Cárdenas. Virtually every other weekend he made a surprise tour of some region of Mexico, visiting the most socially and economically isolated parts of the country in order to talk with peasants and local leaders and get a first-hand view of their problems.

In contrast to the rhythm of work in previous administrations, the new president labored long hours and expected his ministers and aides to do likewise. Government officials were in their offices at 9 A.M., took quick lunches at their desks, and continued working until late into the evening.

In place of the self-congratulatory rhetoric of his predecessor, Echeverría seemed most at ease when elaborating on the shortcomings of the Revolution and attacking what he called "the tragic complacency" of previous regimes. He was sharply critical of past government policy for agricultural and industrial growth, and he was more than ready to acknowledge that the "Mexican miracle" had been produced at the expense of the peasantry, working class, and subproletariat. Throughout his first year in office, the new President continually called for critics of government policy to come forward and express themselves. According to his own spokesmen:

> [Echeverría was working] to dispel the persistent myth developed over many years of the so-called "Mexican Miracle," and not because he is unaware of the real achievements which have been made, but rather because he feels that the persistence of such a myth, in the final analysis, can only favor those sectors that have obtained the greatest benefits from this growth.

> Those who have followed attentively the policy which has developed during the change in attitude of the last 18 months, cannot deny that something important has happened in our system. . . . Complacency has given way to self criticism. . . . An atmosphere has grown in which no one is afraid to denounce errors or to point to unsatisfied demands. . . . The ritualistic exaltation of the achievements of the government is being replaced by a more rigorous analysis of the functioning of institutions.[4]

Beyond this new accessibility and frankness, Echeverría inspired some of his former detractors when he began to attack the laziness, incompetence, and corruption of government bureaucrats in terms far more pointed than had been used by a Mexican official in two decades. He named names; he stressed the fact that corruption could not exist at the bottom of the bureaucratic chain if it did not exist at the top; and he declared himself dedicated to altering the very concept of public office, which he asserted "is regarded by many so-called public servants as booty."[5]

Echeverría's attack on corruption in government was unusually strong and direct, but by no means unprecedented. What was unprecedented—or at least had not been heard since Cárdenas' days—was the attack he launched against the private industrial sector, which he scored as greedy, selfish, unpatriotic, and ultimately "un-Mexican."[6] This charge of "un-Mexican" behavior was a scathing one because since 1940 the term had been reserved for opposition of the left and, very occasionally, for clear-cut neofascist groups. To characterize the most powerful members of the national bourgeoisie in this way was a dramatic and unexpected step for the new president.

Nor was this criticism of the men "who only pursue personal wealth and enrichment"[7] expressed simply in abstract terms. When, for example, Echeverría traveled to the northern state of Chihuahua to preside over the expropriation and distribution of several thousand acres of commercial forests to a group of petitioning peasants, he seized the occasion to publicly humiliate the former owners of these lands, taking them to task for having exploited the forestlands to bring maximum short-term profit at the expense of long-term conservation. In front of a large crowd of peasants and representatives of the press, he addressed the former owners by name, saying:

> We must educate the new generation [of entrepreneurs] so that they comply with their social responsibility. Mexico needs modern entrepreneurs who do not think only in terms of personal profit, but in terms of the general progress of the country and the duty they have to serve society. . . . You must abandon the old entrepreneurial mentality which seeks personal enrichment as an ultimate end. . . . Today we must demand that industrialists do not carry on raping the land as you have done in the past.[8]

The sense that a new political atmosphere now prevailed in Mexico was heightened by the gradual release of the political prisoners of the 1968 movement. While the mass amnesty many hoped for was never granted, men and women originally sentenced to serve 35 or 40 years were freed one at a time or in small groups until more than 100 had been released. Those who, fearing further persecution, had sought exile abroad were encouraged to return to Mexico when the Minister of the Interior, Moya Palencia, broadly hinted, "There is no Mexican who is forced to live outside his country. There are only those who choose to live abroad."[9]

It seems that Echeverría managed to convey to many intellectuals a feeling that greater critical expression would be tolerated. As the Marxist novelist and essayist, Carlos Fuentes, wrote in August of 1971, "Echeverría lifted the veil of fear thrown over the body of Mexico by Díaz Ordaz. Many Mexicans felt free to criticize, to express themselves, to organize without fear of repression."[10] The Magna Carta of the new intellectual freedom was Echeverría's oft repeated assertion that "there is no such thing as ideas which are exotic or alien to the Revolution." This statement struck directly at Díaz Ordaz, who throughout his presidency attempted to touch xenophobic chords by characterizing the ideas of those who disagreed with him as "deriving from foreign philosophies," "exotic," and "alien to the principles of the Mexican Revolution."

A perceptible loosening of government censorship of newspapers and magazines became part of this new period of greater intellectual openness. While far from enjoying complete freedom of the press, journalists felt themselves at greater liberty to write what they saw, to muckrake, and in particular to write serial exposés on neo-latifundism and government corruption and mismanagement.[11]

The Echeverría Reforms

In the first year of his administration Echeverría came forward with 160 legislative initiatives. As one progressive piece of legislation followed another, it became apparent that the new president was operating on the assumption that his regime was the PRI's last chance to reform itself from within.[12]

One of his first reformist efforts was a change in the Agrarian Code designed to improve the credit, marketing, and technical facilities available to peasants and to facilitate the formation of peasant-run cooperatives. Marketing cooperatives were now permitted to export directly abroad without working through a commercial export firm. In addition Echeverría pressured private banks to lend more credit to peasants on more generous terms, and he established a Rural Industries Development Organization to deal with rural over-population by bringing the factories to the countryside. Under Echeverría a number of neo-latifundia owned by old political families were expropriated and distributed (although some question remained about the quality and value of the lands thus seized, and many critics called the distribution a propaganda ploy rather than an effective agrarian reform measure).[13]

The new Agrarian Code strengthened the internal structure of the *ejido* by requiring secret ballots for the election of ejidal officers, a measure that struck at the power of local officials who customarily perpetuate themselves in ejidal office for personal gain. Finally, the new code took ultimate responsibility for ejidal affairs out of the hands of the state governors and their political henchmen, and placed it in the presidency itself.[14]

Constitutional reform was another area in which Echeverría hoped to make his impact felt. In 1971 he sponsored legislation to lower the voting age as well as the minimum age for members of the Chamber of Deputies (21) and senators (30). In addition to this gesture toward young people, the constitutional reform proposed the reduction of the number of signatures required on a petition to form a new political party, and made it easier for opposition parties to achieve representation in the legislature. An opposition party would now need to capture only 1.5 percent of the popular vote to be awarded a seat in the legislature. Of course, nothing in this reform proposal threatened the control of the official party over the Chamber of Deputies and the Senate. The number of seats distributed to opposition parties on the basis of the popular vote would still be limited to 25, and regardless of the reduction in the number of signatures required for the formation of a new party, the PRI-controlled Ministry of the Interior would remain in charge of certifying the validity of the signatures.

Somewhat more politically significant were the educational reforms pushed by Echeverría. Taken as a whole, his policy on education tended to strengthen the legal concept of "university autonomy," the right of the national and state universities to remain independent of outside political control. To give greater force to the "organic law" that protected university autonomy, in 1971 Echeverría threw his weight behind the students and faculty of the University of Nuevo León in their fight to oust a university rector imposed on them by the industrial bourgeoisie of Monterrey and the politicians in their service.[15]

Echeverría's position on population control gradually changed during the time he held office. During his electoral campaign he had clung to the policy established by Díaz Ordaz that population control was not an issue for Mexico. He refused to give government backing to any organized program for family planning, and called instead for more efficient utilization of existing resources and for redistribution of population from crowded to underpopulated areas. During his first three years in office, he modified that stand, and privately sponsored population control programs began to receive official go-ahead: government support in principle if not direct financial aid. By 1973 the Ministries of Health and Social Security were beginning to become officially involved, and by April 1974 Echeverría's position had changed sufficiently so that he was prepared to establish a National Council on Population to disseminate information on family planning practices.

The aspect of Echeverría's reform policy which drew the greatest attention in his first years was his economic program. This program was billed as a shift away from the development priorities of the past thirty years. Income redistribution would be emphasized, even at the cost of slowing the rate of growth of the gross national product. There would be a shift from further industrialization of the urban centers in favor of industrial decentralization and a new emphasis on agricultural development. The new government committed itself to increasing the purchasing power of the poor by creating job opportunities in industry for the large mass of unemployed and underemployed.[16] Further concentration of wealth in the hands of the national bourgeoisie would be halted by raising both personal income taxes and corporate tax, although special incentives for reinvestment would continue. A new capital gains tax and a 10 percent tax on luxury goods would be imposed to reduce speculation and the flow of capital out of the country. Those Mexicans earning more than $24,000 a year would be taxed at 42 percent rather than the 35 percent of the past. In addition, the government would raise the rate of taxation on fixed incomes from bonds and securities.[17]

Early in his administration, Echeverría began to give notice to Mexican industrialists that the rules of the game had substantially altered. He asserted that the industrial bourgeoisie was going to have to change its notion that the best way to conduct business was by turning quick, high profits from over-priced, poor quality goods produced for a limited market behind high protectionist walls. The age of "import substitution" and protectionist policy was over. Import duties originally imposed to protect domestic industries from foreign competition would be reduced in order to force Mexican manufacturers to improve the quality of their goods and increase the productivity of their factories. Subsidies and tax waivers formerly given as a matter of course to expanding Mexican industries would be phased out. Only those Mexican industries producing low priced goods for a popular market would receive help in expanding their productive capacity.[18]

Businessmen were told that they could no longer regard government loans as outright grants. They would have to meet payments on these debts or face takeover by Somex (the Mexican Society for Industrial Credit), a government finance agency. Even the management of the state-run petroleum and electrical industries were told to shape up. These enterprises would have to become self-sustaining, even if it meant raising rates to their industrial consumers. In light of what Echeverría scored as the inefficiency of the private marketing sector, the role of CONASUPO, the state-run retailing agency would be expanded.[19]

An integral part of Echeverría's economic policy was a new attitude toward foreign investment and Mexicanization. Echeverría's program called for a tightening of controls on foreign investors. Foreign-owned industry would have to generate export earnings equal to the profits they take out of the country. Loopholes in the Mexicanization legislation would be closed, and Mexican *presta-nombres* would be sought and exposed. Controls would be imposed on the import of foreign technology. To prevent further abuses, American firms long accustomed to charging their Mexican subsidiaries outrageously inflated sums for patent rights, trademarks, and know-how would be obliged to register all contracts involving the sale of technology with the Ministry of Trade and Industry.[20]

Foreign investment was officially encouraged, but would be more closely subject to Mexican needs. Foreign investors would have to locate their factories in new underindustrialized regions. They would be encouraged to make their investments in fields where they would not come into competition with Mexican-owned enterprises. Investors, both foreign and domestic, would be pressured through fiscal reforms to put their money into industries that create jobs rather than those featuring higher rates of profit. Additional legislation would push industrialists to produce goods for export so that more foreign exchange would enter the country. To further improve Mexico's balance of trade, stricter controls would be imposed on imports and restrictions placed on foreign borrowing.[21]

Echeverría's policy of "economic nationalism" was expressed in his commitment to reduce dependency on U.S. investment and trade with the U.S. market[22] by forging new trade relations with Canada, Japan, China,[23] the Soviet Union, and other markets in both Western and Eastern Europe. To this end, the President circled the globe on official state visits in search of new trade partners. Not only would Mexico seek new markets for her raw materials in advanced industrialized countries, but Torres Manzo, the Minister of Trade and Industry, was dispatched to Latin America to develop a new role for Mexico as a supplier of manufactured goods to relatively less developed countries in Central and South America.[24]

These programs proclaimed by Echeverría as a basic reorientation of Mexican development policy, eventually found their way into law. It was not difficult for the president to draft the legislation to effect his economic program and have it ratified by a Senate and Chamber of Deputies controlled by his party. But the frustrations he suffered when he attempted to implement his reform program indicate some of the parameters of his power. For while the Mexican president may enjoy the awesome status of a national symbol, and while he may possess a certain immunity from direct personal attack, his power is not unlimited. He is, logically enough, subject to pressures from both the right and the left. As we have seen, pressure from the left can be controlled or reduced by the co-optation or the repression of left-wing dissidents. But pressure from the right is exerted by economic interests which are far more costly to buy off and are normally too powerful to successfully harass or threaten with violence. As subsequent events have shown, Echeverría's power and political maneuverability were severely limited by right-wing opposition to his reform program. During his regime, conservative members of the bourgeoisie, acting both inside and outside of the PRI, succeeded in blocking the implementation of the policy changes designed by Echeverría to modify the course of Mexican development.

The Right Strikes Back

Taken as a whole, Echeverría's reform package did not add up to anything like a fundamental transformation of the economic political or social system. Echeverría was not embarking on a new "Mexican road to socialism." Rather, he was trying to modernize and rationalize Mexican capitalism. He was concerned with spreading the fruits of development more widely and fostering a slightly more open, democratic political atmosphere. His goal was to create the climate of social and political stability that would permit further development along capitalist lines. If there is any parallel to be drawn between Luís Echeverría and Lázaro Cárdenas—and the two men were frequently compared at the beginning of Echeverría's regime—it is that Cárdenas' reforms promoted the social peace that formed the underpinning of the rapid economic development of the '40s and '50s, while Echeverría was working to reestablish that social peace, battered and torn as it was by the sharpening economic inequalities and social and political conflicts of the '60s.

Echeverría's efforts to safeguard the long-term future of Mexican capitalism and his efforts to save the national bourgeoisie from their own shortsighted greed were not perceived as such by the most influential and conservative elements of that class. On the contrary, the most powerful Mexican financiers, industrialists, and landowners—

particularly the traditionally conservative group centered in the city of Monterrey—profoundly distrusted Echeverría and responded with fear to his pronouncements. They believed that if this new President were to have his way, the interests of their class would no longer dictate the social, economic, and political policies of Mexico as they had in the past. They were troubled by his political reforms. They were distressed by his attempts to give educators and students more influence over the educational system, curbing their own power over the state universities. They did not like his tampering with an agrarian status quo from which they profited, nor checking the power of local rural bosses dependent on them. Echeverría's efforts to build a broad popular base of support for his regime alarmed them. His surprise visits to the countryside, his talk of "democratic overtures," and his bureaucratic cleanup campaign made them intensely uneasy. Above all, Echeverría's economic nationalism and his determination to gain greater state control over industrial development was frightening to Mexican entrepreneurs whose economic fortunes were closely interwoven with foreign capital. The new president's reforms and his populist appeals were perceived by conservative members of the national bourgeoisie as threatening their privilege and their control over national policy. And so this small but powerful group determined to harass and weaken Echeverría to render him incapable of carrying forward his program for moderate reform.

Conservative Mexican capitalists—the group Echeverría disdainfully referred to as "emissaries of the past"—struck their first blow against his economic program by withholding their investment funds from the market. During the first two years of the new administration, investment by domestic capitalists dropped sharply and the economy went into a serious recession. The annual rate of growth of the gross national product declined from 7.1 to 4.5 percent. Per capita income fell in 1971 for the first time since World War II. Growth in agricultural production dropped to 3 percent per annum, growth in industry to 2.8 percent, and the service sector dropped to 3.3 percent. Confidence in the Mexican economy was severely shaken at home and abroad.

This reluctance of conservative capital to reinvest in the national economy set off a cycle of serious economic repercussions. As industry did not expand at its normal rate, the crisis of unemployment heightened. In addition, a spiraling inflation—the worst in twenty years—began to grip the economy. Exacerbated by food shortages due to droughts and floods, plus the impact of a world-wide inflationary trend, the rate of inflation in Mexico climbed until by 1974 the official statistic had reached 25 percent and the real figure was probably much higher. Prices of popular staples like beans and tortillas rose by as much as 50 percent. Such price increases completely outstripped wage hikes won by the working class. Businessmen resisted government pressure to hold the price of their products steady. Therefore, notwithstanding substantial increases in the minimum wage under the new administration, the domestic market for manufactured goods did not expand as Echeverría had projected, because the purchasing power of peasants and workers was even weaker than it had been during Díaz Ordaz' regime.

Despite the economic reforms designed to redistribute wealth in Mexico, the trend toward higher profits for entrepreneurs and concentration of wealth in the hands of a few continued unchecked under Echeverría.[25] The President's efforts to reverse this trend by levying heavier taxes on the rich failed for the same reason so many of his other economic reforms could not be implemented. Lacking an honest and efficient bureaucracy to collect personal income, luxury, and corporate profit taxes, the government had to continue to rely for its revenue on indirect taxation, which hits the poor harder than any other class and does nothing at all to redistribute wealth.

The same lack of an efficient, honest administrative apparatus hampered Echeverría's efforts to enforce his proposed controls on private industry and to close the loopholes in the Mexicanization legislation. *Prestenombres,* for the most part, were not sought out and exposed. Foreign investors were not effectively subjected to closer supervision and restrictions. Economic relations with the United States continued as they had before, only Mexico's economic dependence on the U.S. was heightened as her trade deficit with respect to the U.S. grew worse.[26] Mexico's unfavorable balance of trade with the U.S. was exacerbated by the 10 percent surcharge attached to imports in 1971 by Richard Nixon. This unilaterally imposed surcharge is estimated to have cost Mexico as much as $200 million in foreign exchange in 1971 alone.[27] Notwithstanding Echeverría's pledge to reduce American control over key Mexican industries, in 1972 Chrysler Corporation bought out Automex after this corporation reported losses of $12 million. Meanwhile, Longoria, the Mexican cotton trading house, was revealed to owe $80 million to foreign banks and was forced to borrow another $12 million just to pay off its back taxes. In addition, the drive to find new foreign markets for the products of Mexican light industry proved largely unsuccessful as these goods could not compete in quality and price with goods produced in Europe, North America and Japan.

Under attack from a threatened landholding class, Echeverría's plans for agricultural renovation fared little better than his program to increase employment, control prices, collect taxes, or control foreign investment. While he pursued illegal landholders with more vigor and probably with more sincerity than had his predecessor, the neolatifundists were mostly successful in blocking his attempts to seize and redistribute their land. According to the Department of Agrarian Affairs, by 1974 the courts had granted 1,700 injunctions restraining the government from expropriating five million hectares of illegally held land. Where the Echeverría administration succeeded in expropriating and distributing illegal land holdings, as in the much publicized case of the Obregón family holdings in Sonora, the land seized was mostly of poor quality and the distribution benefited relatively few landless peasants.

Although Echeverría had focused his agrarian program on providing more economic aid to *ejidatarios* and small holders in order to enable them to raise their productivity, the results were not encouraging. Despite substantial hikes in government funds to agriculture in general and to *ejidatarios* and small holders in particular, the rate of agricultural growth declined, the small increases in income realized by peasant families were wiped out by inflation, and the structure of power remained unchanged in the countryside.

Obviously, not all of Echeverría's economic strategy was blocked by the opposition of conservative capitalists. Factors external to Mexico—worldwide inflation, declining prices for raw materials on the international market, the imposition of the American 10 percent import surcharge—all contributed to the failure of Echeverría's plan to modify the course of Mexican development. Still, the powerful conservative sector of the national bourgeoisie was unrelenting in the economic pressure it exerted, and this group played a determining role in frustrating Echeverría's program. For, when economic pressure alone proved insufficient to thwart the Echeverría reforms, his enemies on the right brought to bear all the political weapons available in their arsenal.

It was dangerous for opposition on the right to strike directly at

Echeverría. Even the most economically powerful hesitated to face off directly against "el Señor Presidente de la República." Instead, his enemies within the national bourgeoisie employed a variety of political techniques designed to undermine his power, and they enlisted a wide range of allies in their effort to oust the president or render him helpless. These allies included conservatives within the official party, politicians whose careers and political fortunes were inextricably linked to Díaz Ordaz and his now discredited policies, the old guard of the CTM whose interests were more closely tied to business and industry than to labor, the government bureaucrats who found the drive for honesty in administration to be a hair-raising prospect, regional and local political strongmen, and others whose power would be undercut by Echeverría's proposed reforms.

The political strategy of the right was simple and unoriginal. Their plan was to exploit the discontent of peasants, workers, students, and other dissidents in order to create a climate of political and social unrest. In so doing they hoped at the very least, to embarrass Echeverría and weaken his hand. Beyond that lay the prospect that continued civil violence might lead to a right-wing military coup of the kind that subsequently did occur in Chile.

To foment the desired atmosphere of chronic violence, the conservative bourgeoisie provided money to recruit, arm, and train paramilitary shock troops. They funded the infiltration of provocateurs into the universities. And they sponsored pseudo-guerrilla groups to carry out terrorist activities in the name of leftist causes. Right-wing gangsterism of this sort had been a factor in Mexican politics long before Echeverría took office. Porristas (paid provocateurs posing as students) had played a part in university politics from the time the universities became mass institutions in the early 1940s.[28] And paramilitary thugs acting under secret orders from conservative politicians within the Department of the Federal District[29] played a key role in provoking violence and army intervention during the 1968 movement.[30] However, when Echeverría began to unfold his reform program in 1970, the activities of armed provocateurs stepped up noticeably. It seems reasonable to assume that these gangs were sponsored by political elements well to the right of the president (both inside and outside of his party), because the activities of the porristas were geared both to repressing left-wing movements and to undercutting the prestige and authority of Echeverría's regime.

From the time the new administration took office, ever greater numbers of provocateurs were infiltrated by the right into the National University in Mexico City and into the state universities in Puebla, Nuevo León, Sonora, Jalisco, Guerrero, and other educational centers. These hired thugs carried out assassinations and provoked riots and pitched battles that cost the lives of hundreds of students and professors and brought these institutions to a standstill for months at a time. While *porristas* became virtually a permanent fixture in university life in the '70s, the clearest case of the right's use of shock troops for the complementary purposes of repressing the left and discrediting a reformist government occurred with an event in 1971, which has become known as the "Corpus Christi massacre."

On Corpus Christi day, June 10, 1971, more than 10,000 students left the Polytechnic Institute in a well organized march to the Monument of the Revolution in downtown Mexico City. The stated object of the demonstration was to dramatize the students' demand for the release of political prisoners held since 1968. However, the underlying motive for calling a mass march at this time seems to have been the desire to reorganize and revitalize the student movement, which had remained in disarray since the slaughter in the Plaza of the Three Cultures in October 1968. The students, led by the remnants of the political organizations that guided the '68 movement, saw this march as a first step toward rebuilding their movement and testing its force in the political arena.

There is considerable evidence that Echeverría viewed the march as an opportunity to demonstrate his willingness to engage in open dialogue with dissidents. It seems that he hoped the march would bring the students to the Plaza of the Constitution, where he planned to emerge on the balcony of the National Palace to greet the demonstrators and invite them to air their grievances and exchange ideas with him.

For its part, the right (both conservative capitalists and Echeverría's enemies within his own party) saw the occasion as an ideal opportunity to politically harass and embarrass the president. Accordingly, the *halcones* ("falcons"), a paramilitary troop sponsored by Monterrey capitalists and equipped and trained by the Department of the Federal District under the authority of a political enemy of Echeverría, Alfonso Martínez Dominguez[31] were dispatched to the scene.

As the march made its way toward the center of the city, roughly

1,000 *halcones* assembled and waited to intercept the students. Out-fitted with knives, pistols, machine guns, and cattle prods, the *hal-cones* passed freely through the lines of uniformed police stationed along the parade route. While 900 special service police sealed off the area and the riot police heightened the confusion by launching tear gas bombs into the crowd, the *halcones* attacked the unarmed demonstrators, killing approximately thirty students and bystanders outright and pursuing the others as they fled through the streets. The *halcones* then rooted students out of the shops, cinemas, and churches where they sought refuge, and proceeded to invade the hospitals where the wounded had been taken, attacking injured students as they lay on the operating tables and in the wards.[32] The toll was high. An estimated fifty students were killed, another fifty "disappeared," and hundreds more were wounded.[33]

Notwithstanding initial attempts by official government spokes-men to portray the events as a "riot" or "clash" between "rival student factions," the truth was hard to conceal—particularly given that many Mexican and foreign newsmen had witnessed both the unprovoked attack and the complicity of the uniformed police squads.[34] Weapons, vehicles, and radio equipment used by the *hal-cones* were readily traced to the department of the Federal District. Official investigations of the massacre were launched and some attempt was made to establish responsibility for the affair. Even-tually the investigation was dropped, although Martínez Dominguez and other conservatives closely linked to him and to ex-President Díaz Ordaz were forced to resign. Yet, despite the resignations of a few key conservatives within the government, it was clear that the right had carried the day. For one thing, the students were forced to abandon mass public demonstrations as a political tactic. For another, Echeverría suffered great political humiliation. He had not been able to turn the demonstration to his own political advantage as he had originally hoped. He was made to appear too weak to main-tain civil order in his own capital city. It was apparent that the police took their orders from authorities other than the president of the Republic. So obvious was the role of the right in provoking disorder that Echeverría was forced to openly acknowledge that the attack had been arranged by reactionaries determined to undermine his power.[35] In an oblique reference to the Monterrey capitalists, Echeverría warned students that they "must not allow themselves to be used as instruments of those who operate in the shade, risking neither their persons nor their economic well-being. . . ," nor should the students "for lack of reflection, lend themselves to the designs of foreign interests and reactionaries."[36] Yet the very fact that Echeverría (and it would seem, just about everyone else in Mexico) was able to identify those who organized and directed the *halcones,* underscored his weak position: he was manifestly powerless to move against these groups, to halt the activities of the provocateurs and their sponsors, much less bring any of these people to justice.

Opposition from the Right and Left

The Corpus Christi massacre provides a clear example of the interaction between opposition of the right and left. In this case leftist opponents of the regime inadvertently played into the hands of the most reactionary elements in Mexico. It is obvious that the right's capacity to make use of the left operated to weaken Echeverría and limit his ability to carry out his moderate reforms.

This dynamic continued to operate for the duration of Echeverría's administration. While Echeverría enjoyed some early success in winning over moderate left-wing dissidents, probably most leftists were never won over, and some who initially supported the president later lost their enthusiasm as it became apparent that the changes Echeverría was working to bring about were very limited indeed.[37] For the most part, leftists remained unimpressed with Echeverría's reform package, which they viewed as nothing more than palliatives. They felt that none of his policies held out any real possibility of fundamentally altering the conditions of social injustice and economic inequality that afflict Mexico. They granted that adjustments had been made, but asserted that these were adjustments geared to preserving the system, adjustments that operated on the principle that the system must be made more flexible if it is to remain essentially unchanged. They noted that Echeverría had appointed large numbers of talented young technocrats to study the economic problem of redistribution of wealth in Mexico. But three years later, these technocrats were still producing reports, pilot projects, and long studies indicating the need for further studies. Echeverría's opponents on the left saw that he lacked the political strength to turn studies into policy. And they felt, in any case, that his policies never came to the root of the problem in Mexico, which was not a question of more or less credit to agriculture or more or less labor intensivity in industry, but rather the fundamental contradictions of capitalist development in a country like Mexico.

In the late 1930s Cárdenas had managed to carry out some basic structural changes in the political and economic system. But to do so he had to mobilize the masses, arm peasants and workers, and risk bringing the country to the brink of civil war. In contrast, Echeverría, for all his populist utterings, was either unwilling or unable to take the steps necessary to organize a mass base of support for his reformist regime. Lacking this kind of popular support, Echeverría had no choice but to bow to the intensifying pressure from conservatives.

Beset by opposition from both the right and the left, Echeverría began to retreat from his initial progressive stand. Since he would not or could not do more to placate, co-opt, or appeal to the left, he began to move to the right. By the end of his third year in office, it seemed that in order to hang onto power, he felt constrained to abandon his "populist" program in all but rhetoric and to adopt policies catering to conservative interests.

Echeverría's steady movement to the right became evident in a number of different areas. The same man who in 1970 had given a small measure of freedom to the press, who in 1971 had ordered the release of several journalists imprisoned for their writings, by 1974 had imposed new government controls over television programming, had clamped down on the press, and had shut down the left-wing weekly, *Porque* and arrested its publishers.[38]

Echeverría's initial efforts to introduce new, young, and progressive blood into the PRI were likewise dropped as party stability and disciplined organization began to take priority over party reform.[39] Of the seven gubernatorial candidates selected by Echeverría in his first three years in power, six were under the age of forty, and all were closely associated with his reform program. In contrast, the average age of the twelve gubernatorial candidates selected by the president in 1974 was sixty, and all of these men were PRI stalwarts, old *politicos* with a power base in conservative state politics.[40]

A number of economic decisions made in 1973 and 1974 can be viewed as concessions to the right designed to reassure the most conservative sector of the national bourgeoisie. For example, in November 1973, Echeverría announced that several companies which had been taken over by the government investment corporation, Nacional Financiera, when they were on the verge of bankruptcy, would be sold to private interests now that government funding had set them back on their feet. Furthermore, private capitalists were pleased to learn in December 1973 that public funds were to be spent to search for new oil deposits and other sources of energy for industry. Clearly this news that the practice of heavy government participation in bottleneck-breaking investments would continue was music to the ears of private capital. In addition, Echeverría made a bid for greater support from Mexican financiers when he publicly promised that he would not move to nationalize the banks, as has been rumored, and capped off this gesture by refusing to let bank employees organize their own union.

This same trend toward concessions to the right was evident in Echeverría's treatment of the conservative labor boss, Fidel Velázquez. Politicians both inside and outside the CTM who were challenging Velázquez's thirty-three year reign over the labor confederation initially enjoyed the support of the president.[41] However, when Echeverría realized that Velázquez was so firmly entrenched that the union leader was likely to win in any showdown between the two, the president quickly revised his policy and provided Velázquez with the concessions he needed to consolidate his control. Given Echeverría's desperate need to curb inflation, he found he was dependent on the labor boss to hold down wage demands. Only a man who enjoyed the iron grip that Velázquez exercised over organized labor could be relied upon to hold popular pressure in check in the face of the soaring cost of living for the working class.[42] To assure his collaboration in this effort, Echeverría effectively increased Velázquez' share of the take by giving him control over a 3.5 million peso fund earmarked for the construction of 100,000 low cost housing units for workers. Furthermore, to strengthen the labor boss' hand in his struggle against the independent labor organizations that had developed as a response to Velázquez' corrupt and authoritarian regime, Echeverría proposed legislation modifying the "right to strike" provision of Article 123 of the Constitution. This modification gave firmer control over strikes to both the government and the CTM central executive by imposing a mandatory conciliation period which effectively outlawed the kind of wildcat strikes which had been undermining Velázquez' power.

Echeverría's attempts to curry favor among conservatives, or at least reduce their hostility, was reflected in his policy toward Chile. In September 1973 the President outraged the Mexican right by denouncing the fascist coup in Chile, calling for three days of national mourning for Salvador Allende, and offering political asylum to his widow and to thousands of other Chilean refugees. However, by May of 1974, Echeverría was citing the Mexican tradition of maintaining relations with all "sister republics" and quietly dispatched his foreign minister to Santiago to restore diplomatic and trade relations with the government of General Pinochet.

With the Chilean coup fresh in everyone's mind, Echeverría apparently perceived his own situation to be so insecure that he felt constrainted to court actively the support of the armed forces. In light of the historical transition in Mexico from military to civilian rule, and in view of the efforts since 1937 to reduce the overt role of the army in political affairs, Echeverría's attempt to bring the army into the limelight, his sudden celebration of the "patriotism," "professionalism," and "popular roots" of the armed forces constituted a significant break in the process of the demilitarization of politics. This suggests that the threat of a military coup weighed on the president's mind.[43] In October 1973, the army received a 15 percent hike in pay. Furthermore, the ambitions of middle ranking army officers, long frustrated by the preeminence of a group of generals in control of the armed forces since they won their spurs in the Revolution of 1917, were at last realized when the president retired 486 of the elderly generals and promoted the middle aged officers to the top ranks.[44] Assuming he might well need their support, Echeverría continued to heap praise upon these "professional patriots," and the army came to enjoy a period of official prestige it had not known in almost forty years.

Perhaps the most significant of the conservative trends emerging in the course of Echeverría's term was the increasing tendency to repress the left in order to pick up support from the right. To placate the conservatives and guarantee its own security, the government took ever harsher measures to halt and silence the student left, while peasant and labor dissidents were met with the same show or use of force. In May 1973, for example, a rally called by students in the Capital to protest police brutality directed against May Day demonstrators in Puebla was met by a force of 10,000 heavily armed riot police and soldiers. In August of '74, another student demonstration in solidarity with a peasant protest caravan and with striking workers was over before it had begun because the march was banned, and thousands of riot police were deployed to enforce that prohibition. After the ill-fated Corpus Christi day march in June 1971, every subsequent effort at organizing public marches and rallies fell victim to the same overkill tactic: the massive threat or application of police and army force.

In light of this trend, the announcement in June 1974 of the arrival of sixty-three officers from the Higher School of War of Brazil did not come as a great surprise. These men were brought to Mexico "to exchange experiences with the Mexican army."[45] In the atmosphere of polarized violence that had come to prevail in Mexico by 1973-4, the invitation to these specialists in urban and rural counter-insurgency and electrified torture only underscored the insecurity of Echeverría's position.

Notwithstanding these attempts to reassure the right, the atmosphere of crisis deepened. By the middle of Echeverría's term there was open speculation as to whether he would manage to complete his six years in office. Conservatives, unimpressed with the president's gestures of conciliation toward them and unmoved by his efforts to guard their economic interests, continued to cast Echeverría as a man too weak—politically and morally—to maintain even a minimal level of law and order in Mexico. Factory owners threatened to arm their own workers in order to protect private property. The conservative national bourgeoisie constantly linked Echeverría's name with that of Salvador Allende, asserting "either we are with the Allendist line of Echeverría, or we are for Mexico and freedom."[46] The implications of this comparison were lost on no one, Allende having been assassinated only two months earlier. Laying aside the tradition of presidential immunity to direct criticism, conservatives began to blast the president for his failure to control "the rising tide of violence," and when Eugenio Garza Sada, a leading member of the Monterrey group was killed during a kidnap attempt, the Monterrey industrialists used the funeral oration to attack Echeverría, even as he stood at the graveside, for creating a climate in which "crime and terror can thrive."[47] At the same time that the right assaulted Echeverría in these terms, it continued to instigate violence through the use of *porristas* and pseudo-guerrillas.

The conservatives' strategy of employing provocateurs to increase the level of civil violence was reenforced by the increasing activity of authentic leftist rural and urban guerillas. These two factors combined to exacerbate the atmosphere of crisis. Echeverría seemed to be caught squarely between these forces of opposition, and his program of reform was bankrupt. [48]

Some Fundamental Contradictions

Echeverría's attempts at reform failed because the problems he tackled were not incidental to the economic system, but rather were the logical and inevitable results of capitalist development in a country like Mexico. As we noted earlier, the development policy that has been pursued in Mexico since 1940 has been based on the "trickle-down" theory. Government economic policy has been intentionally arranged so that enormous profits would accrue to the private industrial sector in the hope that these men would reinvest the accumulated capital in ways that would further the growth of the national economy. Tax exemptions, a regressive tax structure, protectionist legislation, government spending on infrastructure, strict curbs on wage hikes, an agrarian policy favoring the large commercial private agricultural sector were all policies geared toward increasing the income of the national bourgeoisie so that, it was argued, the rate of domestic saving and reinvestment would rise. Over a period of three decades, this policy resulted not only in the "social dislocations," the human suffering detailed in chapter 3, but, at the same time, operated to enhance at every turn the economic and political power enjoyed by the national bourgeoisie. As became evident in the course of the Echeverría administration, the economic strength of the national bourgeoisie has increased over the years to the point where this group can exercise an effective veto power over any public policy perceived as threatening its own interests. By withholding investment funds and encouraging its foreign business partners to do likewise, the national bourgeoisie underscored its position of power and expressed its discontent with Echeverría's policies as it set off or contributed to a series of serious economic problems.

Just as the economic power of the national bourgeoisie has increased over the last thirty-five years, the political influence wielded by this class has grown apace. As we have seen, the national bourgeoisie can shape policy through its influence in the popular sector of the official party, through its control over the appointments of senators, deputies, state governors, university rectors, and its representation at every level of government bureaucracy. It can further effect political decisions through its powerful pressure group organizations like the National Confederation of Industrial Chambers and the National Confederation of Chambers of Commerce, and through its ownership of financial institutions and mass media. If pressure exerted through these various channels is insufficient to obtain desired policy, the Mexican bourgeoisie can count on the cooperation of American partners to pressure Washington for overt and covert U.S. policy designed to push the Mexican president along lines more satisfactory to foreign and domestic capital. Furthermore, in addition to the influence members of the national bourgeoisie have over the police and military apparatus in various Mexican states, we have already seen that important sectors of this class are prepared to organize and equip private armies and paramilitary shock troops to obtain through violent means what cannot be won through political maneuver.

With a national bourgeoisie wielding this degree of power, Echeverría's program for income redistribution was probably doomed from the start. Certainly there are countries where piecemeal, social democratic reform measures have worked to reduce economic inequality and mitigate social injustice within a capitalist system. Northern Europe is a case in point. But the social democratic reforms which have been carried out in northern Europe are set in industrially advanced and economically developed societies. Unlike the Mexican workers, the working classes of northern Europe are well organized, fully literate, homogeneous, and highly productive. The reformist benefits they enjoy were implemented by social democratic parties brought to power by the workers themselves through their own highly articulate labor union movements. The northern European bourgeoisie also contrast sharply with their Mexican counterparts in that they are able to take the longer view on reforms and adjustments to the capitalist system, and are not obsessed with short-term profit maximization. Furthermore, no social democratic reformist regime in Europe has to cope with the problems of a largely agrarian peasant society.

Given the structures and traditions in Mexico, had Echeverría wanted to do more than paste bandages over wounds, he would have needed to carry out a mass mobilization to provide the support for a face-off with the national bourgeoisie. But to the degree that peasants and workers are already organized in the CNC and CTM, such a mobilization would have implied either the creation of parallel

political institutions or the total reconstitution of the CNC and CTM
under new leadership. As it was, Echeverría was unsuccessful in his
attempt to oust or even limit the power of CTM secretary general,
Velázquez. And Bonfil, the progressive secretary general Echeverría
implanted into the CNC to shake up that organization, was myster-
iously killed in an air crash before his more militantly *agrarista* leadership could have any measurable effect. Had Echeverría attempted
to stimulate the creation of new mass organizations under militant
peasant and labor leadership, he would have incurred the hostility
not only of the national bourgeoisie, but of his own PRI machine,
and of CNC and CTM regulars from the level of ejidal delegate and
shop steward right up to the top. It is one thing to give occasional
presidential encouragement to a locally based independent peasant
movement like the Laguna's Central Union as a means of chastising
the regional committee of the CNC for exceeding the normally
acceptable limits of sloth and corruption. It is quite another matter
to attempt a systematic replacement of CNC and CTM functionaries
throughout the Republic with more militant peasant and labor
leaders capable of organizing a political confrontation on a mass scale
with the national bourgeoisie.

But how likely is it that Echeverría actually envisioned a systematic restructuring of the bases of power of the PRI and, by extension,
of the bases of Mexican development? All the evidence suggests that
his aim was to streamline, not to restructure the Mexican economic
and political system. The populist appeal he worked so hard to cultivate was geared more toward building a level of support sufficient
to provide greater leverage and maneuverability vis-á-vis conservative
capitalists, old guard *diazordistas,* the armed forces, and other en-
crusted interests. His goal was not to mobilize the masses to break
the power of the national bourgeoisie, but only to win enough popular support to provide him with greater confidence and leverage in his
role as a reformer operating within the logic of the Mexican system.

Alternatives to PRI Rule

If the record of the Echeverría administration demonstrates anything, it is that radical or even substantial change in the Mexican
system will not come under leadership of the PRI as it is presently
constituted. This conclusion naturally leads us to ask about the
alternatives to continued official party rule. What are the various

forms political change might take in Mexico? What is the likelihood, for example, that transformations might come about through the seizure of power by a revolutionary movement? How probable is it that change will come as a result of a military takeover under the leadership of either reactionary or progressive officers? Let us briefly examine some of these possibilities.

Revolution

The most immediate obstacle to the development of a genuinely revolutionary force in Mexico is that the country has already experienced a great historical upheaval called "The Revolution." That is, a major barrier to radical revolution in Mexico is the existence of the bourgeois revolutionary tradition. There are still people alive today in Mexico who fought in the Revolution of 1917. There are many others around who directly felt its effects or who lived through the turbulent years from 1917 to 1928 that were its aftermath. Succeeding generations of Mexicans have been brought up on the myth of the Revolution. They have had their hopes raised and smashed many times. They have heard countless promises made in the name of the Revolution, and they have seen very few of them fulfilled. They have witnessed the assumption of the revolutionary mantle by political leaders who were representatives of the national bourgeoisie. They have watched these men appropriate the title "revolutionary" for themselves and use that label to manipulate Mexican policy to serve their own class interests.

Mexicans of the popular classes have grown very weary of hearing about revolution. The very words "revolution" and "revolutionary" have lost their meaning. This sense of cynicism and distrust is clearly expressed in the popular folk song, "Juan Sin Tierra" (landless Juan), the tale of a peasant who gave his all in the Revolution of 1917 but had nothing to show for his courageous effort.

> I will sing you the song
> Of a man who went to war,
> Who was wounded in the mountains
> Who just fought to win some land.
>
> Our General told us,
>   "Fight on with great valor
> We are going to give you land,
> As soon as we make the Reform."

Emiliano Zapata said:
"I want Land and Liberty,"
And the government laughed
When they went to bury him.

If they come looking for me
To make another Revolution
I'll tell them, "Sorry, I'm busy
Planting the fields of the landlord."

It is obviously very hard for Marxist or any other revolutionaries to present a program for struggle to people who have had this experience. While the suffering of peasants, workers, and those without jobs is very great, so too is their scepticism about the sincerity and efficacy of self-styled revolutionary leaders of whatever political tendency. Their hopes have been betrayed too many times for them to lend themselves readily to the plans of those who would lead them in struggle.

Committed Marxist revolutionaries in Mexico understand this disaffection only too well. They understand that the problem of building a popular base for revolution is a long-term and complex process. They realize that they first face the task of demystifying the Mexican Revolution. They know that the hope of some day receiving a piece of land has held the landless peasantry in a quiescent state for a very long time. Even when that hope dies, it does not necessarily bring in its wake the desire to fight but, rather, is just as likely to be replaced by a passive mood of resignation. Similarly, the demonstration effect of the great wealth and comfort achieved by a small elite in the cities likewise serves to hold the urban masses in a quiet state of expectation that, at least on a level of individual achievement, they may one day get their share of the pie. When inflation wipes out the small gains made by a working class family, it does not necessarily lead them to pick up the gun. It is just as likely to induce a state of apathetic despair. Serious revolutionaries in Mexico understand that a great deal of political work must go into raising the consciousness of such people and organizing them before their frustrations will be channeled into political action. Furthermore they realize that any effort to build an open political movement is likely to be destroyed by the twin control mechanisms of co-optation and repression. For this reason, more and more revolutionaries have turned to clandestine forms or organization and activity. And the years following the destruction of the 1968 student movement in fact witnessed a steady increase in rural and urban guerrilla activities. Indeed the recent history of Mexican guerrilla struggle can be said to have developed out of the repression since 1968 of open forms of political organization and protest.

As early as 1964, as we have noted, Jénaro Vázquez opened a guerrilla *foco* in the mountains of Guerrero state. His death in February 1972 did not put an end to armed struggle in that region of Mexico. As sporadic guerrilla strikes continued in Guerrero and a new *foco* was established under the leadership of another rural schoolteacher, Lucio Cabañas, other guerrilla bands were in the process of formation and training in various cities and rural areas throughout the Republic. From 1969 through the early '70s, terrorist attacks were registered against banks, government offices, right-wing newspapers, and other sites identified by guerrillas as symbols of the apparatus of repression and reaction. During these years, wealthy Mexican businessmen, politicians, and foreign diplomats became the targets of a spate of kidnappings in which the hostages were generally held for a cash ransom, the promise of the release of political prisoners, and occasionally, the publication or broadcast of the manifesto of the guerrilla group. These guerrillas were pursued and sometimes captured by the army and secret police, but for each arrest made, evidence of new activities by newly formed groups quickly emerged.

In analyzing the significance of these guerrilla activities, many leftists, both Mexican and foreign, have found cause for optimism in what they view as the phoenix-like capacity of the guerrilla movement to rise again out of the ashes of earlier movements that have been suppressed. They point out that 20,000 infantrymen and two airborn companies had to be thrown into the effort to isolate and destroy Cabañas' guerrilla group before the Mexican government could claim to have "pacified" the state of Guerrero. This reading of the "success" of armed struggle is understandable in light of the frustration necessarily felt by leftists when they weigh the possibility of open political mobilization in the context of the co-optive/repressive system that exists today in Mexico. Yet we should bear in mind that Guerrero, the principal setting for guerrilla activities, has a long history of endemic violence, both revolutionary, and more frequently, nonrevolutionary. While it would be inaccurate to characterize Lucio Cabañas' Party of the People as little more than the classic social bandit gang that typically flourishes in inaccessible, impoverished mountain redoubts like Guerrero's Sierra Madre del Sur,[49] neither would it be correct to see this guerrilla band as an incipient National Liberation Front, and Cabañas as another Ho Chi Minh.[50] Lucio Cabañas, like Jénaro Vázquez before him, succeeded in capturing the imagination and respect of dissident Mexicans. But their actions consisted of assaulting or kidnaping *symbols* of Mexico's power structure. In no case can it be said that the activities of the guerrillas genuinely undermined that power structure. Thus, although there was widespread identification with the heroism of these guerrilla fighters, and this identification gave their movements considerable impact beyond the borders of Guerrero, neither leader managed to build a mass movement. Indeed, no guerrilla group has managed thus far to formulate a coherent political program around which large scale support of peasants, workers, and discontented intellectuals might coalesce.[51]

The experience of the Latin American guerrilla struggles of the '60s shows that where such movements lack mass support, they have been isolated and ultimately destroyed by the counterinsurgency force of the government, supported by American aid, advisors, and equipment. If any revolutionary movement. is to take power in Mexico, whether it begins with guerrilla activities in the mountains or the actions of political activists in the cities, its success will ultimately depend on the formation of broad-based and durable organizations of peasants and workers. But the problem of mobilizing this kind of mass support in a system so effectively controlled by a hegemonic party is a dilemma for which revolutionaries have not yet found the solution.

Military Rule

Another potential alternative for radical change is military rule under the leadership of either reactionary, conservative, or even progressive officers. It is somewhat difficult even to pose the question of what form military rule might take in Mexico because the history of "demilitarization" of Mexican politics has long discouraged serious analysis or even speculative discussion along these lines. Studies of direct military intervention in Latin American politics typically begin by excluding Mexico from consideration.[52] And those who have weighed the probability of a military coup have dismissed it as unlikely or impossible. Mexican sociologist Pablo González Casanova wrote as late as 1972, "It is an incontestable fact that Mexico has controlled and overcome the stage of militarism. Militarism no longer represents a permanent and organized threat of a political force imposing its own conditions by coercion. . . ."[53] To support the hypothesis of declining military influence, González Casanova and others cite the decrease in federal spending on the armed forces, the relatively small proportion of the national budget allotted to the military, the stability of the army at a relatively small size, the reduction in the ratio of soldiers to the labor force, and the fact that the last military man to serve as president was Avila Camacho, whose term ended in 1946.[54]

While this argument is persuasive, the recent history of military takeover in virtually every South American republic, including Chile and Uruguay—both countries long believed to have armies "too professional to become directly involved in politics—suggests that no Latin American country is entirely immune to this phenomenon.

It is a truism that in any country which undergoes a prolonged crisis characterized by social unrest and civil violence, the influence of the military will rise. When they are repeatedly brought out of their barracks and into the streets to impose order, the police and armed forces are bound to gain an increased sense of their own importance in the political process and of the incapacity of civilian politicians. Soldiers are always assured by the government they serve that they are performing their duty as patriots when they are called upon to repress a strike or break up a demonstration. But it seems fair to assume that few soldiers or policemen are particularly happy to play a role that requires them to continually strike out at their compatriots. It is often difficult enough to sustain the spirit to kill a foreign enemy. Soldiers who are frequently asked to fire on their own countrymen may grow restive and begin to question why civilian politicians persist in running the country in a way that makes the application of repressive force a constant necessity. They may begin to ask if military technicians might not do a better job. When this attitude prevails among officers as well as enlisted men, it helps to set the stage for military intervention.[55]

Certainly the importance of the military in Mexican politics has diminished as the official party system gained control and brought different classes, interest groups, military and regional strongmen into its fold through a system of co-optive rewards and concessions. But in the event that the techniques of co-optation refined by the official party over the last few decades should break down in the future, the level of coercion employed by the government would inevitably rise. If consistently applied armed force should be required to maintain order in Mexico, the political influence of the military would grow, and the possibility of a military takeover would increase.

In the unlikely but not impossible event that the military would seize power in Mexico, what political character would such a regime have? One pattern is the increasingly common Latin American model of repressive rule by a reactionary military tied to the conservative bourgeoisie and to foreign capital. Another model is provided by the progressive nationalist military regime which directed development in Peru from 1968 until the reformist officers were edged out late in 1975. In Peru, progressive military men, while seriously lacking institutional links to the Peruvian people, nonetheless managed to carry out a series of profound transformations in the economic, social, and institutional structure of their country. Though very much a "revolution from above," these changes included the nationalization of foreign-owned oil and copper industries, an agrarian reform that effectively broke the power of the old landholding oligarchy, the "peruvianization" of financial institutions, the nationalization of all major newspapers, the imposition of state control over the marketing of major export products and the refining of metals, and the gradual transfer of 50 percent ownership to workers in all industries.

Given the conjuncture of class interests between the Mexican officer corps and the national bourgeoisie[56] it seems most likely that if a military takeover were to occur in Mexico, it would follow the more familiar conservative pattern that has marked the military regimes in Argentina, Chile, Brazil, Bolivia, Paraguay, Uruguay, Venezuela, and Colombia.[57] But whether conservative or progressive in orientation, any military junta in power would have to seek the collaboration of like-minded elements from within the official party whose rule had been overturned. The Mexican economy and state appartus are too large and complex to be run by the military alone. An officer corps the size of the Mexican is not large enough to man even a streamlined version of the governmental structure that exists today. An alliance with ideologically compatible members of the PRI would have to be sought to guarantee the participation of sympathetic civilians who would serve as government functionaries under military leadership.

This is not to argue that the scenario set out here is inevitable or even very likely to occur. In the short run a more probable turn of events would be an increase in the relative weight of military influence within the existing political structure of Mexico.

Ronfeldt has pointed out the significant "residual" political roles played by the military within the Mexican political system.[58] In contemporary times, troops have been called in to suppress student movements, squelch guerrilla insurgency, repress peasant demonstrations, break up rural hunger marches, dislodge land invaders, smash strikes, pursue urban guerrillas, maintain order during contested elections, and prop up official party functionaries who face challenges from rival groups at the local or state level. Apart from these overt repressive activities, army chiefs play a key role in the collection of intelligence data: pinpointing subversive activities within their command zones, identifying issues and areas of unrest overlooked by civilian politicians, and helping the government "to secure control over isolated, unruly rural areas."[59]

Over the last several decades these military activities seem mainly to have been directed toward bolstering the PRI in the face of popular pressure for change. It appears likely that, in the short run, army men will continue to perform these functions under civilian orders, but they may extract an ever higher price as compensation for their contribution to propping up this system.

Conclusion

In this chapter we have examined a series of alternatives for change in Mexico: reform under PRI leadership, armed struggle and revolution, and, finally, military rule. The reformist administration of Echeverría is an historical episode which has a record we can evaluate. But we can only analyze the probability of socialist revolution or military rule, and speculate about the characteristics such regimes might display.

It is difficult to predict with any assurance the form that change is likely to take in Mexico. Mexico has a peculiar tradition of bourgeois revolution. Her proximity to the United States sets her apart from other Latin American republics. Mexico's hegemonic single party system—entrenched now for almost half a century—presents a sharp contrast with the unstable political structures characteristic of most Third World countries. The strength of her anticlerical tradition, her foreign policy—always well to the left of her domestic politics—her incomplete, but nonetheless highly visible agrarian reforms, are all features that give Mexico a distinctive political history. This unique combination of characteristics makes it difficult to apply to the Mexican case models derived from the experience of other countries at a similar stage of development.

As Echeverría's term in office drew to a close, Mexicans of virtually every political coloration began to be almost entirely taken up with the choice of the presidential successor. This preoccupation demonstrated the staying power of the PRI and the one-party system. For, in so many respects, the Echeverría years had been difficult and disappointing ones for Mexico. During this administration the indicators of economic growth on which the myth of the "Mexican miracle" were based had begun to slip. The rate of production in both industry and agriculture had slowed, the inflation was the worst Mexicans had known in twenty years, and the country's trade deficit was widening at an increasing rate. The confidence of foreign investors had been shaken both by the poor showing of various economic indicators and by the political violence that appeared to be sweeping the country. The world economic crisis accentuated these trends, and for all the rhetoric that had flown back and forth in 1970 and 1971, the well-being of peasants, workers, and the unemployed continued its steady decline in the face of rising costs of living. Economic inequalities and social injustice were as glaring as ever. But although the Echeverría regime came at the time when the economic and political tensions brewing since the 1940s were finally coming to a head, in 1974 and 1975 the focus of attention and concern even of many left-wing opposition groups turned to the question of the presidential succession. The final two years of Echeverría's administration marked a period of furious politicking in which each political group maneuvered to obtain the presidential nominee who promised to be most compatable with its interests. At this point, opposition movements thought less about changing the system and more about obtaining greater influence over the choice of the successor. Opposition peasant leaders and CNC stalwarts alike carefully examined the agrarian record of the men discussed as presidential material. Labor leaders, from both independent unions and the CTM, studied the labor relations records of the various *presidenciables.* Meanwhile, conservative groups rallied to exert pressure for a nominee who would safeguard their interests. As opposition leaders got caught up in this process, they demonstrated the hold that the PRI has over Mexicans, left, right, and center.

The radical student left was perhaps the only major opposition group, apart from the Communist Party, which stood outside this process. The students' analysis of the political situation generally persuaded them that the choice of the PRI successor would make very little difference to their future or the future of Mexico. The students' cynicism was easy to understand. Nonetheless, the concern with the succession on the part of popularly based opposition organization was neither irrational nor out of place. If one has the task of representing bus drivers or *ejidatarios,* and what one is trying to extract from the system is a higher wage for public transportation workers or more credit from the Ejidal Bank, the line of the nominee on public transport or agricultural credit funding is necessarily a crucial question. For whatever the shortcomings of the official party system, it delivers some payoffs. And it also controls people's lives through the wages it sets, the funds it allocates to social welfare, the amount of money it chooses to channel into ejidal agriculture, the number of jobs it opens in the public sector, and so forth.

As Echeverría entered the lame duck period of his administration and loyal *priistas* scrambled for prominent seats on the bandwagon of his chosen successor, finance minister José López Portillo, political discussion in Mexico continued to focus on Echeverría's policies. The debate centered on the president's capacity to bind his successor to the program of reforms begun during his own term in office. Indeed, there was even serious speculation about Echeverría's ambitions to perpetuate his power after leaving office, by manipulating López Portillo from behind the scenes. In the heat of such discussion, it was all too easy to overlook the fact that Echeverría's reforms had been inadequate to meet the needs of the Mexican people in the early seventies and were likely to prove even less sufficient for the future. Echeverría's urgent desire to commit his successor "to expand and continue" his program suggests that he had a coherent and viable reform policy, but lacked the time to carry it out. It was not, however, for lack of time that the reforms failed. The reforms did not work because they could not work, given the structure of power, the impotence of peasant and workers' organizations, the intransigence of the conservative bourgeoisie, the opposition of foreign capital, and the general alignment of political forces in Mexico.

The combination of radical rhetoric and half-measures that had been the hallmark of Echeverría's administration had not curbed the

power of the bourgeoisie. It had, however, frightened them sufficiently to produce a fall in investments, a massive outflow of capital,
a highly unstable economic situation, and ultimately—as always—
greater suffering for Mexican peasants and workers caught in the
inflationary spiral. The confusion of Echeverría's last months in
office—marked by the devaluation of the peso, fiscal panic, rumors
of military takeover, and a massive land distribution that was vio-
lently opposed by the landholders and eventually halted by the
courts—providing a fitting, if not a happy, end to this contradiction-
ridden administration.

Given the very real sense of crisis that prevailed at the timy he
took office, it seemed inevitable that the administration of López
Portillo would represent one of the periodic "turns to the right" that
had been part of Mexican politics since 1940. Clearly the new president would have to move to regain the confidence of domestic and
foreign capitalists, and to reassure the Mexican middle class that the
value of their savings would not suffer further decline. In addition,
immediate measures were necessary to defuse the growing militancy
of workers faced with wage freezes, and peasants who, tired of waiting for the government to make good on the promise of land reform,
were finally moving throughout the agriculturally rich North and
Northwest to occupy illegally held large estates. The problem for
López Portillo is that within the framework of the system he heads
no *new* options are available to help him cope with the crises produced by capitalist development in Mexico.

Mexico's immediate future under López Portillo promises, at best,
to resemble the Echeverría regime. The extent to which change will
occur will depend, as it always has, on the interplay among the forces
in Mexican politics that have been the subject of this book. The
extent to which the masses will see their condition changed either for
better or for worse will also depend, as it always has, on the interplay
of concession and repression that has kept them on the margins of
Mexican development. It does, however, seem clear that nothing
short of a major upheaval in the Mexican system could genuinely
improve their lot.

Notes

Preface

1. See Robert E. Scott, *Mexican Government in Transition* (Urbana: University of Illinois Press, 1964); Robert E. Scott, "Mexico: The Established Revolution," in Lucian W. Pye and Sidney Verba, eds., *Political Culture and Political Development* (Princeton: Princeton University Press, 1965); and Samuel P. Huntington, *Political Order in Changing Societies* (New Haven: Yale University Press, 1968).

Chapter 1

1. José E. Iturriaga, *La Estructura Social y Cultural de México* (México, D.F.: Fondo de Cultura Económica, 1951), p. 33.

2. Charles C. Cumberland, *Mexico: The Struggle for Modernity* (New York: Oxford University Press, 1968), p. 233.

3. Raymond Vernon, *The Dilemma of Mexico's Development* (Cambridge: Harvard University Press, 1963), pp. 39, 42-43. "Attracted by opportunities in Mexico, United States investments rose from 200 million United States dollars in 1897 to about 1100 million by 1911. The British increased their investments from $164 million in 1880 to over $300 million in 1911. . . ."

4. Barry Carr, "The Peculiarities of the Mexican North, 1880-1928: An Essay in Interpretation," occasional paper, Institute of Latin American Studies, University of Glasgow, no. 4, 1971, pp. 5-6.

5. Richard Roman, *Ideology and Class in the Mexican Revolution: A Study of the Convention and the Constitutional Congress* (Ph.D. dissertation, University of California, Berkeley, 1973), p. 14.

6. Roger D. Hansen, *The Politics of Mexican Development* (Baltimore: The Johns Hopkins Press, 1971), p. 151.

7. Friedrich Katz, "Labor Conditions on Haciendas in Porfirian Mexico: Some Trends and Tendencies," *Hispanic American Historical Review,* vol. 54, no. 1 (February 1974), pp. 34-35.

8. Eric R. Wolf, *Peasant Wars of the Twentieth Century* (New York: Harper and Row, 1969), p. 31. "Among their leaders were women as well as men, *coronelas* as well as coronels."

9. Oscar Lewis, *Pedro Martínez* (New York: Vintage, 1967), pp. 89, 90, 108.

10. Wolf, op. cit., pp. 37-38.

11. Ibid., p. 39.

12. Ibid.

13. Henry Bamford Parkes, *A History of Mexico* (London: Shenval Press, 1962), p. 290.

14. John Reed, *Insurgent Mexico* (New York: D. Appleton, 1914), p. 118.

15. Robert Quirk, *The Mexican Revolution 1914-1915* (Bloomington: University of Indiana Press, 1960), p. 224.

16. Reed, op cit., p. 127.

17. John Womack, Jr., *Zapata and the Mexican Revolution* (New York: Vintage, 1970), pp. 192-193.

18. Wolf, op. cit., p. 36.

19. Parkes, op. cit., p. 278.

20. Roman, op. cit., p. 20.

21. Parkes, op. cit., p. 280.

22. Ibid., p. 281.

23. Ibid., p. 284.

24. It is possible that only the war in Europe saved the Mexicans from a full scale military intervention by U.S. troops. During the entire course of his incumbency, Woodrow Wilson was under heavy pressure from big businessmen with interests in Mexico. Railroad and oil interests, the great cattle barons like William Randolph Hearst, and scores of other immensely powerful men used all the influence they could muster to persuade Wilson to intervene in the Revolution. But common sense prevailed, and even after the troops returned from Europe, Wilson preferred to pursue a policy that permitted him to maneuver from behind the scenes, pulling strings and imposing and lifting arms embargoes. Only toward the end of the Revolution did Wilson give in and send General Pershing on a punitive expedition into northern Mexico.

25. Daniel Cosio Villegas, "The Mexican Left," in Joseph Maier and Richard W. Weatherhead, eds., *The Politics of Change in Latin America* (New York: Praeger, 1964), p. 127.

26. Cumberland, op. cit., pp. 250-253.

27. Ibid., p. 247.

28. Ibid., p. 248.

29. See Andrew Gunder Frank, "Mexico: The Janus Faces of Twentieth Century Bourgeois Revolution," *Monthly Review,* vol. 14, no. 7 (November 1962), p. 374.

30. The Mexican novelist Carlos Fuentes has vividly described both the decline and the economic, political, and social resurgence of the prerevolutionary aristocracy in his novel *Where the Air is Clear* (New York: Noonday Press, 1971). Both this novel and his later book *The Death of Artemio Cruz* (New York: Noonday Press, 1971) deal with the rise of a new industrial elite and ruling class whose wealth and power grew directly out of the Revolution.

31. Jorge Carrión, "Retablo de la Política 'a la Mexicana'," in Fernando Carmona et al., *El Milagro Mexicano* (México, D.F.: Editorial Nuestro Tiempo, 1970), pp. 174-175.

32. Hansen, op. cit., p. 37.

33. Clark W. Reynolds, *The Mexican Economy* (New Haven: Yale University Press, 1970), p. 27.

34. William P. Glade, Jr., and Charles W. Anderson, *The Political Economy of Mexico,* (Madison: University of Wisconsin Press, 1968), p. 87.

35. Frank, op. cit., pp. 383-384. On the emergence of the new bourgeoisie, also see Berta Lerner Sigal et al., *México: Realidad Política de Sus Partidos* (México, D.F.: Instituto Mexicano de Estudios Políticos, 1970), pp. 48-50; and Jorge Graciarena, *Poder y Clases Sociales en el Desarrollo de América Latina* (Buenos Aires: Editorial Paidos, 1967), pp. 161-163.

36. Parkes, op. cit., p. 296.

37. Gerrit Huizer, "Emiliano Zapata and the Peasant Guerrillas," in Rodolfo Stavenhagen, ed., *Agrarian Problems and Peasant Movements in Latin America* (Garden City: Doubleday, 1970), p. 385.

38. An *agrarista* is a person who sympathizes with or fights for the "agrarian cause," for the expropriation of large estates and the distribution of these properties among the landless peasantry.

39. Frank Tannenbaum, *The Mexican Agrarian Revolution* (New York: Macmillan, 1929), pp. 168-170.

40. Marjorie Ruth Clark, *Organized Labor in Mexico* (Chapel Hill: University of North Carolina Press, 1934), p. 27.

41. Codificación de los Decretos del C. Venustiano Carranza (México D.F., 1915), p. 136.

42. Alvaro Obregón was so popular with certain sectors of the working class that when the general lost an arm in battle, the arm was brought in from the field, preserved in formaldehyde, and carried all over Mexico in a large glass container to be displayed as a kind of relic at union meetings.

43. For more information on the House of the Workers of the World, see Clark, op. cit., pp. 22-35; and Luís Araiza, *Historia de la Casa del Obrero Mundial* (México, D.F.: 1963).

44. Richard Roman, op. cit., p. 42.

45. Ibid., pp. 41-42.

46. Cumberland, op. cit., pp. 260-261.

47. Ibid., pp. 263-268.

48. Italics added. Article 123 of the Constitution of 1917. For translated excerpts of the Constitution see Paul E. Sigmund, *Models of Political Change in Latin America* (New York: Praeger, 1970), pp. 11-15; Emilio Portes Gil, *Autobiografía de la Revolución Mexicana* (México, D.F.: Instituto Mexicana de Cultura, 1964), pp. 204-207.

49. Cumberland, op. cit., p. 268.

50. Italics added. Article 27 of the Constitution of 1917. See Sigmund, op. cit., pp. 12-13.

51. See Victor Manzanilla Schaffer, *Reforma Agraria Mexicana* (Colima: Universidad de Colima, 1966), pp. 53-57; and Portes Gil, op. cit., pp. 201-204.

52. Carleton Beals, *Mexico: An Interpretation* (New York, 1923), p. 57.

53. Huizer, op. cit., p. 394.

54. Emiliano Zapata, "Open Letter to Citizen Carranza," March 17, 1919, Morelos, Mexico; quoted in Rene Dumont, "Mexico: The 'Sabotage' of the Agrarian Reform," *New Left Review,* no. 17 (Winter 1962), p. 51. Also see John Womack, Jr., op. cit., p. 319.

55. Notably in the states of Veracruz, Tamaulipas, Michoacán, Durango, México, and Yucatán.

56. Memorial addressed to His Grace the Archbishop of Durango by the Sindicato de Campesinos del Estado de Durango, September 1922. Quoted in Ernest Gruening, *Mexico and Its Heritage* (New York: The Century Company, 1928), pp. 217-218.

57. Ernest Gruening, op. cit., pp. 218-219.

58. Katz, op. cit., p. 30. "There are also indications that the majority of *acasillados* [resident peons] never joined the Revolution. . . . [Among other reasons] the relative security which the *acasillados* enjoyed as well as the paternalism of the *hacendado* may have enhanced their sense of superiority, reinforcing their ties to the *hacienda.*"

59. Eric R. Wolf and Sidney W. Mintz, "Haciendas and Plantations in Middle America and the Antilles," *Social and Economic Studies,* vol. 6, no. 3 (1957), pp. 392-393.

60. Edmundo Flores, *Tratado de Economia Agrícola* (México, D.F.: Fondo de Cultura Económica, 1968), p. 338. In 1920 an estimated 54 million acres of land was held by North American individuals and companies in specific violation of prohibitions on foreign ownership set out in the Constitution of 1917.

61. Flores, op. cit., p. 338.

62. Salomón Eckstein, *El Ejido Colectivo en México* (México, D.F.: Fondo de Cultura Económica, 1967), p. 132.

63. Cosio Villagas, op. cit., pp. 128-129.

64. Ibid., p. 129.

65. For more detailed discussion of the values and goals of the northern dynasty, see Howard F. Cline, *The United States and Mexico* (New York: Atheneum, 1965), pp. 193-194.

66. Interview with Sr. J. Cruz Chacón, reported in Sergio Alcántara Ferrer, *La Organización Colectivista Ejidal en la Comarca Lagunera* (Mèxico, D.F.: Centro de Investigaciones Agrarias, 1967), pp. 20-25.

67. Manzanilla Shaffer, op. cit.

68. Lerner Sigal, op. cit. pp. 52-53.

69. L. Vincent Padgett, *The Mexican Political System* (Boston: Houghton Mifflin Company, 1966), p. 48.

70. Ibid., p. 49.

71. The most important parties and political movements incorporated into the PNR at this time were the Liberal Constitutional Party, the National Co-operativist Party, the Mexican Labor Party, The Mexican Communist Party, the Mexican Agrarian Party, the Socialist Party of the Southeast (centered in Yucatán), and the Frontier Socialist Party (centered in Tamaulipas). Lerner Sigal, op. cit., p. 53n.

72. Padgett, op. cit., p. 49.

Chapter 2

1. Robert E. Scott, *Mexican Government in Transition* (Urbana: University of Illinois Press, 1964), pp. 116-117.

2. William Cameron Townsend, *Lázaro Cárdenas, Mexican Democrat* (Ann Arbor: George Wahr, 1952), pp. 56-58.

3. Anatol Shulgovsky, *México en la Encrucijada de su Historia* (México, D.F.: Fondo de Cultura Popular, 1968), p. 78.

4. Shulgovsky, op. cit., p. 78. Calles' failure to formulate policy designed to cope with the needs of lower class Mexicans was particularly problematic given the disastrous impact of the Depression of 1929 on peasants and workers. Statistics outlining the effect of the Depression on all sectors of the Mexican economy can be found in Arnaldo Córdova, *La Politica de las Masas del Cardenismo* (México, D.F.: Ediciones Era, 1974), pp. 17-19.

5. Shulgovsky, op. cit., p. 82.

6. Ibid. Also see Córdova, op. cit. pp. 41-42.

7. Joe C. Ashby, *Organized Labor and the Mexican Revolution* (Chapel Hill: University of North Carolina Press, 1967), pp. 26-27.

8. Quoted in Verna Carleton Millan, *Mexico Reborn* (Boston: Houghton Mifflin, 1939), p. 94.

9. Ashby, op. cit., p. 26.

10. Raymond Vernon, *The Dilemma of Mexico's Development* (Cambridge: Harvard University Press, 1963), p. 71; Gerrit Huizer, "Peasant Organization and Agrarian Reform in Mexico," in Irving Louis Horowitz, (ed.), *Masses in Latin*

America (New York: Oxford University Press, 1970), p. 469; Victor Alba, *Historia del Movimiento Obrero en América Latina* (México, D.F.: Libreros Mexi-*America* (New York: Oxford University Press, 1970), p. 469; Victor Alba, *Historia del Movimiento Obrero en América Latina* (México, D.F.: Libreros Mexicanos Unidos, 1964), p. 447; Nathaniel and Sylvia Weyl, *The Reconquest of Mexico: The Years of Lázaro Cárdenas* (New York: Oxford University Press, 1939), pp. 235-236.

11. Secretaría de Gobernación, *Seis Años de Servicio al Gobierno de México* (México, D.F.: La Nacional Impresora, 1940), pp. 95-96. According to Lieuwen, the workers militia was eventually to become a determining force in Cárdenas' efforts to ward off a right wing military coup. "On May Day, 1938, a newly organized and uniformed workers' militia, 100,000 strong, paraded en masse through the streets of the capital. Prior to the parade, Cárdenas had warned in a speech that if reactionary forces in the army revolted, they would be obliged to fight these proletarian defenders of his regime." Edwin Lieuwen, *Mexican Militarism: The Political Rise and Fall of the Revolutionary Army, 1910-1940* (Albuquerque: University of New Mexico Press, 1968), p. 127.

12. Confederacíon de Trabajadores de Mexico, *Informe del Comité Nacional* (México, D.F.: 1936-1937), p. 65.

13. Adalberto Tejeda in Veracrúz, Saturnino Cedillo and Gonzalo N. Santos in San Luís Potosí, Emilio Portes Gil in Tamaulipas, Pedro Rodríguez Triana in the Laguna region, and others.

14. For example, the League of Agrarian Communities of Veracrúz, a group of 40,000 armed peasants loyal to and controlled by Adalberto Tejeda, was one of the prime targets of the "unification" effort which preceded the formation of the new peasant confederation by Cárdenas. See Moises González Navarro, *La Confederación Nacional Campesina* (México, D.F.: Costa-Amic, 1968), pp. 134-141; and Emilio Portes Gil, *Autobiografía de la Revolución Mexicana* (México, D.F.: Instituto Mexicano de Cultura, 1964), pp. 706-711.

15. Ashby, op. cit., pp. 33-34, 41.

16. Ministry of Foreign Relations, *The Mexican Government: Tour of the President,* p. 11, cited in Ashby, op. cit., p. 33.

17. Cárdenas' Fourteen Point Program, Monterrey, Feb. 11, 1936, cited in Ashby, p. 34.

18. Córdova, op. cit., pp. 177-178.

19. Ibid.

20. State owned development banks established under Cárdenas (the Banco Nacional de Crédito Ejidal, founded in 1935, and the Banco Nacional de Comercio Exterior, founded in 1937) along with other state banks which expanded their role during his administration, played a key part in the promotion and especially in the orientation of economic development in Mexico. Furthermore, the creation of these banking institutions was consistent with a policy of fostering "a private enterprise system in which the state role would complement, rather than supplant, that of private capital." Nora Louise Hamilton, "Mexico:

The Limits of State Autonomy," *Latin American Perspectives,* vol. 2, no. 2 (Spring 1975), p. 96.

21. Córdova, op. cit., p. 182. "That the Revolution recognized the collaboration of the capitalist class in the progress of Mexico was a principle accepted since the period of armed struggle. It formed part of the revolutionary ideology. Cárdenas said to a group of capitalists in May 1939, 'I cordially invite you to cooperate in the work of national reconstruction. . . . I value your knowledge, your experience and your entrepreneurial spirit; I see you as prominent factors of progress and proponents of our country's culture.' "

22. Albert L. Michaels, "The Crisis of Cardenismo," *Journal of Latin American Studies,* vol. 2, no. 1, p. 59, May 1970.

23. Michaels, op. cit., pp. 53, 55, 70-72, 74.

24. The Mexican right grew steadily more powerful during the Cárdenas years, financially supported in Mexico, as in virtually all Latin American countries, by the European fascist movements. In the mid-30s the national press was heavily subsidized by German agents and was correspondingly sympathetic to the Nazi cause. The Mexican Sinanarchist movement modeled itself after the Spanish falange, and its influence throughout Mexico grew during this period. When Cárdenas came to power, large numbers of fascist sympathizers were holding office in the Chamber of Deputies—a fact reflected by the passage of immigration quotas excluding Jews. In 1937 and 1938 right-wing extremists burned property in Mexico City alleged to belong to Jews. See Nathan L. Whetten, *Rural Mexico* (New York: The Century Company, 1948), pp. 484-522; Weyl, op. cit., pp. 353-366; and Friedrich Katz, ed. *Hitler sobre América Latina: El Fascismo Alemán en Latinoamérica, 1933-1943* (México, D.F.: Fondo de Cultura Popular, 1968), pp. 42-48.

25. Vernon, op. cit., p. 70; L. Vincent Padgett, *The Mexican Political System* (Boston: Houghton Mifflin, 1965), p. 111. Robert J. Alexander, *Communism in Latin America* (New Brunswick: Rutgers University Press, 1957), p. 336.

26. Ibid., p. 131.

27. Ibid.

28. Frank R. Brandenburg, *The Making of Modern Mexico* (Englewood Cliffs: Prentice-Hall, 1964), p. 83.

29. Ibid.

30. Ibid.

31. Notably, the General Workers Confederation (Confederación General de Trabajadores) plus one wing of the divided CROM and independent electricians and miners unions. Scott, op. cit., p. 132.

32. Padgett, op. cit., p. 93.

33. Ibid.

34. For example, in 1947 Lombardo Toledano left the organization he had helped to establish to form a new Marxist oriented Popular Party with its own peasant and labor confederation, the General Union of Workers and Peasants of Mexico (Unión General de Obreros y Campesinos de México, or UGOCM).

35. Padgett, op. cit., p. 99.

36. Ibid.

37. See Roger D. Hansen, *The Politics of Mexican Development* (Baltimore: The Johns Hopkins Press, 1971), p. 116.

38. Robert J. Alexander, *Organized Labor in Latin America* (New York: The Free Press, 1965), p. 195.

39. The traditional relationship between landlord and peon has often been called a "patron-client" relationship. Characteristic of this relationship are arrangements whereby the peasant receives a tiny parcel of land to work for his family's subsistence in return for rendering services to the landlord. The peasant may be obliged to repay the landlord in cash by yielding a portion of his crop to the landlord, by paying rent for the land, or by farming a portion of the landlord's property for him. Typically, the peasant is also obliged to pledge his loyalty to the landlord and to support him in any political conflict that arises. The essential nature of the patron-client relationship is that it is formed by unequal parties: the peasant *needs* what the landlord provides, but the landlord does not need the services of any particular peasant because there are always other landless peasants ready to establish a patron-client relationship with the landlord. See John Duncan Powell, *Peasant Society and Clientelist Politics* (Cambridge, Mass.: Center for International Affairs, 1967), p. 5.

40. A *minifundista* is a peasant who owns a plot of land too small to provide for his family or to require the participation of all family members who are available to contribute their labor.

41. A *colono* is a peasant settled by the government on newly opened territory.

42. An *ejidatario* is a peasant who has received from the government a grant of land in a peasant community called an *ejido*. "The word *ejido* is derived from the Latin verb *exire, exitum,* 'to go out,' 'the way out.' As originally used in Spain, the term was applied to uncultivated land held collectively and located on the outskirts 'on the way out' of agrarian communities. In Mexico the word is used to refer to all types of land which have been restored by agricultural communities under the land reform initiated in 1915. By extension, the word is also used to designate the communities possessing such lands." Elyer N. Simpson, *The Ejido: Mexico's Way Out* (Chapel Hill: University of North Carolina Press, 1937), p. vii.

43. Gerrit Huizer, *The Role of Peasant Organizations in the Process of Agrarian Reform in Latin America* (Washington, D.C.: Inter-American Committee for Agricultural Development, 1968), p. 17.

44. For example, one of the obligations of the CNC State Leagues, according to the statutes of the organization is "to socially and politically orient the peasants in such a way that they invariably act in conformity with the national directives." Estatutos de la Confederación Nacional Campesina, Article 60, V. The model of the CNC as a mechanism for control rather than the articulation of

demands is developed at length in an earlier study. Judith Adler, *The Politics of Land Reform in Mexico* (M.Ph. thesis, London School of Economics, 1970).

45. Leiuwen, op. cit., pp. 85.

46. Ibid., pp. 119-120.

47. Cárdenas, quoted in Leiuwen, op. cit., p. 124.

48. "The present restrictions [against voting] which practically isolate the military from political life . . . are a grave error. . . . Henceforth the members of the army will have, constitutionally, political rights and the duty to exercise them." Ibid.

49. Cárdenas, quoted in Townsend, op. cit., p. 216.

50. Scott, op. cit., p. 131.

51. Pablo González Casanova, *Democracy in Mexico,* (New York: Oxford University Press, 1972), pp. 37-38.

52. Vernon, op. cit., p. 74.

53. Padgett, op. cit., p. 124.

54. Kenneth F. Johnson, *Mexican Democracy: A Critical View* (Boston: Allyn and Bacon, 1971), p. 67.

55. Scott, op. cit., pp. 169-170; Padgett, op. cit., p. 123; Johnson, op. cit., p. 67.

56. Brandenburg, op. cit. (1955), p. 188.

57. González Casanova, op. cit., p. 55.

58. José Luís Cecena, *El Capital Monopolista y La Economía de México* (México, D.F.: Cuadernos Americanos, 1963), cited in González Casanova, op. cit., pp. 49-50. Also see Richard S. Newfarmer and Willard F. Mueller, *Multi-national Corporations in Brazil and Mexico: Structural Sources of Economic and Noneconomic Power* (Washington, D.C.: U.S. Government Printing Office, 1975), pp. 45-94.

59. González Casanova, op. cit., p. 50.

60. Ibid., p. 52.

61. Ibid.

62. Joseph C. Goulden, "Mexico: PRI's False Front Democracy," Alicia Patterson Fund Reprint, December 1966, p. 7.

63. Ibid.

64. Political leaders in Mexico often describe this process as "auscultation." Asucultation is really a medical technique in which the doctor uses a stethoscope to listen to sounds within the human body in order to detect those sounds which provide clues for a diagnosis. In Mexico, the term is used to describe the way in which the president listens for indications of the health of the body politic. In a way, auscultation is similar to a public opinion poll in which the only opinions that are registered are those of "opinion makers,"—political bosses, the leaders of influential sectors of society, etc. Jaime Plenn, *The News,* México, D.F.: January 3, 1969, p. 5.

65. Hansen, op. cit., p. 111.

66. Peter Lord, *The Peasantry as an Emerging Political Factor in Mexico, Bolivia and Venezuela* (Madison, Wisconsin: The Land Tenure Center, 1965), p. 25.

Chapter 3

1. Banco de Mexico, S.A., Departamento de Estudios Económicos, 1973.
2. In real terms.
3. Melville J. Ulmer, "Who's Making It in Mexico?" *The New Republic,* September 25, 1971, p. 21.
4. Fernando Carmona et al., *El Milagro Mexicano* (México, D.F.: Editorial Nuestro Tiempo, 1970), p. 20.
5. Ulmer, op. cit., p. 21.
6. Roger D. Hansen, *The Politics of Mexican Development* (Baltimore: Johns Hopkins Press, 1971), p. 41.
7. *La Economía Mexicana en Cifras* (México, D.F.: Nacional Financiera, 1970).
8. Secretaría de Hacienda y Crédito Publio.
9. Hansen, op. cit., p. 1.
10. David Barkin, "The Persistence of Poverty in Mexico: Some Explanatory Hypotheses," paper delivered to the Latin American Studies Association, Washington, D.C., April 1970.
11. Ibid.
12. Hansen, op. cit., p. 3.
13. See Diego G. López Rosado and Juan F. Noyola Vásquez, "Los Salarios Reales en México, 1939-1950," *El Trimestre Económico,* vol. 18, no. 2, April-June 1951. Ifigenia de Navarrete, "Income Distribution in Mexico," in Enrique Pérez López, ed., *The Recent Development of Mexico's Economy* (Austin: University of Texas Press, 1967).
14. Hansen, op. cit., p. 50.
15. United States Agency for International Development, *A Review of Alliance for Progress Goals* (Washington, D.C.: U.S. Government Printing Office, 1969), p. 62.
16. Pablo González Casanova, *Democracy in Mexico* (New York: Oxford University Press, 1972), p. 139.
17. Hansen, op. cit., pp. 48-49. Also see Rafael Izquierdo, "Protectionism in Mexico," in Raymond Vernon, ed., *Public Policy and Private Enterprise in Mexico* (Cambridge: Harvard University Press, 1964), pp. 243-289.
18. Barkin, op. cit., p. 10.
19. Hansen, op. cit., p. 49.
20. Barkin, op. cit., p. 8. Clark W. Reynolds, *The Mexican Economy: Twentieth Century Structures and Growth* (New Haven: Yale University Press, 1970).

21. Ibid., p. 10.

22. Preliminary results of a study of the psychology of Mexican businessmen, carried out by psychologists and psychiatrists of the Instituto Mexicano de Psicoanálisis, tend to confirm the existence of highly ambivalent feelings toward collaboration with American capitalists. The study, which included the analysis of the dreams of Mexican enterpreneurs, suggested that even among Mexicans whose business interests are strongly linked and intertwined with business interests of American capitalists, it is common to find overwhelming feelings of fear and repugnance for their foreign partners.

23. North American Congress on Latin America, *Mexico 1968: A Study of Domination and Repression* (New York: NACLA, 1968), p. 29.

24. Harvey Levenstein, "A Lesson in Foreign Control from Mexico," *Toronto Star*, April 4, 1973.

25. Ibid.

26. North American Congress on Latin America, *Yanqui Dollar* (New York: NACLA, 1971), p. 29.

27. Ibid.

28. Ibid. p. 29. *Business Latin America*, August 12, 1971, p. 250.

29. Carlos Fuentes, *The Death of Artemio Cruz* (New York: Noonday, 1964), pp. 20-21. Also see pp. 53, 80, 111, 135.

30. NACLA, op. cit. (1971), p. 29.

31. *Journal of Commerce*, April 26, 1971.

32. NACLA, op. cit. (1968), p. 26.

33. NACLA, op. cit. (1968), p. 25.

34. Between 1946 and 1965 the U.S. Export-Import Bank loaned Mexico $862 million at 12.6 percent interest. This loan, on which $108 million in interest was paid, was specifically earmarked for the purchase of U.S.-made machinery and equipment. Since 1945 this same bank loaned $270 million to finance the purchase of American equipment for the Mexican railways. Ibid., p. 26.

35. Barkin, op. cit., pp. 12-13. A hair-raising account of the consequences of the rush to buy foreign-made industrial equipment is provided by Leo Fenster, "At Twice the Price: The Mexican Auto Swindle," *The Nation*, June 2, 1970. In this article Fenster indicates that the new and expensive capital equipment supplied to the Mexican auto industry by American, British, French, Italian, German, and Japanese parent firms is, in fact, obsolete by advanced industrial standards.

36. Saul Trejo Reyes, "El Incremento de la Producción y el Empleo Industrial en México, 1950-1965," *Demografía y Economía* vol. 4, no. 1, 1970, p. 102-120.

37. Barkin, op. cit., p. 2.

38. Barkin, op. cit., pp. 11-12.

39. Hansen, op. cit., pp. 43-45.

40. Barkin, op. cit., p. 7.

41. Ibid., p. 9.

42. Hansen, op. cit., p. 85.

43. Ibid.

44. Ibid., pp. 85-86.

45. Judith Adler, "The Politics of Land Reform in Mexico" (M. Phil. thesis, London School of Economics, 1970), p. 90; Paul Nathan, "México en la Epoca de Cárdenas," *Problemas Agrícolas e Industriales de México,* vol. 7, no. 3 (1955), p. 26; also see Nathaniel and Sylvia Weyl, *The Reconquest of Mexico: The Years of Lázaro Cárdenas* (New York: Oxford University Press, 1939), pp. 279-281.

46. Rodolfo Stavenhagen, "Social Aspects of Agrarian Structure in Mexico," in Stavenhagen, ed., *Agrarian Problems and Peasant Movements in Latin America* (Garden City, N.Y.: Doubleday, 1970), pp. 225-227.

47. The organization of the Laguna *ejidos* into collectives was only partially the result of Cárdenas' preference for collective forms of farming. It should be noted that the Laguna region became a principal site of land distribution under Cárdenas precisely because it had over the previous 30-35 years been the scene of a continuous political struggle for land, and the home of a large number and variety of socialist and communist-led peasant leagues, unions, syndicates, and the like. These leftist *agraristas* played an important part in pressuring for collective forms of agricultural exploitation.

48. Salomón Eckstein, "Collective Farming in Mexico," in Rodolfo Stavenhagen, ed., *Agrarian Problems and Peasant Movements in Latin America* (Garden City, N.Y.: Doubleday, 1970), p. 276.

49. Liga de Agrónomos Socialistas, *El Colectivismo Agrario en México: La Comarca Lagunera* (México, D.F.: Editorial Cultura, 1940), pp. 133-136. Salomón Eckstein, *El Ejido Colectivo en México* (México, D.F.: Fondo de Cultura Económica, 1967), p. 140; Salomón Eckstein, op. cit., (1970), pp. 292-294; Juan Ballesteros Porta, *Explotación Individual o Colectiva?: El Caso de los Ejidos de Tlahualilo* (México, D.F.: Centro de Investigaciones Agrarias, 1964), p. 46.

50. Ballesteros Porta, op. cit., p. 46.

51. Eckstein, op. cit. (1970), pp. 277-281.

52. Ibid.; Nathan L. Whetten, *Rural Mexico* (New York: The Century Company, 1948), pp. 220-224.

53. Whetten, op. cit., pp. 221-222.

54. Ibid.

55. The Decree of October 6, 1937.

56. Landowners were generally compensated for their land in government bonds, and for their capital goods (wells, pumps, etc.) in cash.

57. Jesús Silva Herzog, *El Agrarismo Mexicano y la Reforma Agraria* (México, D.F.: Fondo de Cultura Económica, 1959), p. 453.

58. See Friedrich Katz, *Hitler sobre América Latina: El Fascismo Alemán en*

Latinoamérica 1933-1943. (México, D.F.: Fondo de Cultura Popular, 1968), pp. 42-48.

59. Vicente Lombardo Toledano, "Los Intentos de Revisión del Marxismo durante la Guerra," in *La CTAL ante la Guerra y ante la Post-Guerra* (México, D.F.: 1945), pp. 65-80.

60. Manuel Avila Camacho, *Unidad Nacional: Pensamiento Político del Señor General de División Manuel Ávila Camacho, Presidente Constitucional de Los Estados Unidos Mexicanos* (México, D.F.: 1945), pp. 157-158.

61. Compendio Estadístico, Departmento Agrario, México, D.F., 1948.

62. Frank R. Brandenburg, *The Making of Modern Mexico* (Englewood Cliffs: Prentice-Hall, 1964), pp. 102-103.

63. Raymond Vernon, *The Dilemma of Mexico's Development* (Cambridge: Harvard University Press, 1963), pp. 102-103.

64. Ibid.; Hansen, op. cit., p. 81.

65. From 1946 to the present the legal maximum holdings have been either 247 acres of irrigated land, 494 acres of seasonal rainfall land, 1,976 acres of pasture land, or 3,952 acres of arid mountain land. In addition, special exceptions to this formula were made to stimulate the production of certain cash crops. So called "small private properties" given over to the cultivation of cotton may reach a legal 370 acres of prime irrigated land, while the limits on irrigated land devoted to bananas, sugar cane, henequen, vanilla, rubber, olives, cocoa, and fruit trees have been revised upward to 740 acres. For those landowners who raise cattle, the limit is set as "the amount of land necessary to support 500 head of cattle." Some cattle ranches in northern Mexico have as much as 50,000 acres.

66. Even during the second half of the Cárdenas regime, an agrarian law was introduced which favored private commercial farmers over landless peasants and *ejidatarios.* The Law of Livestock Development (*Ley de Fomento Ganadero*), issued March 1, 1937, declared unaffectable as much cattle land as was needed for the breeding of five hundred head of cattle or the equivalent in small livestock. The law intended to stimulate investment by cattle owners who, fearful of expropriation, had ceased to make further investments in cattle. In fact, the law stimulated neolatifundism, as large landowners simulated cattle breeding on a large scale to protect illegally large properties.

67. Edmundo Flores, *Tratado de Economía Agrícola* (México, D.F.: Fondo de Cultura Económica, 1968), p. 311.

68. François Chevalier, "The *Ejido* and Political Stability in Mexico," in Claudio Veliz, ed., *The Politics of Conformity in Latin America* (New York: Oxford University Press, 1967), p. 175.

69. Adler, op. cit., pp. 167-185.

70. Eckstein, op. cit. (1966), pp. 146-147.

71. Hansen, op. cit., p. 81.

72. To the extent that the government has brought a small number of

ejidatarios into the green revolution program, the results have not been happy ones for the peasants involved. Under the program, *ejidatarios* have been forced to invest heavily in chemical and mechanical inputs, and the resulting increases in productivity have not covered the money laid out for equipment, wells, insecticide, fertilizer, etc. Cynthia Hewitt Alcántara, unpublished manuscript, "The Green Revolution," chapter 5.

73. Hansen, op. cit., p. 81.

74. Ibid.

75. Ibid.

76. Chevalier, op. cit., p. 179.

77. Rodolfo Stavenhagen, op. cit., p. 249. Here are some of the figures Stavenhagen uses to demonstrate the equal productive capacity of ejidal and private agriculture: According to the 1960 agricultural census, the relative proportion of the value of crops grown on *ejido* land, (43 percent of total value of all crops) corresponds roughly to the relative proportion of cultivable land in the *ejido* sector (41 percent of all irrigated land in the country). In other words, the *ejido* contributes to the country's agricultural product in direct proportion to its participation in the resource land.

According to the same source, the private farms possess 70 percent of all capital in agriculture (excluding the value of the land itself), whereas the *ejidos* possess only 30 percent of all agricultural capital. Yet they contribute, as noted, 43 percent of the value of all crops. This suggests that the *ejidatarios* use the few capital resources they have at their disposal more intensively and efficiently. Indeed, for every $1,000 in capital, the *ejido* sector produces crops in the value of $955 while the private farms of more than five hectares produce only $763.

It has been stated that in the private farms of over five hectares, 28 percent of the agricultural labor force is employed. These same farm units possess 62 percent of all capital in agriculture. On the other hand, the *ejidos* avail themselves of 45 percent of the labor force and possess 30 percent of the capital. Nevertheless the value of agricultural production in these two groups corresponds roughly to the relative amount of cultivable land they possess. This means that the higher concentration of capital in the larger private farms (of over five hectares in size) does not contribute significantly to an increase in production but does contribute to displace manpower.

Other studies that demonstrate the high productive capacity of ejidal and minifundist agriculture include: Salomón Eckstein, *El Marco Macroeconómico del Problema Agrario Mexicano* (México, D.F.: Centro de Investigaciones Agrarias, 1968); Sergio Reyes Osorio, "El Desarrollo Polarizado de la Agricultura Mexicana," *Comercio Exterior*, 19 (March 1969); Hansen, op. cit., pp. 60-64.

78. Rodolfo Stavenhagen, op. cit., pp. 250-251.

79. Carlos Tello supplies these figures on land concentration in the 1960s: 50 percent of the land is in the hands of only slightly more than 1 percent of all landowners. In some states (Guerrero and Oaxaca, to name only two), 75-95

percent of all private land is held by less than 1.5 percent of private owners. Thirty-six percent of all cropland is in the hands of 1.4 percent of all owners, while 50 percent of all those in agriculture have less than 12 percent of croplands. Carlos Tello, *La Tenencia de La Tierra en México* (México, D.F.: Instituto de Investigaciones Sociales, 1968).

80. Chevalier, op. cit., p. 167. Also see Eric Wolf, *Peasant Wars of the Twentieth Century* (New York: Harper & Row, 1969), p. 45.

81. See Rodolfo Stavenhagen et al., *Neolatifundismo y Explotación: De Emiliano Zapata a Anderson Clayton & Co.* (México, D.F.: Editorial Nuestro Tiempo, 1968).

82. Chevalier, op. cit., p. 189.

83. Ibid.

84. Alan Riding, "Mexico: No More 'Miracle,' " *New York Times,* Special Economic Report on Latin America, January 28, 1972, p. 69.

85. Official government figures in 1974 showed inflation at 22 percent.

86. Hansen, op. cit., pp. 72-77.

87. Centro de Investigaciones Agrarias, *Estructura Agraria y Desarrollo Agrícola en México* (México, D.F.: CDIA, 1970), vol. I, p. 175.

88. Ibid.

89. Ibid.

90. Ibid.

91. Ibid.

92. *Excelsior*, November 30, 1971, pp. 1, 22. A recent study of employment carried out by the government Department of Hydraulic Resources indicates that 67 percent of the economically active population receives less than the minimum wage. *Latin American Profile,* CENCOS, 1:73, p. 21.

93. Centro de Investigaciones Agrarias, op. cit., vol. II, p. 38. According to the 1960 census, in all of Mexico there were only 54,000 tractors and about three million handplows. By 1968 the number of tractors had increased to 70,000, but these were concentrated in the hands of large commercial producers. See R. S. Abercrombie, "Mecanización Agrícola y Ocupación en América Latina" in Ernest Feder, ed., *La Lucha de Clases en el Campo* (México, D.F.: Fondo de Cultura Económica, 1975), p. 230. Ironically, while peasants are seriously underequipped in most areas of Mexico, in the commercialized agricultural regions of the North and Northwest they are often "overequipped," i.e., they are encouraged or obliged by the government to buy on credit agricultural machinery which is too highly mechanized for their needs. Hewitt Alcántara, op. cit.

94. Centro de Investigaciones Agrarias, op. cit., vol. 2, p. 38.

95. Ibid., p. 52-53.

96. For a discussion of the utility of census material as an indicator of social welfare in the period 1910-1960 see James W. Wilkie, *The Mexican Revolution: Federal Expenditure and Social Change since 1910* (Berkeley: University of California Press, 1967), pp. 204-232.

97. González Casanova, op. cit., pp. 73-74.

98. Ibid.

99. Ibid., pp. 72-74.

100. Hansen, op. cit., p. 78.

101. There is an important and ongoing dispute in Mexico among politicians, agronomists, and economists as to just how far land resources might be stretched. On the one side are those who believe that the natural resources of Mexico would prove insufficient to support even the present agricultural population even if every square inch of land now held in illegally large land concentrations were distributed in accord with the land reform law. On the other side are agrarian experts who assert that the land resources of Mexico would be sufficient to support all future generations of peasants who wish to remain on the land *if* other models of agricultural development (particularly the labor intensive model employed in the People's Republic of China) were applied in Mexico, while further industrialization draws surplus rural population into an urban job market. Either way, this dispute is over an essentially moot point. The present Mexican government would not and could not institute a Chinese model in the agricultural sector. Therefore, in this discussion we have considered only the real-life effects of ongoing agricultural policy.

102. For a lengthy description and study of *bracero* working conditions s e Ernest Galarza, "Trabajadores Mexicanos en Tierra Extranjera," *Problemas Agrícolas e Industriales de México* (January-June 1958), pp. 1-84. Also see Máximo Peón, *Como Viven los Mexicanos en los Estados Unidos* (México, D.F.: B. Costa-Amic, 1966); and Myrtle R. Reul, *Territorial Boundaries of Rural Poverty: Profiles of Exploitation* (East Lansing: Center for Rural Manpower and Public Affairs, Michigan State University, 1974), pp. 125-136, 459-472.

103. In 1958, for example, when an economic recession in the United States forced cuts of up to 60 percent in *bracero* contracting, this kind of violence occurred at the *bracero* induction centers in Enpalme, Sonora, and elsewhere throughout the North of Mexico.

104. "The seasonal emigration of *braceros* ... far exceeds the number quoted in statistics. About 800,000 every year seems a likely figure." Chevalier, op. cit., p. 185.

105. The official estimate is $200 million for the period from 1958 to 1964. However, for political reasons this figure was set quite low and the actual remittance to Mexico during this time was probably more in the neighborhood of 750 million to one billion dollars. Donald D. Brand, *Mexico: Land of Sunshine and Shadow* (Princeton: D. Van Nostrand, 1966), p. 129.

106. In 1972, 100,000 seasonal and 43,000 daily laborers received permits to work in the U.S. The number of people who cross the border illegally to seek work is, of course, much higher.

107. The *bracero* remittances had been the third largest earner of foreign exchange after tourism (including border transactions) and cotton.

108. The population of Mexico City has tripled in the last decade. In 1971 the population of greater Mexico City reached eleven million. The official projection for the year 2000 is twenty-nine million.

109. Enrique Padilla Aragón, *Mexico: Desarrollo con Pobreza* (México, D.F.: Siglo XXI Editores, 1970), p. 42.

110. *Journal of Commerce,* March 1, 1972.

111. Saul Trejo, op. cit., pp. 21-24.

112. *Excelsior,* México, D.F., July 31, 1971, p. 9.

113. The tenement neighborhood described by Oscar Lewis in his study of the urban poor, *The Children of Sánchez* (New York: Vintage, 1961), was located in this area behind the National Palace and the main cathedral of Mexico.

114. *Excelsior,* Mexico, D.F., July 31, 1971, p. 9.

115. Ibid.

116. "México, uno de los cinco paises más matones del mundo," *Siempre!* México, D.F., October 28, 1970, p. 39. The *Siempre!* article was based on data from a 1970 United Nations report on criminality.

117. Manuel Mejido, *Excelsior,* August 2, 1971, p. 14.

118. When it received official status, Netzahualcoyotl became the fourth largest "city" in Mexico after the Capital, Guadalajara, and Monterrey.

119. *The Daily Worker,* New York, October 21, 1970.

120. *The New York Times,* News of the Week, June 11, 1972.

121. Ibid.

122. While there are some regulations that prohibit selling goods on city buses, the bus drivers, whose lot is extremely difficult and whose workday frequently runs fourteen hours, are usually sympathetic enough to allow hundreds of vendors to jump on and off their buses each day without paying the fare.

123. *Journal of Commerce,* February 3, 1972.

124. Ibid., "La Basura, Negocio de Choferes del D.D.F.," *Excelsior,* August 3, 1971.

125. *Excelsior,* February 2, 1972.

126. *Excelsior,* August 4, 1971.

127. The average number of children in these families is 5.2

128. 1970 census.

129. Hansen, op, cit., p. 86.

130. Mexico derives only 13 percent of her gross national product in taxes, most of which falls on the salaried workers. Barkin, op. cit., p. 6.

131. *Gaceta UNAM,* vol. 18, Nueva Epoca, no. 3, March 1969. Only 2.8 percent of students enrolled at the National University come from peasant backgrounds.

132. Fernando Carmona et al., op. cit.

Chapter 4

1. Pablo González Casanova, *Democracy in Mexico* (New York: Oxford University Press, 1972), p. 23-24.

2. Ibid.

3. Ibid., p. 17.

4. For example, in an earlier study of electoral violence during the period 1957-1959, on the basis of newspaper reports *alone* I noted 124 separate incidents of electoral violence, all associated directly or indirectly with the presidential elections of 1958. These incidents included the breakup of opposition party rallies, violence over disputed elections, physical attacks on the candidates and supporters of opposition parties, physical coercion at the polls, riots over the imposition of PRI candidates where an opposition party victory was generally believed to have occurred, and the destruction of opposition party headquarters by army and/or police forces. The figure 124 is probably low, given that it was based *only* on events reported in the Mexican press. These incidents occurred in 23 of the 32 federal states and territories, and were particularly frequent and virulent in the states of Baja California, Veracruz, Zacatecas, Chiapas, and Chihuaha.

5. González Casanova, op. cit., p. 12.

6. Ibid.

7. Ibid.

8. To the best of my knowledge the term was first used with specific reference to Mexico in James Cockcroft and Bo Anderson, "Control and Cooptation in Mexican Politics," in Irving Louis Horowitz et al., eds., *Latin American Radicalism* (New York: Random House, 1969), p. 366-389, especially p. 376ff. A second case study of cooptation in Mexican politics was developed by Robert F. Adie, "Cooperation, Cooptation and Conflict in Mexican Peasant Organizations," *Inter-American Economic Affairs,* vol. 24 (Winter 1970), pp. 3-25. I am using the term in a broader sense than it is employed in either the Cockcroft and Anderson or Adie articles. See Judith Adler, *The Politics of Land Reform in Mexico* (M. Phil. thesis, London School of Economics, 1970), pp. 228-232.

9. Adler, op. cit.

10. Mexican economist Miguel Wionczek writes, "One of the things that the capitalist and socialist countries have in common is that both (for different reasons) offer the scientist and technician a margin of liberty for research and a decent standard of living. In Mexico, on the other hand, until very recently this group has faced the humiliating alternative of living a life of sacrifice and self-denial, or accepting unconditionally the rules of the political game. Among the other reasons for this situation [are] the anti-intellectual attitude . . . of the postrevolutionary elites which is the result of the rise to national, regional and local power of poorly educated leaders, the incorporation into the political apparatus of 'cooptable' intellectuals, and the profound suspicion of this apparatus toward

those who are not disposed to sell their independence in exchange for immediate politcal gain." Miguel S. Wionczek, "El Subdesarrollo Científico y Technológico: Sus Consecuencias," in Wionczek, ed., *Disyuntivas sociales* (México, D.F.: SEP/SETENTAS, 1971), pp. 185-186.

11. Henry A. Landsberger and Cynthia N. Hewitt, "Ten Sources of Weakness and Cleavage in Latin American Peasant Movements," in Rodolfo Stavenhagen, ed., *Agrarian Problems and Peasant Movements in Latin America* (Garden City: Doubleday, 1970), pp. 569-573.

12. Ibid., p. 573.

13. A recent work that makes this same important distinction between individual and group cooptation is Susan Eckstein, "The Irony of Organization: Resource and Regulatory," *The British Journal of Sociology,* vol. 27, no. 2 (June 1976), pp. 150-164.

14. For example, the UGOCM, an independent peasant organization led by Jacinto López, agitated throughout the late 1950s to focus attention on illegal land holdings in the states of Sonora, Sinaloa, Nayarit, and Colima. In 1957 and 1958 the peasant movement carried out a series of land invasions on huge estates illegally owned by foreign nationals, including the million acre Cananea Cattle Company of the American Greene family. The invasions of the Greene estate began in late spring of 1957, and UGOCM members tell of being removed by federal troops and returning to occupy the land as many as eighteen times. Finally the government responded and the estate was expropriated and divided into seven huge cattle raising *ejidos.* However, among the 853 peasant families who formed part of the new *ejidos,* less than one-third were UGOCM members. The rest were CNC affiliated peasants who had not participated in the land invasions.

15. *Charro* is the term popularly used to describe corrupt union leaders.

16. *Tamales* are baked corn meal cakes, often prepared with a filling of hot chili peppers. They are a typical peasant dish.

17. The full name of the organization is the Unión Central de Sociedades de Crédito Colectivo Ejidal (Central Union of Collective Ejidal Credit Societies).

18. Gerrit Huizer, *The Role of Peasant Organizations in the Process of Agrarian Reform in Latin America* (Washington, D.C.: Comité Inter-Americano de Desarrollo Agrícola, 1968), p. 132.

19. The Ejidal Bank acts as an agent in the sale of crops produced by most of the *ejidatarios* affiliated with the CNC. As the Ejidal Bank in most regions of Mexico is notorious for its corruption, peasants who are forced to rely on the Bank to act as their sale agent normally receive lower profits than peasants, like the Central Union members, who are able to avoid dealing with the Ejidal Bank representatives. Even when the Central Union sells its members' cotton on the world market at exactly the same price obtained by the Ejidal Bank, members come out ahead financially because they have not had to underwrite or subsidize the kickbacks, rake-offs, etc., enjoyed by Ejidal Bank functionaries.

20. "Rapid industrialization, an Alemán fetish, required low wages and the sacrifice of the labor force to capital accumulation. . . . Continuous protests from . . . labor made no perceptible change in Alemán's philosophy or conduct. . . . For Alemán, the sacrifice of a generation of workers and peasants was a small price for making his nation materially strong, industrialized, modernized, advanced." Frank Brandenburg, op. cit., pp. 102-103.

21. Ruíz Cortines received 74 percent of the vote. By PRI standards, he had only just "squeaked by."

22. Gustavo Díaz Ordaz, quoted in *La Opinión*, Torreón, Coahuila, Feb. 24, 1947.

23. The full page advertisement in a local or national daily is a political tactic employed with great frequency by Mexican organizations of every political coloration. Full page ads are used to promulgate political manifestos, the proceedings of party or union congresses, to applaud or denounce legislative initiatives or newly announced policies, and so forth. Often they are used to declare an organization's solidarity with the president and his party. In the height of the student movement crisis in 1968, Mexican newspapers were bursting with paid announcements of solidarity with the president and his regime placed there by official party organizations such as unions and associations affiliated with the CTM, CNC, or CNOP, as well as by certain opposition organizations that wished to disassociate themselves from the "disorders."

24. *Oposición*, vol. 3, no. 43 (June 1972), p. 13.

25. "Informe que rinde la Unión Central al quinto congreso, febrero 1947," Archives of the Central Union, Torreón, Coahuila.

26. Here is a typical example of this approach from the archives of the Central Union: "It is known to all that the widespread desire for liberation made possible the Revolution of 1910. Emiliano Zapata, with profound wisdom pointed out the necessity of giving land to those who had none, and in 1917 defeated the usurpers who had risen up against our Revolution, motivated by the same interests as those who today ask for the revision of Article 27 of the Constitution. . . . Is it inconsequential that after the loss of so much blood, after so many vicissitudes and sacrifices have been endured for the country, a group of playboys [*señoritos*] try, with one feather, to wipe away the entire Agrarian Reform, and in so doing, to halt all progress in the agrarian field?"

27. The *vía chilena*, the Chilean road to socialism, was a slightly different case. Official relations between Mexico and Chile had long been very cordial and remained warm after the socialist government of Salvador Allende came to power in 1970. In the summer of 1971, for example, when large areas of Chile were devastated by earthquakes, the wife of President Luís Echeverría, Ester Zuno de Echeverría traveled to Santiago and toured the earthquake damaged regions to deliver emergency aid donated by the Mexican government. When Allende made an official state visit to Mexico, Echeverría took the occasion to join the Chilean leader in denouncing American imperialism, and to praise

Chile's "peaceful road to socialism." Allende responded graciously by stressing the importance of the Mexican Revolution as a symbol for the other Latin American nations.

Thus, it was fairly safe for opposition groups on the left to come out in praise of the Allende regime and in favor of the Chilean road to socialism. However, the emphasis had to be on the *Chilean* road to socialism, clearly implying that it was not the Mexican road.

28. Militant movements of the left are not the only organizations that claim Zapata as their inspiration. The CNC has appropriated Zapata as their symbol, and they play on the Zapata image continually. Zapata's face and words appear on the cover or letterhead of a large proportion of CNC publications, and his portrait is prominently displayed in CNC headquarters. Often CNC artists go so far as to use drawings and woodcuts of the *agrarista* hero with gun in hand and a murderous expression in his eyes.

In 1971 an "urban guerrilla group" called the Zapatista Urban Front, kidnapped Julio Hirschfeld, a wealthy businessman, and held him for $240,000 ransom. However, it now appears that these latter-day *zapatistas* may have been right wing extremists trying to provoke a government crackdown on the left.

With so many different organizations simultaneously claiming Zapata as their inspiration, a certain amount of confusion develops in the minds of many Mexicans as to what it was that Zapata really stood for. But nonetheless, most opposition organizations continue to identify their struggle with that of Zapata.

29. Not only are some regimes more tolerant of political dissidence than others, but there are periods during each six-year administration when the government is more willing to deal with opposition. Generally, the first year or two of each new administration is a time of greater openness, during which the new chief executive seeks reconciliation with the groups most severely damaged by the policies of his predecessor. A brief period of "self criticism" and "reassessment of achievements" at the beginning of a new regime signals a moment in which moderate opposition is safe. At times a new president finds it convenient to shake up or throw out a hierarchy of bureaucrats and politicians he finds already entrenched at the time he takes office. To hasten this process he may, for example, make substantial concessions to an independent organization like the Central Union in order to find in the political resurgence of that organization an excuse to "rennovate" the CNC.

30. The cases in which the activists of an opposition organization are wiped out together with the leadership occur, generally speaking, in the countryside. Sometimes the army or the police forces play a direct role in the slaughter, while at other times, "private armies" of thugs hired by landowners whose interests are threatened will carry out the massacre of peasant families involved in the struggle.

31. Rubén Jaramillo was a leader of peasants in Morelos State from his youth, fighting under Emiliano Zapata, to his death on May 23, 1962 when he

was taken from his home by soldiers and assassinated along with his wife, two stepsons and a nephew. The disfigured bodies were riddled with bullets marked with the symbol of the Fabrica Nacional de Municiones, which produces arms and ammunition exclusively for the army and police forces. See Froylan Manjarrez, "Matanza en Xochicalco," in Jaramillo and Manjarrez, *Rubén Jaramillo: Autobiografía y Asesinato* (México, D.F.: Editorial Nuestro Tiempo, 1967), pp. 126-131. Jénaro Vázquez, a rural schoolteacher turned guerrilla, was killed in an auto accident while fleeing army troops on February 2, 1972. Lucio Cabañas, another rural schoolteacher, likewise led a peasant band in the mountains of Guerrero State and evaded capture for almost a decade until he was shot and killed by army troops in the Sierra Madre near Acapulco in December 1974. A more detailed discussion of the significance of these *guerrilleros* follows in chapter 6.

32. The big Mexico City dailies, as well as local newspapers, carry frequent accounts of violent conflict in the countryside. However, often what is reported as a "shootout between rival peasant factions" or an "individually motivated homicide" turns out, upon careful investigation, to be an instance of armed repression of an opposition movement or leader by hired assassins.

33. See José Santos Valdes, *Madera* (México, D.F.: Imprenta Laura, 1968).

34. "The Mexican Struggle," *Nacla's Latin America and Empire Report,* vol. 6, no. 3 (March 1972), p. 5.

35. Michael Klare, "The Pentagon's Counterinsurgency Research Infrastructure," *Nacla Newsletter,* vol. 4, no. 9 (June 1971), p. 9.

36. U.S. Department of Defense, *Military Assistance Facts* (Washington, D.C., 1969), pp. 16-17.

37. Ibid., p. 21.

38. U.S. Agency for International Development, Statistics and Reports Division, *Operations Report,* June 30, 1961-June 30, 1969.

39. For example, the total U.S. Military Assistance Program expenditures for the fiscal years 1950-1969 was $425.6 million for Brazil, $163 million for Chile, $128.8 million for Argentina and $105.4 million for Venezuela. U.S. Department of Defense, Office of the Assistant Secretary of Defense for International Security Affairs, *Military Assistance and Foreign Military Sales Facts* (Washington, D.C.: 1970). Cited in Michael T. Klare, *War Without End* (New York: Random House, 1972), p. 376.

Chapter 5

1. A good English source on these events is North American Congress on Latin America, *Mexico 1968: A Study in Domination and Repression* (New York: NACLA, 1968). In his study, Kenneth F. Johnson, *Mexican Democracy: A Critical View* (Boston: Allyn and Bacon, 1971), pp. 148-164, the author provides an analysis that focuses on behind-the-scenes, inter-elite maneuverings

in high political circles. A more recent publication, Evelyn P. Stevens, *Protest and Response in Mexico* (Cambridge, Mass.: The MIT Press, 1974), pp. 185-240, provides an excellent, detailed analysis of the events in comparative perspective with other Mexican protest movements. In writing this account, I relied on contemporary newspaper accounts, interviews with participants, an unpublished report by Cuauhtemoc Reséndez Nuñez, the NACLA documents cited above, and, in particular, my own experience with the movement.

2. Jean Louis M. de Lannoy, "Student Political Activism in Mexico," paper presented to the Canadian Sociology and Anthropology Association, May 30, 1973, p. 5.

3. Ibid.

4. The most important groups represented in Mexican high schools and universities at the time were the Communists, Christian Democrats, Trotskyists, Maoists, Sparticus League, Guevarists, and Socialists. Ramón Ramírez, *El Movimiento Estudiantil de México*, vol. 1, (México, D.F.: Ediciones ERA, 1969), p. 24.

5. The unification of these groups was particularly significant because the government had long promoted division, if not direct confrontation between liberal arts and technical students as a means of containing potential political opposition on the campuses. (Hiber Conteris, "The New Outbreak of the Student Rebellion" in NACLA, op. cit., p. 8).

The preparatory schools and the UNAM into which they channel their graduates are the prestige institutions of Mexican education. "The UNAM complex, with headquarters at the specially constructed University City, consumes 3/4ths of the total federal budget assigned to Mexican universities. Its student body is drawn primarily from the urban middle and upper middle classes. Since 1928, the campus has enjoyed 'autonomy', i.e. freedom from military and police intervention."

"The technical schools, on the other hand, draw their students primarily from worker and peasant backgrounds, enjoy a much lower budget, do not have 'autonomy' and are consequently from time to time the scenes of brutal military and police intervention.

"These and other differences, coupled with PRI manipulations have tended to produce antagonisms and rivalries which have traditionally divided the Mexican student movement." NACLA, op. cit. p. 24.

6. Jean Louis M. de Lannoy, op. cit., p. 17.

7. Ibid., p. 18.

8. "In order to practice direct democracy, the students organized multiple seminars and meetings, assemblies, teach-ins and mass demonstrations. In all those forms of meeting the principle of free speech was strictly enforced; no regulation on speech was accepted. . . . But the refusal of any organizational restraint leaves the door open to all possible manipulations. The paradox is that the principle of direct democracy gets defeated when it allows the least

democratic minded people to take advantage of it at the expense of the majority. Appeals to collective enthusiasm for all prepared motions do not favor the formation of a responsible, accountable electorate at the grass root level." Ibid., p. 22.

9. In the period when Daniel Cohn-Bendit ("Dany the Red") and other student leaders were turned into international celebrities almost overnight by media anxious to reduce ideological movements to individual personalities, this concern on the part of the Mexican students is understandable.

10. This account is based on personal observation, interviews, and Mexico City daily newspapers for the period July-October. 1968.

11. See Luís González de Alba, *Los Días y los Años* (México, D.F.: Biblioteca ERA, 1971); and Ramón Ramírez, op. cit.

12. University and secondary school faculty formed their own organization, the Coalition of Middle and Higher Education Teachers for Democratic Freedom.

13. CTM Bulletin, Sept. 3, 1968.

14. Labor and peasant organizations that came out in support of the movement were the Sindicato de Electricistas, the Comisión Organizadora de Telefonistas, the Sindicato Revolucionario de Trabajadores de la Fábrica de Loza "El Anfora," the Consejo Nacional Ferrocarrillero, the Unión de Choferes Taxistas de Transporte Colectiva and the Central Campesina Independiente.

15. John Womack, Jr., "The Spoils of the Mexican Revolution," *Foreign Affairs*, vol. 48, no. 4 (July 1970), p. 683.

16. Jean Louis M. de Lannoy, op. cit., p. 11.

17. Articles 145 and 145[b] define the crime of "social dissolution," providing sentences of 2 to 12 years for any Mexican or foreigner who meets with a group of 3 or more individuals (Mexican or foreign) to discuss ideas or programs that tend to disturb the public order or affect Mexican sovereignty. Sentences of up to 12 years are given those convicted of spreading ideas that "tend to produce rebellion, sedition, riot, or insurrection," and sentences of up to 20 years are given to any Mexican or foreigner convicted of carrying out acts "which prepare morally or materially for the invasion of national territory or the submission of the country to any foreign government."

Articles 145 and 145[b] were passed during World War II when it appeared that stiff legislation was needed to control the rampant activities of Nazis and fascist sympathizers in Mexico. However, since their passage, the articles were almost exlusively employed to persecute figures on the left: communists, socialists, and radical student, labor, and peasant leaders.

18. Hiber Conteris, op. cit., p. 9.

19. In 1971, the existence of paramilitary shock troops was finally publicly acknowledged, although the government refused to take responsibility for their acts, which cost hundreds of lives in 1968, and hundreds more since that time.

20. Hiber Conteris, op. cit., p. 9.

21. In the Plaza of the Three Cultures the sixteenth century Spanish colonial

Church of the Apostle Santiago stands directly adjacent to the recently exca-
vated Aztec ruins and the ultra-modern headquarters of the Ministry of Foreign
Relations. Hence the Plaza is named for the Aztec, Spanish, and modern Mexican Cultures.

Throughout the summer, the Plaza had been the scene of some of the most
violent clashes between students and police. Here students had repeatedly asked
and received the moral and material support of the working class and middle
class residents of the surrounding neighborhood. From the wall-to-wall windows
of their apartments, the people of Tlatelolco had rained down streams of eggs,
tomatoes, shoes, clods of dirt, and even boiling water on the soldiers who
seemed almost continually to be milling about in the streets below. They provided the students with food, bottles, rags and gasoline, or with a hiding place,
according to the strategic needs of the moment. Because the Italian film "Battle
of Algiers" was showing in local theaters that summer, people had begun to
speak of Tlatelolco as "the Mexican Kasbah," although two urban centers could
hardly be less similar than the narrow, twisting alleys of the Algerian "native
quarter," and the glass and steel buildings of Tlatelolco, each one set apart from
its neighbor by a broad, flat esplanade. There was, however, this similarity: both
neighborhoods were quickly identified by the government as a focal point of
agitation, and both were made to pay for the resistance they had mounted.

22. Oriana Falacci, an Italian journalist, received four bullet wounds, was
dragged from a balcony overlooking the plaza by her hair, and was left bleeding
on the ground after having been robbed of her watch and all her money. An
English journalist was forced to lie under fire for two hours with a gun at his
head.

23. National Strike Council, Bulletin, October 6, 1968, reproduced in
NACLA, op. cit., p. 19. For good coverage of these events in English, see the
Sunday Times and the *Observer,* both October 6, 1968. For further detail see,
Jorge Carrión et al, *Tres Culturas en Agonía* (México, D.F.: Editorial Nuestro
Tiempo, 1969); and Elena Poniatowska, *La Noche de Tlatelolco* (México, D.F.:
Ediciones ERA, 1971).

24. There is little agreement on the precise number of people killed on
October 2. Some estimates go as high as 500, while naturally the official government figures are very low: some 37 killed and wounded. My own estimate
coincides with the figures given by John Womack, Jr., op. cit., p. 684. Although
I was in Tlatelolco on the night of the massacre, I am in no position to supply
accurate details based on my own observations. I was approaching the Plaza at
the moment when the soldiers surrounded the area. I managed to reach one of
the buildings facing the Plaza when the shooting commenced. When the Plaza
had been "cleared" the buildings came under fire. Several direct hits were scored
killing at least two people on the lower floors of the building. Thus, given the
precarious nature of the observation point, my experience is more that of an
earwitness than an eyewitness.

25. The government claimed that the students had been armed and offered

the army fatalities as evidence that the "exchange" of fire had been initiated by the students. However, autopsies on the army casualties later confirmed that the soldiers had been shot by military issued weapons.

26. Typical of the abuses was the January 1, 1970, assault at Lecumberi Prison in Mexico City. Fifty-odd "common" prisoners armed with clubs and chains were turned loose by the warden in the political prisoners' wing of the penitentiary. The political prisoners were beaten and their cells sacked while their jailers looked on.

Another abuse vigorously protested by the students was the fact that after more than a year in jail, the political prisoners were neither offered bail nor brought to trial. The Mexican Constitution guarantees a fair and open trial within one year of arrest.

27. Everyone was in accord that the movement had to agitate for the release of the prisoners, but conflicts arose between those who insisted that the political prisoners be absolved of all guilt at an open trial, and others (including a majority of the prisoners themselves) who were content to see the prisoners released under a general amnesty, even though they realized that the government would score valuable propaganda points from this sort of "humanitarian gesture."

28. The word literally means "cheerleaders." The different paramilitary groups go under a variety of names: the Falcons (*halcones*), the Pancho Villas, the Olympic Battalion (active since '68), and others.

Chapter 6

1. John Womack, Jr., "The Spoils of the Mexican Revolution," *Foreign Affairs* vol. 48, no. 4 (July 1970).

2. Ibid.

3. This is often framed in terms of a "clean sweep" or a cleanup of the corruption tolerated or even promoted by the preceding president. The clearest case was the cleanup campaign of Adolfo Ruíz Cortines, who succeeded Miguel Alemán in 1952. Ruíz Cortines faced a grave problem upon assuming office. The dignity of the presidential office had deteriorated so rapidly during the last years of Alemán's incumbency that Ruíz Cortines was hard pressed to restore its prestige. Flagrantly corrupt activities of Alemán and of *alemanistas* at all levels of the government had been carried on in a manner so cavalier as to become distressing if not to say intolerable to even the least idealistic of their countrymen. "Exposures of graft and fraud during the Alemán administration," wrote Clarence Senior, "started exploding immediately after it went out of office in the fall of 1952. The amounts pocketed by the government clique must be astronomical for a poverty-stricken country like Mexico, even if they do not reach the frequently quoted figure of $800 million." Clarence Senior, *Land Reform and Democracy* (Gainsville: University of Florida Press, 1958), p. 141.

4. Porfirio Muñoz Ledo, Undersecretary of the Ministry of the Presidency, from a speech delivered April 27, 1971, quoted in *Excelsior,* 28 April 1971.

5. Ibid., and *Excelsior,* Mexico City, August 7, 1971, p. 1.

6. See Echeverría's State of the Nation Address, Sept. 1, 1972.

7. *Excelsior,* April 18, 1971.

8. Ibid.

9. *Excelsior,* México, D.F., May 25, 1971.

10. Carlos Fuentes, *Tiempo Mexicano* (México, D.F.: Cuadernos de Joaquín Mortiz, 1973, p. 166.

11. León Roberto García, "Democracia: real o fascismo?" *Excelsior,* México, D.F., April 1971, p. 13.

12. *Latin America,* London, March 19, 1971.

13. Ley Federal de Reforma Agraria, Presidencia de la República, *El Gobierno Mexicano,* México, D.F., Dec. 1-31, 1970, pp. 167-170.

14. Address of the chief of the Department of Agrarian Affairs to the Chamber of Deputies, Feb. 2, 1971, quoted in *El Nacional,* México, D.F., Feb. 3, 1971.

15. *Excelsior,* México, D.F., May 4, May 19, 1971.

16. Jorge Eduardo Navarrete, ed., *México: La Política Económica del Nuevo Gobierno* (México, D.F.: Banco Nacional de Comercio Exterior, 1971), pp. 16-18, 83-86.

17. Ibid., pp. 71, 87.

18. Ibid., pp. 95-100, 119-122.

19. Jorge Eduardo Navarrete, ed., *México: La Política Económica para 1972* (México, D.F.: Banco Nacional de Comercio Exterior, 1972), pp. 26-33.

20. Jorge Eduardo Navarrete, op. cit., (1971), pp. 127=128.

21. Ibid.

22. The U.S. buys two-thirds of Mexico's exports and provides three-fourths of Mexico's imports. Mexico is the United States' largest trading partner in Latin America. U.S. investment represents 80 percent of the $3.5 billion worth of foreign investment in Mexico.

23. Mexico established relations with the Peoples Republic of China in Feb. 1972. Notwithstanding the huge potential of the Chinese market, in Asia Mexico's most promising trade agreement was made with Japan, a country whose economy is nearly perfectly complementary to Mexico's, a country eager to supply Mexico with technicians and know-how, and a country whose interests in expanding its economic influence in Latin America coincide perfectly with Mexico's desire to move away from dependency on the United States.

24. Luís Echeverría, "The President of Mexico's Report on his Trip to Three Continents," *Comercio Exterior,* vol. 19, no. 6, June 1973, pp. 7-11; and Jorge Eduardo Navarrete, op. cit. (1971), pp. 145ff.

25. Ifigenia de Navarrete, study cited in CENCOS, National Center for Social Communication, Mexico, May 15, 1974.

26. Mexico's purchases from the U.S. rose to $2.6 billion in 1973, while her sales to the U.S. were only $1.7 billion. This trade deficit represented an increase of 90 percent over 1972.

27. Alan Riding, "Recession Interrupts Mexico's 20 Years of Growth," *Globe and Mail*, Toronto, Feb. 1972.

28. The most important groups active since 1968 are the *halcones* ("falcons"), *aquarios, Pancho Villistas*, MURO, and the *brigada olímpica* ("olympic brigade").

29. The governing authority for Mexico City and its environs.

30. The role of *porristas* is confusing for precisely this reason. Since the '40s, provocateurs and shock troops in the pay of local, regional, or national politicians, or responsible directly to certain ministries and departments within the government, have been used on occasion in place of conventional law enforcement agents to squelch leftist activities in labor and peasant movements or on the university campuses. By the same token, hired thugs controlled by conservative capitalists have attacked the same sectors of the population, but have done so as much to undermine government authority as to repress leftist movements. It is often difficult to determine who controls or commands any particular band of political gangsters. These troops may be directed by political strongmen within the official party, by elements of the national bourgeoisie, or by both acting in concert. Often it is equally hard to tell if the left is under attack from political forces intent on simply suppressing leftist activities, or if the attack is also an attempt to embarrass the government. Obviously, from the point of view of the left wing group under attack, the effect is the same in either case. It is important to note, however, that in whatever country they are found, it is the nature of such political thugs, recruited as they are from the ranks of unemployed and unemployable street toughs, that they can be bought and utilized as political tools by any sector of the society that has the money necessary to sponsor paramilitary operations. In Mexico this restricts the use of political gangsterism to the right.

31. Martínez Domínguez was named president of the official party in 1968, a post from which he hoped to launch a campaign to win his party's nomination for the presidency of the Republic. Díaz Ordaz himself may well have preferred to name the conservative Martínez Domínguez as his successor, but was forced by internal party pressures to give the nod to Echeverría. When Echeverría edged him out for the PRI nomination for President, Martínez Domínguez was "kicked upstairs" to the post of regent (in effect, mayor) of the Federal District. On both personal and ideological grounds. Martínez Domínguez regarded Echeverría with implacable hostility.

32. *Excelsior*, México, D.F., June 11, 1971.

33. As is usual in these events there are no absolutely reliable figures on the number of casualties, but the estimates given here are gleaned from newspaper reports and eye-witness accounts.

34. *Excelsior,* México, D.F., June 11, 12, 13, 1971. The fact that journalists themselves were physically assaulted by the *halcones* probably contributed, together with a temporary lifting of press censorship, to the accuracy of the report on this event.

35. *Excelsior,* México, D.F., June 16, 1971.

36. Ibid.

37. For example, in August 1971, Carlos Fuentes wrote an article expressing qualified approval of the new President and his policies. Even then, however, Fuentes noted that Echeverría, "had not complied with one basic condition without which the policy of democratization could not be carried out: He did not dismantle the repressive apparatus created in 1968." Only two months later Fuentes had joined poet and essayist Octavio Paz, university leaders Herberto Castillo and Cabeza de Vaca, railroad workers' union leader Demitrio Vallejo and electricians' union leader, Rafael Galvan in the formation of what they hoped would become the core of an opposition movement of the left. See Fuentes, op. cit., pp. 166, 192-193.

38. In July 1976, the progressive group of editors who had brought the Mexican daily *Excelsior* to hemispheric prominence as the leading independent newspaper in Latin America, was ousted from control of the paper in a rigged general assembly of the cooperative that owns the daily. Led by Julio Scherer, the progressive editors had pursued an editorial line of critical support for Echeverría. Toward the end of the Echeverría regime, as *Excelsior*'s support on domestic issues turned increasingly to criticism, the *Excelsior* editors lost their access to high government officials and came under attack for their "lack of patriotism." The conservative takeover of *Excelsior* is generally seen as a significant turn to the right in the Echeverría regime. However, the question of who might have engineered it—Echeverría, a large investor in Organizción Editorial Mexicana, which owns a chain of 27 newspapers in competition with *Excelsior,* or President-elect José López Portillo, who had not enjoyed *Excelsior*'s endorsement during his precandidacy—remains unclear. For details see *Latin America,* London, July 23, 1976.

39. *Latin America,* London, August 30, 1974.

40. Ibid.

41. In 1971 Echeverría gave the word to the Ministry of Labor to recognize Rafael Galvan's independent (non-CTM affiliated) electricians' union as a legitimate representative of the workers in contract negotiations.

42. For example in 1974, Velázquez "won" a 20 percent across the board wage hike for CTM members, but the cost of living was up 42 percent in the same year, and the original demand had been for a 35 percent wage increase.

43. David F. Ronfeldt, "The Mexican Army and Political Order since 1940," in Abraham F. Lowenthal, ed., *Armies and Politics in Latin America* (New York: Holmes & Meier, 1976), argues that the Mexican army, "may not be so inactive nor the political system as highly demilitarized as it often appears" (p. 294).

Ronfeldt asserts that the army has important "residual political roles" which should not be overlooked "just because they are exercised in subordination to civilian ruling groups and strong political institutions" (ibid.). I believe that the significance of Echeverría's appeal to army leaders lies not in the fact that he recognized the army's importance, but in the open and effusive quality of the courtship he pressed.

44. Alan Riding, "Mexican Army, Amid Rumors, Insists It Steers Clear of Politics," *New York Times,* Feb. 5, 1974.

45. *Latin America,* July, 1974.

46. *New York Times,* November 7, 1973.

47. *Excelsior,* México, D.F., October 23, 1973.

48. As potential allies in his reform efforts, Echeverría possibly could have counted upon the support of Sergio Mendes Arceo, powerful bishop of Cuernavaca as well as other progressive churchmen. However the constitutional prohibitions on political activity by the clergy was successfully invoked by the right to neutralize the potential alliance between the reformist *echeverristas* and the leaders of the Catholic left.

49. "Social banditry, a universal and virtually unchanging phenomenon, is little more than endemic peasant protest against oppression and poverty: a cry for vengeance on the rich and the oppressors, a vague dream of some curb upon them, a righting of individual wrongs. . . . Social banditry, though a protest, is a modest and unrevolutionary protest. It protests not against the fact that peasants are poor and oppressed, but that they are sometimes excessively poor and oppressed." Eric J. Hobsbawm, *Primitive Rebels* (New York: W. W. Norton, 1959), pp. 5, 24. Also see, Hobsbawm, *Bandits,* (New York: Dell, 1969), p. 16. "Federal officials estimate that Guerrero's 1.5 million people account for at least 2,500 homicides a year but admit that the figure is only an estimate. None but the more sensational killings attract attention outside the lawless backlands." *Los Angeles Times,* December 19, 1971.

50. For an analysis of the class base and national character of the Vietnamese NLF, see Eric Wolf, *Peasant Wars of the Twentieth Century,* (New York: Harper and Row, 1969), chapter 4.

51. Marlise Simons, *Washington Post,* June 30, 1974. The political program of Jénaro Vázquez and Lucio Cabañas can be found in English in NACLA, "The Mexican Struggle," *Latin America and Empire Report,* vol. 6, no. 3, March 1972. Also see *Porqué?* no. 160, July 22, 1971 and no. 161, July 29, 1971.

52. See, for example, the opening sentence to a chapter on the military in Robert F. Adie and Guy E. Poitras, *Latin America: The Politics of Immobility* (Englewood Cliffs, N.J.: Prentice-Hall, 1974), p. 189. "The military in Latin America, except in countries like Costa Rica and Mexico, plays a pivotal role in the various political systems of the area."

53. Pablo González Casanova, *Democracy in Mexico* (New York: Oxford University Press, 1972), p. 37.

54. Ibid., pp. 36-37. On the recent increase in the size of the military Ronfeldt writes, "The armed forces total about 80 thousand members, which is small for such a large populous country. The army accounts for 65 thousand, up from 55 thousand five years ago." Ronfeldt, op. cit., p. 310.

55. For a discussion of political polarization of a so-called "professional" army, see Liisa L. North, "The Military in Chilean Politics," in Abraham F. Lowenthal, op. cit., pp. 165-196.

56. González Casanova describes "the concurrence of military and entrepreneurial interests: the old parasitical military underwent a process of bourgeoisification. In part this was a result of certain political measures by which the financial power of the military as a whole was reduced while contracts were signed and the military chief was provided with necessities to become an entrepreneur." González Casanova, op. cit., p. 38.

57. For analysis of potential divisions and tendencies within the military (left, right, and center), see Liisa L. North, op. cit.

58. Ronfeldt, op. cit., pp. 294-299.

59. Ibid., p. 296.

Bibliography

Abercombie, R. S. "Mecanización Agrícola y Ocupación en América Latina." In Ernest Feder, ed., *La Lucha de Clases en el Campo.* México, D.F.: Fondo de Cultura Económica, 1975.

Adie, Robert F. "Cooperation, Cooptation and Conflict in Mexican Peasant Organizations." *Inter-American Economic Affairs,* vol. 24, 1970.

Adler, Judith. "The Politics of Land Reform in Mexico." M. Phil. thesis, London School of Economics, 1970.

Alba, Victór. *Historia del Movimiento Obrero en América Latina.* México, D.F.: Libreros Mexicanos Unidos, 1964.

Alcántara, Cynthia Hewitt. "The Green Revolution." Unpublished manuscript, 1973.

Alcántara Ferrer, Sergio. *La Organización Colectivista Ejidal en la Comarca Lagunera.* México, D.F., 1967.

Alexander, Robert J. *Communism in Latin America.* New Brunswick: Rutgers University Press, 1957.

—— *Organized Labor in Latin America.* New York: The Free Press, 1965.

Almond, Gabriel A., and Sidney Verba. *The Civic Culture.* Boston: Little, Brown, 1965.

Araiza, Luís. *Historia de la Casa del Obrero Mundial.* México, D.F., 1963.

Ashby, Joe C. *Organized Labor and the Mexican Revolution Under Lázaro Cárdenas.* Chapel Hill: University of North Carolina Press, 1967.

Avila Camacho, Manuel. *Pensamiento Político.* México, D.F.: 1945.

213

Banco de México. *Encuesta Sobre Ingreso y Gastos Familiares en México.* México, D.F.: Banco de México, 1967.

——. *La Distribución del Ingreso en México.* México, D.F.: Fondo de Cultura Económica, 1968.

Barkin, David. "The Persistence of Poverty in Mexico: Some Explanatory Hypotheses." Paper delivered to the Latin American Studies Association, Washington, D.C., April 1970.

Beals, Carleton. *Mexico: An Interpretation.* New York, 1923.

Brandenburg, Frank R. *The Making of Modern Mexico.* Englewood Cliffs: Prentice-Hall, 1964.

——. "Mexico: An Experiment in One Party Democracy." Ph.D. dissertation, University of Pennsylvania, 1955.

Carmona, Fernando et al., *El Milagro Mexicano.* México, D.F.: Editorial Nuestro Tiempo, 1970.

Carr, Barry. "The Peculiarities of the Mexican North, 1880-1928: An Essay in Interpretation." Occasional Paper, Institute of Latin American Studies, University of Glasgow, no. 4, 1971.

Carrión, Jorge. "Retablo de la Política 'a la Mexicana.' " In Fernando Carmona et al., *El Milagro Mexicano.* México, D.F.: Editorial Nuestro Tiempo, 1970.

——et al., *Tres Culturas en Agonía.* México, D.F.: Editorial Nuestro Tiempo, 1969.

Ceceña, José Luís. *El Capital Monopolista y la Economía de México.* México, D.F.: Cuadernos Americanos, 1963.

Centro de Investigaciones Agrarias. *Estructura Agraria y Desarrollo Agrícola en México.* México, D.F.: CDIA, 1970.

Chevalier, François. "The *Ejido* and Political Stability in Mexico." In Claudio Veliz, ed., *The Politics of Conformity in Latin America.* New York: Oxford University Press, 1967.

Clark, Marjorie Ruth. *Organized Labor in Mexico.* Chapel Hill: University of North Carolina Press, 1934.

Cline, Howard F. *The United States and Mexico.* New York: Atheneum, 1965.

Cockcroft, James, and Bo Anderson. "Control and Cooptation in Mexican Politics." In Irving Louis Horowitz et al., eds., *Latin American Radicalism.* New York: Random House, 1969.

Confederación de Trabajadores de México. *Informe del Comité Nacional.* México, D.F., 1936-1937.

Córdova, Arnaldo. *La Política de las Masas del Cardenismo.* México, D.F.: Ediciones ERA, 1974.

Cosio Villegas, Daniel. "The Mexican Left." In Joseph Maier and Richard W. Weatherhead, eds., *The Politics of Change in Latin America.* New York: Praeger, 1964.

Cumberland, Charles C. *Mexico: The Struggle for Modernity.* New York: Oxford University Press, 1968.

Dovring, Folke. "Land Reform and Productivity: The Mexican Case, Analysis of Census Data." Madison: The Land Tenure Center, 1969.

Easton, David. *A Systems Analysis of Political Life.* New York: John Wiley and Sons, 1965.

Echeverría, Luís. *Praxis Política,* vols. 1-23. México, D.F.: Editorial Diana, 1970-1975.

Eckstein, Salomón. *El Ejido Colectivo en México.* México, D.F.: Fondo de Cultura Económica, 1967.

Eckstein, Salomón. *El Marco Macroeconómico del Problema Agrario Mexicano.* México, D.F.: Centro de Investigaciones Agrarias, 1968.

Eckstein, Shlomo. "Collective Farming in Mexico." In Rodolfo Stavenhagen, ed., *Agrarian Problems and Peasant Movements in Latin America.* Garden City: Doubleday, 1970.

Eckstein, Susan. "The Irony of Organization: Resource and Regulatory." *The British Journal of Sociology,* vol. 27, no. 2, (June 1976).

Edelman, Murray. *The Symbolic Uses of Politics.* Urbana: University of Iliinois Press, 1967.

Fagen, Richard R., and William S. Tuohy. *Politics and Privilege in a Mexican City.* Stanford: Stanford University Press, 1972.

Fenster, Leo. "At Twice the Price: The Mexican Auto Swindle." *The Nation,* June 2, 1970.

Flores, Edmundo. *Tratado de Economía Agrícola.* México, D.F.: Fondo de Cultura Económica, 1968.

Frank, Andrew Gunder. "Mexico: The Janus Faces of Twentieth Century Bourgeois Revolution." *Monthly Review,* vol. 14, no. 7 (November 1962).

Fuentes, Carlos. *The Death of Artemio Cruz.* New York: Noonday Press, 1971.

——. *Tiempo Mexicano.* México, D.F.: Cuadernos de Joaquín Mortiz, 1973.

——. *Where the Air is Clear.* New York: Noonday Press, 1971.

Galarza, Ernest. "Trabajadores Mexicanos en Tierra Extranjera." In *Problemas Agrícolas e Industriales de México,* January-June, 1958.

Galeano, Eduardo. *Open Veins of Latin America.* New York: Monthly Review Press, 1973.

Glade, William P., and Charles W. Anderson. *The Political Economy of Mexico.* Madison: University of Wisconsin Press, 1968.

González Casanova, Pablo. *Democracy in Mexico*. New York: Oxford University Press, 1970.

González de Alba, Luís. *Los Días y Los Años*. México, D.F.: Ediciones ERA, 1971.

González Navarro, Moisés. *La Confederación Nacional Campesina*. México, D.F.: Costa-Amic, 1968.

González Ramírez, Manuel. *La Revolución Social de México*. vol. 3, *El Problema Agrario*. México, D.F.: Fondo de Cultura Económica, 1966.

Goulden, Joseph C. "Mexico: PRI's False Front Democracy." Alicia Patterson Fund Reprint, December 1966.

Graciarena, Jorge. *Poder y Clases Sociales en el Desarrollo de América Latina*. Buenos Aires: Editorial Paidós, 1967.

Gruening, Ernest. *Mexico and Its Heritage*. New York: The Century Company, 1928.

Hamilton, Nora Louise. "Mexico: The Limits of State Autonomy." *Latin American Perspectives*, vol. 2, no. 2 (1975).

Hansen, Roger D. *The Politics of Mexican Development*. Baltimore: The Johns Hopkins Press, 1971.

Hobsbawm, Eric J. *Bandits*. New York: Dell, 1969.

———. *Primitive Rebels*. New York: W. E. Norton, 1959.

Horton, D. E. "Land Reform and Economic Development in Latin America: The Mexican Case." *Illinois Agricultural Economics*, vol. 8, no. 9 (January 1968).

Huizer, Gerrit. "Emiliano Zapata and the Peasant Guerrillas." In Rodolfo Stavenhagen, ed., *Agrarian Problems and Peasant Movements in Latin America*. Garden City: Doubleday, 1970.

———. "Peasant Organization and Agrarian Reform in Mexico." In Irving Louis Horowitz, ed., *Masses in Latin America*. New York: Oxford University Press, 1970.

———. *The Role of Peasant Organizations in the Process of Agrarian Reform in Latin America*. Washington, D.C.: Comité Inter-Americano de Desarrollo Agrícola, 1968.

Iturriaga, José E. *La Estructura Social y Cultural de México*. México, D.F.: Fondo de Cultura Económica, 1951.

Izquierdo, Rafael. "Protectionism in Mexico." In Raymond Vernon, ed., *Public Policy and Private Enterprise in Mexico*. Cambridge: Harvard University Press, 1964.

Jaramillo, Rubén. *Autobiografía*. México, D.F.: Editorial Nuestro Tiempo, 1967.

Johnson, Kenneth F. *Mexican Democracy: A Critical View*. Boston: Allyn and Bacon, 1971.

Katz, Friedrich, ed. *Hitler sobre América Latina: El Fascismo Alemán en Latinoamérica 1933-1943*. México, D.F.: Fondo de Cultura Popular, 1968.

———. "Labor Conditions on Haciendas in Porfirian Mexico: Some Trends and Tendencies." *Hispanic American Historical Review*, vol. 54, no. 1 (February 1974).

Kautsky, John H. "Patterns of Modernizing Revolutions: Mexico and the Soviet Union." *Sage Professional Papers in Comparative Politics*, vol. 5, no. 01-056, 1975.

Kirk, Betty. *Covering the Mexican Front*. Norman: University of Oklahoma Press, 1942.

Klare, Michael. "The Pentagon's Counterinsurgency Infrastructure." *Nacla Newsletter*, vol. 4, no. 9 (June 1971).

———. *War Without End*. New York: Random House, 1972.

Landsberger, Henry A., and Cynthia N. Hewitt. "Ten Sources of Weakness and Cleavage in Latin American Peasant Movements." In Rodolfo Stavenhagen, ed., *Agrarian Problems and Peasant Movements in Latin America*. Garden City: Doubleday, 1970.

Lerner Sigal, Berta, et al. *México: Realidad Política de Sus Partidos*. México, D.F.: Instituto Mexicano de Estudios Políticos, 1970.

Lewis, Oscar. *The Children of Sánchez*. New York: Vintage, 1961.

———. *Pedro Martínez*. New York: Vintage, 1967.

Lieuwen, Edwin. *Mexican Militarism: The Political Rise and Fall of the Revolutionary Army, 1910-1940*. Albuquerque: University of New Mexico Press, 1968.

Liga de Agrónomos Socialistas. *El Colectivismo Agrario en México: La Comarca Lagunera*. México, D.F.: Liga de Agrónomos Socialistas, 1940.

Lombardo Toledano, Vicente. "Los Intentos de Revisión del Marxismo durante la Guerra." In *La CTAL ante la Guerra y ante la Post-Guerra*. México, D.F.: 1945.

López Rosano, Diego G., and Juan F. Noyola Vásquez. "Los Salarios Reales en México, 1939-1950." *El Trimestre Económico*, vol. 18, no. 2 (April-June 1951).

Lord, Peter. *The Peasantry as an Emerging Factor in Mexico, Bolivia and Venezuela*. Madison: The Land Tenure Center, 1965.

Maccoby, Michael. "Love and Authority in a Mexican Village." In Jack M. Potter, May N. Diaz, and George M. Foster, eds., *Peasant Society*. Boston: Little, Brown, 1967.

Manzanilla Schaffer, Victór. *Reforma Agraria Mexicana.* Colima: Universidad de Colima, 1966.

Michaels, Albert L. "The Crisis of Cardenismo." *Journal of Latin American Studies,* vol. 2, no. 1, May 1970.

Millan, Verna Carleton. *Mexico Reborn.* Boston: Houghton Mifflin, 1939.

Nacional Financiera. *La Economía Mexicana en Cifras.* México, D.F., 1970.

Nathan, Paul. "México en la Epoca de Cárdenas." *Problemas Agrícolas e Industriales de México,* vol. 8, no. 3, 1955.

Navarrette, Ifigenia M. de. "Income Distribution in Mexico." In Enrique Pérez López, ed., *Mexico's Recent Economic Growth.* Austin: University of Texas Press, 1967.

Navarrete, Jorge Eduardo, ed. *México: La Política Económica del Nuevo Gobierno.* México, D.F.: Banco Nacional de Comercio Exterior, 1971.

Newfarmer, Richard S., and Willard F. Mueller. *Multinational Corporations in Brazil and Mexico: Structural Sources of Economic and Noneconomic Power.* Washington, D.C.: U.S. Government Printing Office, 1975.

North American Congress on Latin America. *Mexico 1968: A Study of Domination and Repression.* New York: NACLA, 1968.

———. *Yanqui Dollar.* New York: NACLA, 1971.

North, Liisa, L. "The Military in Chilean Politics." In Abraham F. Lowenthal, ed., *Armies and Politics in Latin America.* New York: Holmes and Meier, 1976.

Olizar, Maryoka. *Guía de los Mercados de México.* México, D.F.: 1974.

Padgett, L. Vincent. *The Mexican Political System.* Boston: Houghton Mifflin, 1966.

Padilla Aragón, Enrique. *México: Desarrollo con Pobreza.* México, D.F.: Siglo Veintiuno Editores, 1970.

Parkes, Henry Bamford. *A History of Mexico.* London: Shenval Press, 1962.

Paz, Octavio. *The Labyrinth of Solitude: Life and Thought in Mexico.* New York, Grove Press, 1961.

———. *The Other Mexico.* New York: Grove Press, 1972.

Peón, Máximo, *Como Viven los Mexicanos en los Estados Unidos.* México, D.F.: B. Costa-Amic, 1966.

Pérez López, Enrique, ed. *The Recent Development of Mexico's Economy.* Austin: University of Texas Press, 1967.

Poniatowska, Elena. *La Noche de Tlatelolco.* México, D.F.: Ediciones ERA, 1971.

Portes Gil, Emilio. *Autobiografía de la Revolución Mexicana.* México, D.F.: Instituto Mexicano de Cultura, 1964.

――. "Novecientos Mil Campesinos en una Sola Confederación." In *La Unificación Campesina.* México, D.F.: Ediciones del PNR, 1935.

Powell, John Duncan. *Peasant Society and Clientelist Politics.* Cambridge: Center for International Affairs, 1967.

Pozas, Ricardo. *Juan the Chamula.* Berkeley: University of California Press, 1971.

Quirk, Robert. *The Mexican Revolution 1914-1915.* Bloomington: University of Indiana Press, 1960.

Ramírez, Ramón. *El Movimiento Estudiantil de México.* vols. 1, 2. México, D.F.: Ediciones ERA, 1969.

Ramos, Samuel. *Profile of Man and Culture in Mexico.* Austin: University of Texas Press, 1962.

Reed, John. *Insurgent Mexico.* New York: Appleton, 1914.

Reul, Myrtle R. *Territorial Boundaries of Rural Poverty: Profiles of Exploitation.* East Lansing: Center for Rural Manpower and Public Affairs, Michigan State University, 1974.

Reyes Osorio, Sergio. "El Desarrollo Polarizado de la Agricultura Mexicana." *Comercio Exterior,* March 1969.

Reynolds, Clark W. *The Mexican Economy.* New Haven: Yale University Press, 1970.

Richmond, Patricia McIntire. "Mexico: A Case Study of One-Party Politics." Ph.D. dissertation, University of California, 1965.

Riding, Alan. "The Death of the Latin American Guerrilla Movement." *World,* July 3, 1973.

Roman, Richard. "Ideology and Class in the Mexican Revolution: A Study of the Convention and the Constitutional Congress." Ph.D. dissertation, University of California, Berkeley, 1973.

Ronfeldt, David F. *Atencingo: The Politics of Agrarian Struggle in a Mexican Ejido.* Stanford: Stanford University Press, 1973.

――. "The Mexican Army and Political Order Since 1940." In Abraham F. Lowenthal, ed., *Armies and Politics in Latin America.* New York: Holmes and Meier Publishers, 1976.

Santos Valdes, José. *Madera.* México, D.F.: Imprenta Laura, 1968.

Schmitt, Karl M. *Communism in Mexico.* Austin: University of Texas Press, 1965.

Scott, Robert E. *Mexican Government in Transition.* Urbana: University of Illinois Press, 1964.

Secretaria de Gobernación. *Seis Años de Servicio al Gobierno de México.* México, D.F.: La Nacional Impresora, 1940.

Secretaria de Industria y Comercio. *Censo General de Población 1970: Resumen General*. México, D.F.: Dirección General de Estadística, 1972.

Shulgovsky, Anatol. *México en la Encrucijada de su Historia*. México, D.F.: Fondo de Cultura Popular, 1968.

Sierra, José Luís. *El 10 de Junio y la Izquierda Radical*. México, D.F.: Editorial Heterodoxia, 1972.

Sigmund, Paul E. *Models of Political Change in Latin America*. New York: Praeger, 1970.

Silva Herzog, Jesús. *El Agrarismo Mexicano y la Reforma Agraria*. México, D.F.: Fondo de Cultura Económica, 1959.

Simpson, Eyler N. *The Ejido: Mexico's Way Out*. Chapel Hill: University of North Carolina Press, 1937.

Solis, Leopoldo M. *Controversias sobre el Crecimiento y la Distribución*. México, D.F.: Fondo de Cultura Económica, 1972.

Stavenhagen, Rodolfo. "Social Aspects of Agrarian Structure in Mexico." In Rodolfo Stavenhagen, ed., *Agrarian Problems and Peasant Movements in Latin America*. Garden City: Doubleday, 1970.

———. et al., *Neolatifundismo y Explotación: De Emiliano Zapata a Anderson Clayton & Co*. México, D.F.: Editorial Nuestro Tiempo, 1968.

Stevens, Evelyn P. *Protest and Response in Mexico*. Cambridge, Mass.: MIT Press, 1974.

Tannenbaum, Frank. *The Mexican Agrarian Revolution*. New York: Macmillan, 1929.

Tello, Carlos. *La Tenencia de la Tierra en México*. México, D.F.: Instituto de Investigaciones Sociales, 1968.

Townsend, William Cameron. *Lázaro Cárdenas, Mexican Democrat*. Ann Arbor: George Wahr Publishing Company, 1952.

Trejo Reyes, Saul. "El Incremento de la Producción y el Empleo Industrial en México, 1950-1965." *Demografía y Economía*, vol. 4, no. 1 (1970).

———. "Industrialization and Employment Growth: Mexico 1950-1965. Ph.D. dissertation, Yale University, 1971.

Tucker, William. *The Mexican Government Today*. Minneapolis: University of Minnesota Press, 1957.

Tuohy, William S. "Psychology in Social Science: The Case of Mexican Politics." Paper delivered at the Latin American Studies Association meeting, Madison, Wisconsin, May 1973.

Ulmer, Melville, J. "Who's Making It in Mexico?" *The New Republic,* September 25, 1971.

Unikel, Luís. "Urbanización y Urbanismo: Situación y Perspectivas." In Miguel S. Wionczek, ed., *Disyuntivas Sociales: Presente y Futuro de la Sociedad Mexicana.* México, D.F.: SEP/SETENTAS, 1971.

United Nations Economic Commission for Latin America. "Income Distribution in Latin America." *Economic Bulletin for Latin America,* October 1967.

Vernon, Raymond. *The Dilemma of Mexico's Development.* Cambridge: Harvard University Press, 1963.

Warman, Arturo. *Los Campesinos: Hijos Predilectos del Regimen.* México, D.F.: Editorial Nuestro Tiempo, 1972.

Weyl, Nathaniel and Sylvia. *The Reconquest of Mexico: The Years of Lázaro Cárdenas.* New York: Oxford University Press, 1939.

Whetten, Nathan L. *Rural Mexico.* New York: The Century Company, 1948.

Wilkie, James W. *The Mexican Revolution: Federal Expenditure and Social Change Since 1910.* Berkeley: University of California Press, 1967.

Wionczek, Miguel S. "El Subdesarrollo Científico y Tecnológico: Sus Consecuencias." In Miguel S. Wionczek, ed., *Disyuntivas Sociales: Presente y Futuro de la Sociedad Mexicana.* México, D.F.: SEP/SETENTAS, 1971.

Wolf, Eric R. *Peasant Wars of the Twentieth Century.* New York: Harper and Row, 1969.

Wolf, Eric R., and Sidney W. Mintz. "Haciendas and Plantations in Middle America and the Antilles." *Social and Economic Studies,* vol. 6, no. 3 (1957).

Womack, John Jr. *Zapata and the Mexican Revolution.* New York: Vintage, 1970.

———. "The Spoils of the Mexican Revolution." *Foreign Affairs,* vol. 48, no. 4 (July 1970).

Periodicals

Business Latin America

Comercio Exterior

El Nacional

El Siglo de Torreón

Excelsior

Journal of Commerce

La Opinión Torreón

Latin America

Nacla Newsletter

Index

DATE DUE

GAYLORD PRINTED IN U.S.A.